CORPORATE REPUTATION, THE BRAND & THE BOTTOM LINE

CORPORATE REPUTATION, THE **BRAND** & THE BOTTOM LINE

THIRD EDITION

POWERFUL PROVEN COMMUNICATION STRATEGIES FOR MAXIMIZING VALUE

ROGER HAYWOOD

The Chartered
Institute of Marketing

KOGAN PAGE

London and Sterling, VA

First published in 1994 by McGraw-Hill as *Managing Your Reputation: How To Plan and Run Communications Programmes that Win Friends and Build Success*
Second edition published by Kogan Page as *Manage Your Reputation: How to Plan Public Relations to Build and Protect the Organization's Most Powerful Asset* in 2002
Third edition published by Kogan Page in 2005 as *Corporate Reputation, the Brand and the Bottom Line*

Kogan Page Limited
120 Pentonville Road
London N1 9JN
UK

Kogan Page US
120 Quicksilver Drive
Sterling VA 20166–2012
USA

The views expressed in this book are those of the individual authors and are not necessarily the same as those of the Chartered Institute of Marketing.

British Library Cataloguing in Publication Data

A CIP record for this book is available from the British Library.

ISBN 0 7494 4408 8

Library of Congress Cataloging-in-Publication Data

Haywood, Roger, 1939–
  Corporate reputation, the brand and the bottom line : powerful proven
communication strategies for maximizing value / Roger Haywood.— 3rd ed.
    p. cm.
  Previous ed. published as: Manage your reputation. London : Kogan Page,
c2002
  Includes bibliographical references and index.
  ISBN 0-7494-4408-8 (alk. paper)
  1. Public relations. 2. Corporate image. 3. Organizational
effectiveness. I. Haywood, Roger, 1939– Manage your reputation. II. Title.
HD59 H32 2003
659.2—dc22
                                2005009330

Typeset by Jean Cussons Typesetting, Diss, Norfolk
Printed and bound by Creative Print and Design (Wales), Ebbw Vale

Contents

with brand marketing 136; Marketing promotion versus
corporate projection 136; Using brands to project
corporate values 137; Develop communications
strengths as insurance 138; Leading marketing with
public relations 139; Condition the market through
communications 140; Get public relations and advertising
together 141; Control the marketing specialists 142;
Advertising versus public relations personnel 144;
Some observations, in summary 149

Preface

THE MANAGEMENT OF REPUTATION IS A WONDERFUL CONCEPT BUT, TOO OFTEN, IT DOES NOT WORK

What organization would want a poor or, even worse, a shabby reputation? So why do so few managements pay serious attention to what should be a powerful and positive asset? The reason is that a good reputation does not happen by accident; it requires bold, visionary managers with commitment and integrity. And, despite legislation, guidelines and best practice standards, too many managements are not driven by the vision of what could be, but by expediency.

This is not entirely the fault of management. Many of the influential observers of organizations (whether commercial or not) do not understand the imperative that behaving properly is the only way to behave profitably. Just look at some of those observers: say, for example, the regulators, the media, the financial sector.

The government is run and policy is set by people who, almost entirely, have never been in business and often have never had to make management decisions. Civil servants with similarly limited management experience often advise them; the last business people in government that some might be able to name would be the ennobled David Young and Michael Heseltine. Most ministers, in most administrations, would struggle to win a position on a 'third division' company board.

Few journalists have worked in management, even if they are supposed to be business correspondents; often, if they try to look at the bigger picture, the pressures from their editors are all about what is news today – and tomorrow can look after itself.

In the business sector, the City and its constituent elements in the analysis, banking, investment and other financial sectors, are still several steps away from believing that good behaviour is profitable behaviour. For example, companies may announce investment plans and see the share price drop; analysts make noises about integrity but promote investments that give the best return, almost regardless of what they may be doing to the community or the planet; the tobacco sector rides high despite making and promoting products that enslave and ultimately kill customers; even well-intentioned environmental aspirations may not enhance the attractiveness of chemical companies; high street names trade on the basis that they hope the public never find out the truth about their products and sales methods – all without risking censure from the investment community. That is unless the management is foolish enough to do anything that attracts attention. The rich get richer and the poor work harder.

Reputation enhances short- and long-term performance

No wonder it pays to have a keep-your-heads-down mentality. Expediency is seen as wise management judgement. Some big companies follow policies of ignoring sensitive issues; professional advisers advance the case for letting others take any flak; and managers tend to do anything that enhances short-term profits. This policy would be understandable if it did not often mean that it risks running the operation into trouble once managers have stepped out with their bonuses and have cashed in their share options.

Perhaps this is harsh but there is too much truth in it to be comfortable. Certainly, the financial and business establishments are a long way from recognizing and rewarding managers for caring, responding and doing more, not less, for the good of their fellow citizens, their communities, the environment and *all* their stakeholders, not just their shareholders. Ironically, there is growing evidence that companies that treat their customers and employees well find this offers the maximum benefit to their investors. But attitudes are slowly changing, and this book will be a small part of this change.

For there are two bright lights in the panorama; first the leading trade and professional bodies, and second, of course, the public. Trade and professional bodies are often leading the way to a more enlightened approach that can benefit the stakeholders far more than battening down the hatches. Many of the better ones have some seasoned managers in key positions such as John Sunderland, Sir John Egan and Sir Digby Jones at the Confederation of British Industry, and Christopher Beale and Miles Templeman at the Institute of Directors. Such bodies (and the supporting specialist management institutes in export, human resources, business law, marketing, communications and other sectors), work hard to set the standards. If only the broader business community could be more positive about the value of these visionary initiatives – not today but hopefully tomorrow.

But maybe there is more than just hope at work, for the public is learning it has the power to change the behaviour of those who seek their understanding, goodwill and support. Customers, neighbours, shareholders, employees and many others do not like companies that do not behave well. They can buy the products and services of the competitors, object to planning permissions, take their investments elsewhere, look for different jobs and, even, talk to the media – who often may not be interested in enlightened management but still enjoy reporting rows and protests.

The three key assets: reputation, reputation and reputation

Therefore, the whole contention of this book is that reputation matters at corporate, at brand, at *all* levels. And a good reputation pays. The factors that shape reputation can be managed. The investment in these management initiatives can reap major dividends. And a failure to address reputation issues can be a painful, expensive and even terminal error.

A second contention of this book is that the management of reputation must be, ultimately, the responsibility of the chairman, the chief executive and the board – or their equivalents in non-commercial organizations.

Consider an analogy with another totally established discipline: this book will argue that the chairman is the chief financial officer. But he or she will delegate to a finance director the responsibility for advice, management, control and implementation of agreed sound financial policies. So, similarly, the chairman is the chief reputation manager, and he or she should delegate comparable responsibilities to the reputation director.

Of course, virtually no companies have such a person. But all serious managements include in their senior ranks (or should do) an executive responsible for managing relationships, a communications expert, someone who, above all, cares about what the organization does and not just what it says. And that person is (or should be) the public relations director. He or she should be entrusted with these responsibilities. Sometimes this might need a bolder, more responsible brief for the public relations professional. And, in turn, this might mean a bolder, more responsible person in this role.

The case for good, proactive, bold public relations is clear. Surely the idea of organizations listening to those they depend on for success, shaping policies to meet their best interests and informing the public and all stakeholders, must be good? Such organizational policies should be central to the information democracy in which we now live. But in reality, often public relations is seen as (and sometimes is) spin – manipulation of the facts, economy with the truth and even 'burying the bad news'.

The case for good proactive, bold public relations may be clear, but the problem might be the quantity and quality of professionals with the skills to handle this challenge. The new generation of brighter, tougher, better educated young people coming into the business will mean that organizations will have no problems, in a decade or two, recruiting and retaining the best possible. However, today they may have to trawl through sad mediocrity to find the stars. But the good guys and gals do exist. Find one – and accept the importance of the role is such that he or she should be rewarded at finance director level, and given similar resources, access, responsibilities and position on the board. Not down the corridor. Do not accept a less experienced person and give him or her a less responsible role to match. Neither should you be tempted by a good journalist who usually will not have the management and strategic experience that the role demands; you could pay a high price and get substandard advice while he or she is learning the corporate ropes.

Appoint the best and expect the best

In appointing the ideal candidate, remember he or she is being paid to tell you what you need to know, not what you want to hear. One unforgivable failing in a public relations professional is timidity. Good public relations people must have integrity, vision, imagination, analytical capabilities, communications skills, commitment, staying power and courage; some chairmen can be intimidating, particularly when they are hearing what they do not want to hear. Also, the public relations job can be very lonely when all is going wrong: the whole board may have failed to pay attention to the public relations advice before chaos erupted, then it turns to the adviser for an instant solution to an impossible situation.

Communications can only be effective if it is supported by good corporate policies. The weakness can be when the public relations becomes a means of selling the message not a strategy for involving the stakeholders and building a better future. A Fleet Street editor said to me that there was no difference between good and bad public relations. As he put it, 'at the heart of every public relations disaster on which we report, there is always a highly paid professional'.

Organizations in trouble are frequently the authors of their own problems. A study by the Public Relation Standards Council (confirmed by US research) suggests that over 70 per cent of major public relations problems that make the news were either created by the organization or, with suitable issues planning, could have been predicted and avoided. Indeed at least half the disasters could have been anticipated if the right questions had been asked of the right executives. Examples of this include the Barclays banking left-hand/right-hand confused strategy over branch closures; the sinking of the *Herald of Free Enterprise*; Shell's challenge to environmental thinking over its plans to dump oil platforms in the deep sea; the Railtrack domino safety problems; the collapse of the credibility of engineering firm Jarvis; the criticisms of Dyson whose boss berated lack of investment in UK manufacturing then, just weeks later, announced he was moving his factories to the Far East; the product problems of Coca-Cola (over the low countries contamination incident, plus the backfire over the expensive launch of its tweaked tapwater, Dasani); the hammering that McDonald's got over health aspects of its products, plus the drama of the *Super Size Me* film.

At the very least, all such examples suggest poor judgement, a flawed understanding of likely public opinion, an inability to deal effectively with the media, weak issues monitoring, or above all, timid management. Sometimes they suggest a combination of all of these.

There are many more such self-inflicted injuries, which have caused immense damage to reputations and sales, and in some cases share values; there will be more, as many managements do not seem to learn from the problems that have hit other organizations.

The key to reputation management is issues analysis

A good public relations professional should have helped management to avoid the damage to reputation and the bottom line. The fact that most of the companies facing such nightmares have a public relations professional at the heart of the organization is no criticism of public relations – but more a condemnation of the structure, perhaps of their reporting lines, responsibilities or capabilities.

In most cases, the senior public relations person simply does not have the right access at board level, and his or her views are rarely considered significant enough to affect policy decisions. More often, he or she is down the corridor issuing manipulated news stories rather than in the boardroom advising on the public relations implications of policies that are under discussion. Strong professionals will not accept such terms, which may explain why some organizations suffer serial disasters.

There are some excellent examples of public relations departments headed by great professionals doing a first-class job, such as in BP, Cadbury Schweppes, Lloyds TSB, Royal & Sun Alliance, Tesco, Virgin and Vodafone. Indeed, at its best, public relations is fundamental to building both the reputation of the organization and good relations between it and those it depends upon for success. Such goodwill and support can only be won by the company developing and promoting policies that will win public approval.

When Jo Moore recommended burying the bad news on 11 September 2001 she was guilty of much more than insensitivity. She displayed a breathtakingly cynical approach to the news. The idea that trumpeting the good news and hiding the bad news will win any conviction is completely ludicrous. A story that is hidden becomes twice as powerful and damaging as one that is promoted. When I was interviewed by the *Today* programme on the Jo Moore saga, I made the point that the good public relations professional handles the bad news with as much boldness and confidence as he or she does the good news. I was severely criticized by Sarah Montague who suggested that I did not live in the real world.

Perhaps she has a point. If living in the real world means dropping your values, not speaking out when you need to speak out, not having the courage to tell those who pay your fees or salaries what it is vital that they know and understand, fudging the truth, lying to journalists – then perhaps she was right. But many in public relations do care about standards. Such professionals may not be the majority yet but they do represent the future.

Standards are rising. There are professional bodies promoting best practice. For example, the Chartered Institute of Public Relations is doing a magnificent job in promoting and developing the craft. It has a professional code, which clearly identifies unacceptable and unprofessional behaviour. In developing this, some argue that it has paid less attention to developing policies for expecting members to perform their duty, unlike the medical, accountancy, legal and other professional bodies. As the business matures, many professionals hope the emphasis will shift from what a practitioner should not do to what he or she should do. Ultimately, there could be censure for members not offering the right advice to management at the right time.

Not only will this book argue that reputation matters *immensely*, but also it will also suggest practical ways to set reputation policies and to implement them to the benefit of the organization, all stakeholders and the world in which we and our successors will live. Reputation is an asset and the management of it is a mission.

Acknowledgements

This book is the second edition with the publisher Kogan Page. My appreciation goes to the many professionals at McGraw-Hill who backed the earlier venture, which followed *All About Public Relations*, the top-selling text in this sector in the world. This earlier book remains the number one required reading for many college and university public relations, marketing, media and related courses.

My special thanks to the team at Kogan Page, particularly Pauline Goodwin who had the conviction that this was the right book at the right time, and urged me to produce this revised and updated edition.

Also, I would like to expresss my appreciation to the many colleagues who either offered helpful observations on the contents of this book or who kindly provided useful examples and allowed me to quote their experience.

I am also indebted to those who generously allowed me to be less than kind about their public relations efforts – often examples of when it went wrong. I hope their tolerance lasts and that the next time I see them it will not be in court. Should they feel I am being superior, may I say that I have made more mistakes in this daft business than I care to remember. But that's another book for another time...

Introduction

REPUTATION AND ITS CONTRIBUTION TO THE BOTTOM LINE

Why bother about the corporate reputation? If the price and quality of the products are right who cares about anything else? Once, in the midst of a contract I was undertaking for the food industry, a director of Sainsbury's (long since moved on) said to me that all the customers care about is price, quality and convenience. But as we discussed the approach of the study, he kept raising, seemingly unconsciously, issues that were not directly about price, quality and convenience yet affected sales – animal rights, Third World labour conditions, e-numbers, salt content, food-miles (the distance foods had travelled to the store), employment conditions, genetically modified foods, directors' pay and several others.

I asked him if he felt people cared about the values of companies they deal with, and whether it mattered that customers trusted the managers. He felt trust was essential. Surely, I suggested, trust is an essential element in any relationship, and most companies need to build relationships to succeed. And if customers (and any other stakeholder group) trusted the managers, surely they were making decisions based on their perceptions of the reputation of the organization?

He laughed and told me never to offer to play him at chess or, even worse, poker. Customers care about price, quality, convenience and how the company behaves, he smiled. And how they relate to them? I wondered.

'Yes,' he corrected himself. 'Price, quality, convenience, relationships and communications. This is getting like that Monty Python sketch about whatever the Romans did for us. You win! Reputation matters.'

Of course, companies can benefit from a good reputation. They get the reputation they deserve and, therefore, the trust and relationships they deserve. Of equal importance, damage to a corporate reputation can cause an immense collapse in confidence. This can create a potentially severe decline in sales, share price or both. When Coca-Cola mishandled a contamination incident in Belgium, it failed to recognize the potential damage to the brand. A major reason for the media interest generated was the idea of the managers of a global brand, priding themselves on its quality reputation, yet behaving in an indifferent, even cavalier manner. The end result was a massive loss of share value, an immediate decline in sales, and sadly, long-term damage to the corporate reputation.

MANAGEMENT BEHAVIOUR AFFECTS CUSTOMER ATTITUDES

The reputation of the management of Rover (which had bought the tattered company from BMW) was similarly seriously affected. The new team had published a glowing report on how they were to rescue the company, rebuild its fortunes through new efficiencies and expanded sales. Some of their product moves were indeed excellent, including the creation of the Rover 75 and its award-winning design and performance. Yet the behaviour of the managers was seen as not matching the vision that they had presented both to the City and to the local Midlands community where their factories were located. The directors had invested their own capital and taken some risk in the purchase. Most people believed that they should get a fair reward for this. However, figures that came out later showed that the chief executive was one of the best-paid motor industry executives in Europe. This was at a time when sales were in steep decline. A special pension fund had been set up into which the company put £13 million to benefit a handful of directors. This was at the same time as the company pension fund, supposed to provide for the employees, was estimated to be some £60 million short.

The public had been enthused to support the reborn company; research suggested they had been impressed by the ambition and plans of the rescuing directors. However, the rewards to this group were judged by the media and many opinion leaders to be out of proportion to the rewards to others – and certainly counter to the disappointing sales and financial performance of the company. The media and opinion leaders may be just one group – but market performance seemed to suggest that customers were no more impressed. Sales declined to a point where they were barely more than half that forecast at the time of the takeover.

Consider another example. Jarvis is a UK public company with capabilities in construction and maintenance, particularly in handling public contracts. The company was implicated in a rail crash on a section of line where it had the responsibility for maintenance. Early news reports suggested that there could have been problems with the quality of this maintenance. The company was slow to respond and failed to provide satisfactory answers to journalists trying to find out what had happened.

Someone, somehow made the decision to suggest that the company was considering the reason for the crash was sabotage. This, of course, was a major development and generated major media coverage. However, it was not long before this claim was being questioned; it rapidly came to be seen as a smokescreen, as there appeared to be no evidence for the assertion of criminal activity by unknown saboteurs. Later, an enquiry into the accident certainly implicated the company, and a year or more after the accident, management admitted some liability for the rail crash.

The seriousness of the accident and the failure of management to handle the situation was one of the key factors in the subsequent declining fortunes of Jarvis. From being a growing and prosperous company it moved rapidly to one that was substantially in debt. At the same time, its share price dropped to just 6 per cent of its peak level, within a little more than two years.

REPUTATION IS WHAT THE STAKEHOLDERS PERCEIVE

It has been argued with much justification that reputation is not something the company manages, *because it is the perceptions in the minds of those observing the organization*. In truth, although the board

3

may be charged with the responsibility of managing the reputation, they can really only manage those factors that might influence the reputation. That is close but not the same thing. Certainly, the board will be held responsible for the corporate reputation (good or bad) even if they cannot manage it, let alone control it. But they should worry, argues UK reputation strategist, Garry Honey. He believes that a key factor will be any gap between stakeholder perceptions and company performance. In his view, a reputation can be enhanced, protected, damaged or destroyed by company actions.

Clearly, how the company behaves will be a major factor in how stakeholders view its performance and so, to that extent, this directly affects the reputation that it earns. Therefore, if reputation is in the minds of the stakeholders, how does the company actually manage this important yet intangible asset? Why would it allocate personnel and resources to such a management function?

One reason it might be worthwhile is that an estimated 90 per cent of incidents that damage corporate reputation were avoidable, predictable or self-inflicted. Therefore, if the company has in place programmes to identify those risks that could result in damage to the reputation, it is more likely to be able to develop and follow policies that minimize such risks. For the same reason, it is wise for the board to allocate a professional to be responsible for all the factors that impact upon reputation. This executive must sit on the board of management; he or she needs to be involved in every business discussion where a decision might be taken that will have an influence upon corporate reputation.

REPUTATION MANAGEMENT *IS* PUBLIC RELATIONS

Who should this executive be? Why would many argue for trusting the management of reputation (or those factors that influence reputation) to the public relations professional? The validity of this suggestion depends on how the company defines public relations. Does it see public relations working as a strategic management discipline? If public relations is an information service down the corridor – or is merely a gathering of duties to do with relationships with the media and other commentators – then it is simply not a strategic function. These are tactical roles. If, on the other hand, public relations is seen as being all about those factors that build trust and upon which relationships depend, then the professional responsible for this area needs to be involved in every policy decision. There is unlikely to be anybody on the board who has such a broad view of all the stakeholder relationships as the public relations professional. This does not mean communications alone is central to good reputation policies. It is what the company does, not just what it says, that ultimately shapes the perceptions in the minds of stakeholders that manifest themselves as the corporate reputation.

Of course, the chief executive and chairman are the ultimate custodians of the reputation – or so it will be judged by the stakeholders. However, with financial, legal, human resource and marketing functions, the chief executive and chairman need a seasoned professional not only to look after these areas but to offer strategic advice to the board. So it is with public relations, and therefore reputation. Theoretically, the responsibilities could be allocated to the legal, financial, human resources or marketing professional on the board. Certainly the legal and financial professionals have a similar broad view of the company, but they are unlikely to have the human relations, sensitivity and communications skills that might be necessary for the job. Theirs is a more rigid and prescribed discipline. The human resources professional may well have the sensitivity and communications skill, but the nature of his or her work is that it is focused largely internally; those in this role will not necessarily have a good perspective or feeling for other audiences such as the financial community, the communities within which the organization works, local and national government and the trade and professional sectors.

The marketing professional will also have the human relations skills, the sensitivity and communications capability. However, his or her work is largely focused on development and delivery of products and services that are designed to exceed customer expectation. This is more than a full-time job, and would allow very little time to take responsibility for issues outside the sales, markets, distribution, and product and service promotional arenas.

This is not to denigrate the roles of these professionals; indeed it is completely the reverse. The demands on these executives and the skills they need to deploy should not be diluted. It would seem logical to have a professional who is focused specifically on reputation. As public relations covers all stakeholders and the whole of the effort is related to the development of reputation, this becomes a natural extension of the role of the public relations professional. Alternatively, the board could consider appointing a reputation professional. But there are no such people, except those who have learnt their skills through the world of public relations.

This assumption that reputation management is part of the broader public relations role runs through many aspects of this book. However, should the management decide to allocate this responsibility outside the public relations role, the techniques, skills and approaches recommended in the following chapters are still relevant.

IF REPUTATION MATTERS, THEN MEASURE IT

If the organization is to avoid the severe damage to its balance sheet and trading results that can be caused by a dent in its reputation, then it becomes very valuable to be able to measure its reputation. It is simple to make a comparative rating of the reputation of one organization alongside those of others, say competitors. A reasonably simple study can be run which asks a representative sample of stakeholders to rate their perceptions of the company alongside a number of others to which it might bear comparison. As noted, these could be direct competitors, or they could be companies in unrelated fields, but similar in size and position within their respective sectors. This study could ask questions along the lines of: which organization the respondents would trust; which they would feel best able to deal with problems; which they believe are most honest and so on. A section elsewhere in this book looks at such a study run by MORI. However, such studies, though interesting, might only show that company A has a better reputation than company B. Some measure could be put against this that might rate company A as being 30 per cent better than B. However, it does not give an actual value of the reputation.

The valuation of reputation is not yet an exact science, but it inevitably will become so over the coming years. Indeed, it is possible that reputation will become an asset on the balance sheet which may be only slightly less precise than the valuation that has traditionally been given for goodwill.

During the 1980s, Rank Hovis McDougall challenged conventional thinking by putting a valuation on its brands so it could add these to its balance sheet. Other companies followed. The original thinking was that to explicitly value such an asset made the company less liable to aggressive takeover bids, which were common at that time.

At the same time, the brand valuations enhanced the value of the company, which could be seen to be beneficial should the company decide to put itself up for sale, or even as a measure of the performance of the directors. Marketing professionals – traditionally among the biggest spenders around the board table – also liked the concept because it changed the classification of their operational spending from an overhead (which some considered came out of profits) to an investment in enhanced brand value.

There will be a similar development with reputation evaluation – just as soon as the accountancy profession has developed a method that is broadly acceptable to all, and that will conform to the statutory and best-practice guidelines by which they are bound.

THE FACTORS THAT INDICATE A GOOD REPUTATION

Currently there is some debate about the factors that need to be appraised in measuring reputation, or as Garry Honey says, quoting Ted Levitt from his milestone book *Marketing Myopia*, 'tangibilising the intangible'.

Honey is an independent consultant who has worked in the marketing and brand management field for some 25 years. He was a key member of the team at KPMG when that firm developed its brand valuation model, which was soon followed by other major accountancy and management consultancy firms. He is a research fellow with the Centre for Stakeholding and Sustainable Enterprise of the Kingston Business School (part of Kingston University) in Surrey, UK, and also says, 'Stakeholder concerns must be the ultimate reputation drivers. It is essential that the board take these seriously and make stakeholder engagement both a priority and a reality. Indeed, it must be part of the company ethos.'

Honey also believes that the key factor will be an agreement on the parameters to be measured, which he calls key performance indicators. He notes that Charles Fombrun, an adviser based in New York, introduced the concept of reputational capital in 1996, which inevitably led to a business interest in quantifying corporate reputation. Fombrun ranked US corporations on three key reputation drivers: whether they had a higher than average share value (this equates to market confidence), whether they could recruit readily (this related to employee attraction, and to some extent, to employee satisfaction and performance), and whether they could command premium prices for their products or services (an indication of market leadership).

However, Honey points out that there have been a number of other indicators suggested since that earlier work, including quality of stewardship, the sustainability of operations, attention and association. The director at the centre at Kingston Business School, Professor Charles Jackson, has commented, 'reputation is based on how well a company performs against stakeholder expectations, so any measurement tool must logically include expectation and here the critical factors are attention and association'.

The centre defines attention as that factor that reflects the amount of interest the organization attracts, which could be because of its sector or its profile. Association relates to the link between the names and values, particularly at the brand and corporate levels. He would argue that the distance an organization puts between its corporate name and consumer brands reflects both its communications strategy and its segmentation.

Some would argue with the concept that the bigger the distance, the greater the safety, which he summarizes as the ability of the organization to distance itself rapidly from negative incidents: 'if there is mud flying about, to what does it stick and why?' It is certainly true that if the brand name and the corporate name are the same, then poor performance, mishandling of any area or damage to reputation in one will impact directly on the other. Equally, it could be argued that simply having a different name will not be enough these days for there to be a real distance. Many public relations professionals would argue that the company should not be in the business of creating such a distance, as good relations are built upon trust, which is built upon transparency – not upon techniques to cloud responsibilities or create a smokescreen around business links. Honey does not agree.

The fact that there is no agreed formula or approach for measuring reputation does not mean that management can risk sitting back and waiting until one is developed. As already noted, damage to the reputation will cause very serious damage to the brand or to the corporation, and in some cases this may well be terminal, as was seen in companies noted elsewhere in this book, such as Townsend Thorenson, Ratner, and in this section, Jarvis.

REPUTATION MUST BE A BOARD ISSUE

What is far more important than waiting until the accountancy profession has sorted out its approach to this central issue is the fact that reputation should be considered as a board agenda item. Somebody must be appointed to take primary responsibility for this, reporting to the chief executive or directly to the chairman. The current state of reputation must be researched and evaluated, all policies that impact upon this should be reviewed, and the topic debated, not just occasionally but on a regular basis.

Some recent moves towards best practice and reporting both in the United States and the UK are likely to be followed around the world. These are defining ever stricter parameters for reporting on what some consider to be 'soft' elements that none the less can have an impact upon financial performance. For example, the Operational Financial Review (OFR) regulations in the UK will require major public companies to disclose all relevant risks for investors. These are described as specifically material risks which would significantly affect the decision to invest in the company. The vulnerability of the company to damage through poor risk management or activities that could impact on reputation would clearly fall into this area.

The message to management has to be to take reputation seriously and use best-practice processes to put some level of measurement upon this. Whether any attempt should be made to put a value on the balance sheet is a matter to be discussed between the board and the auditors. Clearly, reputation can be viewed as an element within goodwill. However, the minimum requirement is to have in place processes that anticipate where problems could arise, and processes to prevent problems from becoming damaging crises. Enlightened companies – similar to those that pioneered the development of brand management – may well want to shift from the purely protective area of risk management into the proactive opportunity that is created by initiatives that generate a good reputation that will help sales, investment, employee goodwill, and add trust and value to all relationships with all stakeholders.

REPUTATION IS THE ULTIMATE BUSINESS ASSET

Public opinion can close a company, or remove a government; stop a war, or build an international brand. Public relations is everywhere.

Public relations is life. Organizations need to create awareness of their activities and their ambitions. They need to create understanding. They need to convert this understanding into goodwill. They need to nurture this goodwill to become the positive support that stimulates positive action. Customers buy. Shareholders invest. Employees work. Neighbours support. Unions cooperate. Governments legislate.

That is the role of public relations: evaluating public perceptions; developing the policies that will win approval; projecting these to win the reputation the organization deserves; and generating the support that it needs, among all key audiences.

And the reputation that is built helps to set public expectations. Would you expect CNN or the BBC to carry deliberately misleading news reports, General Electric or IBM to knowingly compromise public safety through selling dangerous products, or Disney to be covertly financing a porn channel?

Sadly, too many companies that should have worked harder on their reputations have failed such tests. In an earlier edition of this book just a few years ago I suggested the public could trust companies like Ford, Nike and Exxon, mainly because of their apparent concern with open communications. Events have since proved that these companies were cynical or grossly ineffective in their operations, or that I was naive. Equally, questions have been asked about the authority and integrity of the public relations advisers in such companies. It makes it ever more difficult to advance credibly the argument that companies understand the importance of reputation and therefore behave in the best interests of the audiences they serve and depend upon for success.

Perhaps the truth is that some organizations operate on the basis that profit will allow them to get away with anything, even cynicism. Maybe today, but not tomorrow.

And give anyone the choice, what would they choose? To be a hero by working to standards they can defend with anyone, anywhere; or to pursue short-term profitability that depends on no astute journalist finding out the truth and blowing them out of the water? Some will still choose short-term profits. And they will pay the price when they are caught out.

For ease, much of the comment in this book is in the context of companies. However, as all who work in the coyly named 'non-profit' sector will confirm, these principles apply equally in all organizations, such as charities, trade and professional bodies, societies, associations, clubs, local and national authorities, public bodies, trade unions and even governments – though few would guess it about the latter on the evidence of their everyday behaviour! Yet this step-by-step approach applies to the non-profit sector as well, Amnesty International, the reborn government department Defra, the National Trust, Oxfam and Save the Children have all admirably demonstrated.

This book attempts to plot a way through this vital but confusing and ill-charted area. It is not an academic treatise; it is based on practical experience, some of it painfully gained through making embarrassing and public mistakes. Nor is this a textbook. There are plenty of those, including the author's own *All About Public Relations*.

This book is intended to be a friendly, anecdotal journey through the worlds of reputation, goodwill and public opinion – more a travelogue than a route map.

Reputation matters. It makes work worthwhile and it adds quality to all aspects of the organization. And not least, it add profitability to the bottom line. You must, dear reader, accept this proposition or you would not be reading these words. But, you ask, how do you manage reputation? Kindly turn the page.

Author' note
As each chapter is written to be self-contained, certain key points may be covered more than once.

1

Basic principles
Understand this reputation business

*Organizations can work to win the reputation they wish;
whatever they do, they will get the one they **deserve***

Key factors discussed

- The link between reputation and trust.
- How trust reinforces relationships.
- Relationships and the bottom line.
- Reputation management and public relations.
- Deploying skilled professionals.
- Setting policy and strategy.
- Performance criteria and reporting.
- Wins synergy through integrations.

THE ESSENCE OF REPUTATION AS PERCEIVED BY THE PUBLICS

As individuals we all get the reputation we deserve. Why? Because our reputation is decided by others who observe the way that we behave.

So what is the difference with companies? And does reputation matter? Why do some companies behave in ways that suggest that their reputation is of no consequence? Do they feel that reputation has no influence on their success?

Irrefutable evidence confirms that reputation is a major factor in deciding the attitudes towards the organization of those that it depends upon for its success – its customers, its employees, its shareholders, its neighbours, its trade and professional peers, its suppliers and all the other stakeholders. Many of these groups have a significant impact on the trading success of the organization. And, of course, the difference between a good and bad reputation can be measured.

Who in the organization has the best claim to manage the reputation: that is, who should be responsible to the chairman, the chief executive and the board for advising on and setting policies for all those organization activities that shape its reputation? As noted in the introduction, the professional responsible for public relations must be the prime candidate.

But can reputation be managed? Some would argue that reputation is an inevitable by-product of the activities, the operations, the processes, the products and services, the policies and the management of the organization. And of course, reputation is not owned by the managers of the organization. It really exists only in the perceptions of its stakeholders. However, the managers do control many of the factors that influence and shape reputation.

Of course they do. But then the profitability of the organization and its capital value is the result of an equally diverse set of financial factors. No one can imagine an organization of any consequence that does not have a financial director to coordinate and manage these financial aspects: nor one where he or she does not report directly to the chairman who is, in both law and practice, the chief financial officer.

So it must be similar with public relations and its role in managing reputation. A professional reputation manager (the public relations practitioner) manages and coordinates all influences on the many relationships that help to create the reputation across all the publics with which the organization interacts. The reputation cannot be managed effectively unless the chairman sees himself or herself as the chief public relations officer.

It takes effort, it takes planning, it takes vision, it takes commitment, it takes energy, it takes resources and professionalism to build a good reputation.

In the public relations industry there has been much debate about whether this descriptive phrase 'public relations' really spells out what the discipline is all about. Some have argued that it should be changed to 'communications'. However, the author strongly believes that public relations is much more than communications. Indeed, 'communications' suggests it is what the organization says rather than what it does; communications suggests talking rather than listening. Yet listening to people's views is what helps shape policies. Only policies that can win the public's goodwill will win public goodwill.

Some people, both inside and outside the business, may think that public relations is all about 'the public'. But 'the public' in public relations really refers more to *publics* than the *general public*. In other words, one 'public' in a programme might be the scientific community or leaders of local councils or investment analysts. Therefore, this business really should be called *publics* relations – but this is rather cumbersome and pedantic.

To try to avoid this confusion, some people talk about audiences, though this is a less than satisfactory phrase. Audiences are usually sitting and listening. But the whole essence of public relations is that it is a two-way process that requires much more than speaking out – it builds upon asking questions and listening to what people say.

So although this book uses the terminology 'public relations' and refers to both publics and audiences, it should be clearly understood that these two words are simply shorthand to describe individuals or groups of individuals with whom the organization wishes to develop relationships.

In truth, there are no such things as the public, audiences or readers. All of these are a way of describing groups of people who, at that moment and on that topic, seem to have something in common. We happily talk about ramblers or football fans but every single member of these groups is an individual who may have nothing in common with all the others apart from their particular interest or involvement in that outdoor pursuit or that particular football club.

This shorthand may be necessary but it should never be allowed to cloud judgement. No programme should treat individuals as if they were simply a group.

CONTROL ALL ACTIVITIES THAT SHAPE REPUTATION

Should public relations be managing the corporate reputation? There is logic in this, as argued in the approach recommended. Even should the board decide otherwise, it is vital that one executive should take these responsibilities, probably reporting to the chief executive, and certainly with close and regular reviews with the chairman.

For this argument, let us assume that the public relations director is allocated this reputation responsibility; he or she has been given the brief, the resources, is on the board and has access across the organization. As in other parts of the book, examples and structures are related to commercial companies but the approaches are similar for non-profit bodies.

The comparison between the finance director and the reputation director, noted elsewhere, can be extended. Everyone at every level in the organization will have financial responsibilities; no one in the organization could drive a lorry or post a letter without it being within some agreed financial policy. All need to understand the need to control costs and to behave responsibly, reporting anything that might cause a problem or appears to be outside agreed policies.

The finance director may not be monitoring or controlling every tiny financial aspect of operations. But he or she will be setting the policies and agreeing all income and expenditure budgets which cascade both down and up the organization. Therefore, every executive and member of the staff with any element of financial responsibility in their role will be working within such policies and reporting to his or her boss, who will integrate such figures within those from other in his/her team, ensuring these are within budget and policy, and reporting up to his/her boss, and so on up to the figures collated by the finance director's department. In a sense, when the finance director reports to the board or prepares the figures for the annual report and the AGM, he or she is reporting on the financial performance of everyone in the organization.

So it must be with the reputation director. Everyone at every level in the organization will have reputation responsibilities; no one in the organization could drive a lorry or post a letter without it being within some agreed performance policy that relates to the management of reputation. All need to understand the necessity to respect and exceed customer expectations and to behave responsibly,

15

reporting anything that might cause a problem or appears to be outside agreed policies.

TURNING CONCEPTS INTO PRACTICAL POLICIES

Therefore, although this book focuses on the public relations initiatives that manage those factors that shape reputation, the executive charged with this responsibility has a company-wide duty. Of course, as with finance, the management of reputation is a responsibility of all managers and the heads of all operational areas, and indeed their staffs. However, once managers are aware of and familiar with the reputation policies, this should only represent a tiny percentage of their time. Good reputation practices rapidly become second nature. The board might need to allow a 6- or 12-month period for the concepts to be presented, reviewed, discussed and adopted; this could be done overnight, but developing familiarization and ownership of such a significant new area of strategy is best achieved with an allowance of time for managers to adjust their thinking and departmental practices.

The steps can be summarized in 20 key actions, most of which involve much of the company, and some of which involve all of the company and external audiences of significance. The role should allow and require the reputation director to:

1. Research stakeholder perceptions of the corporate reputation.
2. Regularly collate senior colleagues' views on related strategies.
3. Check these against the views of external observers/influencers.
4. Undertake an issues audit to maximize reputation options.
5. Identify areas of potential risk and recommend remedial action.
6. Evaluate anything external that might impact on the reputation.
7. From this information, recommend reputation policies.
8. Present such draft policies for refining/approval by the board.
9. Ensure reputation is core to all human resources policies.
10. Produce guidelines to be adopted across the organization.
11. Brief all discipline heads in their role in supporting these plans.
12. Develop briefing processes for internal/external audiences.
13. Set up procedures to monitor and report on progress.
14. Provide the necessary advice and support to colleagues.
15. Particularly, agree policies with the marketing director.

16. Ensure policies link corporate and brand reputation strategies.
17. Ensure these are followed by all with market responsibilities.
18. Benchmark and measure progress in the perceptions.
19. Report these changes to appropriate stakeholders and regulators.
20. From these studies, recommend amendments to policy.

REPUTATION AS A PUBLIC RELATIONS RESPONSIBILITY

This book reviews the corporate activities that can shape reputation. This is presented on the basis that reputation is an integral factor within the remit of public relations. However, should the organization structure the function differently, the processes detailed will still need to be managed.

The criterion for this third edition of *Corporate Reputation, the Brand and the Bottom Line* has been to ensure that any reader should have sufficient information to participate fully and confidently in a serious discussion on any aspect of the craft.

For each of us, our personal reputation is one of our most precious qualities. So it is with companies and other organizations. If you manage an organization, then you must manage your corporate reputation. It is your top responsibility. Ultimately everything – particularly sales and, therefore, profit – is dependent on how you are regarded. Your corporate reputation may well be your most valuable asset. To paraphrase George Washington: *With a reputation you can do anything – without one, nothing.*

If you do not give the management of this factor the highest priority, then you are leaving to chance what reputation you will enjoy – or, more likely, not enjoy. In the absence of positive action, you are allowing circumstance to shape this vital business asset. In effect, you are saying: 'I will leave others, many of whom may not be sympathetic to our aims, to decide how we are viewed by all those upon whom we depend for success.'

Do not imagine that you have some 'right' to goodwill and support. You will only win these if you work for them... and are seen to work for them. If a good reputation is not your priority, do not be surprised if you find it is being shaped by such factors as your competitors' unchallenged assertions; a (yet another) superficial evaluation by an ill-informed analyst; some *no-smoke-without-fire* gossip recycled by a headline-hungry journalist; another business-bashing report from a consumer group; privileged point-scoring by politicians; the rabble-raising, distorted complaints from an un-elected pressure group; or the totally reasonable fears of your confused factory neighbours.

Why complain if these groups and their views are inaccurate, or biased, or even malicious? You have control both over the information they receive... and the company actions they observe which shape their attitudes.

It is an infallible rule. The company that has a poor reputation has poor management. Good managers build good reputations. The company that has a good reputation may deserve it, but the managers will have worked hard to ensure that they *win* proper recognition.*

The principles of 'private relations' and of 'good relations with the public one serves' are the same, asserted the late Lord Forte, founder of the major international hotels group. 'Reputation and respect can only be built on foundations of honesty and trust. Honesty can conceivably get you into trouble but it remains the best policy. Anything less can destroy in a day what may have taken years to achieve.'

He was right then. And it is true today.

ATTITUDE: A VITAL FACTOR IN ALL DECISIONS

There is a truth they certainly do not teach you at Harvard or Henley or the LSE. The attitude of someone making a decision can be more important than all factual elements. In business, there is an understandable pressure to focus only on the tangible factors that make business sense – for example, is our price competitive; are the working conditions acceptable; will this earn the right return for the shareholders; might the factory neighbours accept this planning application?

We tell ourselves that if we get these right then all ensuing decisions will be in our favour. But many of those on whom we depend for our business success are not *in business* with us. They often have a

---

*Thse factors apply to one-person businesses, partnerships and global corporations – as well as institutions and non-profit bodies. For simplicity, all commercial bodies in this text are referred to as companies.

very different agenda, but one that matters; employees may be looking at security or career options; shareholders comparing invest-ments for their pensions; local politicians seeking a vote-winning business/community alliance.

Often, as managers, we apply all our skill to make ours the best offer – yet still find that the customers buy someone else's dearer product; that the best graduates do not always recognize the oppor-tunities we offer; that the share price goes down despite the company reporting good results; that the local community rejects our plans, though they need the jobs.

Sometimes, managers rely too much on logic and believe that all decisions are made on a rational basis alone. The factor they may overlook is that decisions are influenced by opinions and attitudes. It matters significantly what people *feel* about our products, services and, indeed, our organizations.

One of the prime functions of public relations is to manage company policies to build the regard in which the organization is held. Favourable attitudes can be critical to success, taking ages to nurture. However, it would be unwise to believe that attitudes are not logical; they are built on observation, influential comment and personal experience. And therefore attitudes have a powerful influ-ence on decisions and actions.

GOODWILL CAN BE A POWERFUL BONUS

In business communications, attitudes spell the difference between success and failure. For example, when we choose where we work, in which companies we invest and what products we buy, our attitude to each organization plays a part... and often, this is the single most significant factor.

For example, studies show that many graduates put social respon-sibility even ahead of salary when deciding where they will pursue employment opportunities.

When Coca-Cola misjudged a product contamination scare in Belgium and the Netherlands or Nike ignored concerns over Third World labour conditions, in each case, one of the first measures of the impact was a collapsing share price. Why? This was long before any real damage to the trading positions could be calculated. It was simply that people are frightened by food contamination and they don't like cynicism.

TRY THE 'PUB TEST'

The attitudes of key publics to your organization are shaped largely by the attitudes of the organization, towards *them*. It is easy to spot-check such attitudes. Positive or negative, we all reflect our innate view of the likely attitudes of these companies towards their audiences.

Consider this spontaneous appraisal of public relations effectiveness. You are introduced in the bar or club to someone you have not met before. He or she naturally asks, 'What do you do? Who do you work for then?' You answer, 'ABC.' And the response you get to that is a rough but valid test of ABC's public relations: either, 'Oh dear, ABC have been in trouble recently. That consumer report did you no favours. Got any solution to the pollution problems?'; or 'You did well to win that great export order. Saw your chairman on *Newsnight* talking about global investment... very impressive. I even bought a few of your ABC shares myself.' Or even 'Who are ABC?'

Its not corporate 'image' but corporate personality that counts. Public relations both helps to create the 'personality' of the organization... and to project this to the audiences it depends on for success.

We all demonstrate our rating of organizations' public relations every day, usually unconsciously. Some people may survive in some walks of life without concerning themselves with personality. Yet, few organizations can hope to prosper without a sympathetic, favourable personality, unless they enjoy a monopoly or some other form of protection that means they can afford not to bother about making friends and influencing people. A few fortunate people may have such a natural, positive personality that they never need to think about their behaviour. Perhaps an occasional company falls into this category.

Usually, the strongest corporate personality will be much more than the personality of one individual, though it will be shaped by the input of many managers. A company that is closely linked to one individual may have only a 'reflected' personality – consider Sir Richard Branson and Virgin; or Bill Gates and Microsoft. Do such companies have their own personality separate from that of the founder and prime mover? If not, then growth, diversification and succession can become difficult.

THE MANAGEMENT OF CORPORATE REPUTATION

One view of public relations describes the craft as the projection of the personality of the organization. The corporate personality is what the organization is, reflects the values it believes are important, determines where it is heading. But, above all, the personality can be developed and controlled by the management, to become the underpinning factor in the building of the corporate reputation. Perhaps the most practical description of public relations is that it is *the management* of *corporate reputation*.

One quality of good management is that it is thoughtful and consistent. These are also qualities in corporate personalities that are likely to bring success. Just as we can anticipate how someone with a developed and balanced personality will behave, we should be able to predict how corporations will handle themselves.

Of course, there are many other factors that are essential to success. The best public relations will not compensate for weaknesses in customer care, production, quality, service or personnel and other important business areas. Indeed, it is likely that an active public relations programme would expose rather than hide such weaknesses.

A request that many advisers get from their bosses or clients is to develop a public relations plan to fix *management* problems. For example, a manufacturing company complains that the public do not appreciate the quality of its products. If that is because the quality is not up to standard, then that is a management problem. However, if the products are excellent and the message has not been conveyed (or the competition is stealing all the 'quality' kudos), then that may identify a legitimate area for public relations attention.

Mutual understanding

The Chartered Institute of Public Relations says, 'public relations is about reputation – the result of what you do, want you say and what others say about you'. It adds that public relations is the planned and sustained effort to establish and maintain goodwill and mutual understanding between an organization and its publics.

Effective public relations is much more than communications: it should be fundamental to the organization. Public relations should begin before the decision-making stage when issues are being debated by management and policies are being formulated.

My own definition is:

Public relations is the discipline responsible for creating the optimum environment within which the organization operates, through evaluating the attitudes of those upon whom it depends for success, then developing both the policies and the supporting communications to earn their under-standing and support.

Clearly, any definition should stand alone but it may be helpful to add a few comments. 'Discipline' is convenient shorthand for management function or role, emphasizing the planned and struc-tured approach that is necessary. The 'optimum environment' is clear in meaning but does not limit the many factors that might apply in each case. The phrase 'policies and supporting communications' confirms that public relations is a management function and that communications is but *part* of the process.

This definition avoids the weakness of 'goodwill' in the CIPR defi-nition but opts for 'understanding and support'. This is because public relations must not just create an atmosphere, mood, attitudes or even (important though it is) *reputation* – it must also produce some sort of action, as *support* identifies.

You do not necessarily have to feel warmth towards an organiza-tion to be able to support it. *Goodwill* is perhaps too emotive while *understanding* is neutral. For example, you might vote for the ABC political party (but reluctantly) because they have won your under-standing and support, though not necessarily your goodwill; you might understand and support the need for nuclear power genera-tion, security systems in shops and offices, price rises for your elec-tricity, without having any goodwill towards them.

REPUTATION AND PUBLIC RELATIONS POLICY

As reputation is an essential top management responsibility, so is public relations – not an optional extra, nor a function that can be delegated to administrators. Policy must be decided – and supported – from the top.

International businessman, the late Lord Hanson, built one of the world's largest and most diversified corporations over the course of his career, starting from virtually nothing. Effective public relations was central to this; indeed, many journalists rate him as one of the all-time greatest personal practitioners.

One of his key abilities was to be accessible. Part of this secret was the organization of his office support staff; journalists and other commentators who received a call from the great man were never certain from where he was calling. Ring any of his offices and an efficient personable secretary would take the message, as if he had just popped out for a moment. In fact he would often return the call, sometimes in minutes, from halfway round the world.

He believed that the basis of good public relations is 'do it yourself':

> Do not delegate the key elements. You may get a Tim Bell or a Roger Haywood to give you the advice or set up the procedures – but never let them become the spokesmen for your organization. That is the job that senior executives must undertake themselves. Creative people may be able to develop great advertising for you, but this principle should not be applied to public relations. This is essentially a personal skill and a senior responsi-bility.
>
> Winston Churchill said something about accountants which I think applies to all consultants and particularly those in public relations – *have them on tap but never on top.*

Business people sometimes ask whether their company should have public relations. It is a meaningless question. No director would ask if the company needs a reputation. Companies have both reputations and public relations whether they are aware of it or not. The real question they should ask is: Do we want to plan, control and manage our reputation... or rely on chance and the uncoordinated activities undertaken by whoever wants to get involved?

The best public relations policies to manage reputation will not be developed by instinct alone, though it may play a helpful role; there is no room for the enthusiastic amateur in the sensitive and critical area of human relations.

Good public relations needs thought, planning and organization. No manager can claim to have 'natural' public relations skills any more than a natural talent for law, personnel, finance or production. The development of a worthwhile public relations policy needs as much thought, attention and professional skill as does the financial, personnel or any other business discipline.

Public relations must be a two-way activity: listening to what the publics think, as well as projecting the organization's messages. It follows that public relations efforts can only be effective where the aims of the organization are compatible with the expectations of the public. The concept of the *hidden persuader* in public relations is nonsense.

THE MANAGER AND COMMUNICATIONS

Sir Denys Henderson was once the most successful chairman of ICI, one of the largest chemical manufacturing companies in the world. He later moved to chair the Rank Group and Crown Estates, confirming his reputation as a businessman who saw communications as a strategic tool for change. In his ICI days he built the company to be a world leader, then oversaw a dramatic reorganization of its operations when the bioscience activities were successfully separated out as Zeneca; this bold move created two distinct and buoyant companies able to concentrate on their different markets.

Public relations was an essential element in the changes that had an impact on all stakeholders in the company. Sir Denys demonstrated that integrity in communications is central:

> The most skilful use of 'smoke and mirrors' can disguise fundamental problems for no more than a limited period. In the end, there must be substance behind the promise – truth will undoubtedly out, regardless of any camouflage efforts by the most expert 'spin' doctor. Management has to accept responsibility not only for the success or otherwise of the message but also for the facts behind it. It is for this reason that I view the professional management of communication as an essential tool for business success.

> The ability to communicate key messages, with fluency and integrity, is a vital skill which managers must acquire if they are to succeed in today's complex, ever-changing business world. The audiences to be addressed may well cover employees, customers, shareholders, politicians, local communities and the general public, often, both at home and across the world. The different concerns of each group must be met sensitively. The relevant messages, whether dealing with good or bad news, must be communicated with consistency, clarity and honesty.

As top leaders confirm, strength of character is essential for a good communicator. It is the responsibility of the chairman and chief executive (and other senior executives) to ensure that the company behaves properly; one of these managers must also take the role of top spokesperson.

However, the public relations professional may act as the normal day-to-day voice of the company and plan the public presentations by his or her senior executives. A prime responsibility will be to advise management colleagues on how to review and change any proposed policies that are not in the best public interest.

Certainly, if the organization does not take control, its reputation is at risk of being shaped by others, possibly working to a hostile agenda. Visiting lecturer in international marketing at Cranfield Business School, Richard Yallop, recalls the observation that the right to be heard does not automatically include the right to be taken seriously. Everything we say or do is public relations, and should reflect serious business strategy designed to project reputation. If companies do not take control of their public relations, more and more, in this increasingly competitive world, their futures will be in the hands of their major competitors.

Enlightened policies tend to be profitable policies

In a commercial democracy, a perverse organization may deceive some of the public all of the time and all of the public some of the time, but never all of the public all of the time.

The company that decides that only the highest standard of corporate behaviour is acceptable will find that the best behaviour is always the most profitable behaviour. Certainly, cut corners on corporate standards and you risk serious damage to reputation, credibility and commercial success when (rarely *if*) this behaviour is exposed.

Behaving well should be a happier, more comfortable, responsible position. This argument may not be sufficient, alone, for a doubting management. Far more persuasive is the demonstrable fact that good behaviour can be measured on the bottom line. Ethics can be profitable!

THE REQUIREMENTS OF COMMUNICATIONS

We all communicate. It is one of the joys (and frustrations) of the public relations business that, because everyone can communicate, to a greater or lesser extent, everyone can understand the importance of this ability.

Difficulties arise when managers believe that communications is no more than a natural ability. The reality is that communications is a sophisticated and complex process; in business it is a discipline and can be practised well or badly. As with any discipline, it has rules, can be tested, measured, learnt and examined. Why would practitioners spend three or four years full time, or seven or eight years at night classes, to gain qualifications (followed by the lengthy and painful apprenticeship involved in making all the concepts work in practice) if this gives no advantage over an enthusiastic amateur?

Of course, there are matters of judgement and a good public relations amateur may be better, sometimes, than a poor professional. But a good professional should always be worth listening to and his or her advice should not be rejected lightly, without considering the possible outcome.

A good public relations professional gains no satisfaction from being proved correct when recommendations are ignored and everything goes wrong. We all have too many horror stories of disasters. Too many of them begin with the boss or the client saying something like 'Everything's going so well that the last thing we need to worry about is good relations', or 'I think we can tackle this as we go along without wasting money or time on any fussy complex plan', or 'Believe me, I'm a natural communicator. There's no advice I need from some public relations person', or 'Let me play this off the cuff. We don't want to spoil our spontaneity with any briefing or rehearsal', etc.

Ask a public relations professional to stop going on about past successes and talk candidly about some failures. Here is one of mine.

Redirecting a skilled workforce

Build confidence, be honest – and be sure to say what you mean to say

Mike MacIntosh (not his real name) was a tough Scot, an engineer and a no-nonsense manager. He was my boss at the time that the group board of the aerospace company for which we both worked asked us to plan the redirection of an unprofitable division. An excellent team, under his direction, looked at the problem and identified that the operation needed to change methods and move into new markets. This would require substantial investment and complete retraining for several hundred of the division's technical people.

The responsibility of public relations was to build, project and protect the reputation through managing internal and external communications around the reorganization. Everything in this area was carefully planned and coordinated with our personnel, production and marketing colleagues. As part of the plan, I organized an internal briefing for all top managers. This would be followed immediately by a briefing to the entire 500 members of the division's staff. Bulletins, newsletters and briefing meetings were planned to cover other audiences such as the managers and employees of other divisions, customers, shareholders, overseas associates, the local and specialized trade media, the unions, professional bodies and so on. All clicked together smoothly into one coordinated plan.

Mike knew the importance of the decisions and the need for careful communications; he had approved the plan. He accepted the discipline – on everyone, that is, except himself. He felt he was a persuasive communicator and resisted all my efforts to get him to run through his talk to the employees, which would be the keystone of the whole operation.

Early in the planning stages, he had outlined to me what he intended to say and, later, accepted my draft of how he could best express it. He refused to rehearse this presentation. I should have insisted but he bullied me – a junior and less experienced practitioner then – into reluctant submission.

The end result was a disaster. Eventually most of the staff either left or were made redundant. The division, a shadow of what it should have been, was sold to a competitor for a giveaway price. The sad irony was that Mike also lost his job after he had finished the closure forced on him. What had gone wrong?

It would not be fair solely to blame Mike. It was my fault. I should never have allowed him to speak without that dummy run. The test of my capabilities proved that, at the key point, I lacked an essential quality – courage. I made a mistake I vowed I would never make again. I should not have been cowed.

The briefing notes were fine. The media coverage was great. The excitement and anticipation as the employees took their places in the canteen – the only room in the division large enough to take them all – was exactly what was needed to build a new joint-venture spirit between management and a dedicated, skilled workforce.

But, within seconds, the anticipation had turned to worry; the best craftsmen and women had decided to look for new employment. The weaker ones could do little but keep their heads down. The spirit of the team was irreparably broken and any hope of building a new future was out of the window.

You could not fault Mike's intention, but the effect of his impromptu first sentence was exactly the opposite of what he intended. He had smiled and gave them all a thought that, I am sure, from the excited atmosphere that day, had never occurred to anyone there:

'Now, I don't want you to worry about your jobs.'

THE USE OF SKILLED PROFESSIONALS

There are right ways and wrong ways of doing things. There are times when a newsletter is appropriate and times when a video will be the best method, times for a meeting, times for a new page on the website. Some techniques will help win approval while others, used at the wrong time or in the wrong way, will antagonize. There are problems that demand face-to-face discussion when no other substitute will do. Sometimes that might require 10 minutes over coffee with the right person – and other times where a global matrix of top conferences might be right.

If the aim of communications is to get people to do something differently (and if it is not, then what is the point?), it is critical to realize that information alone will rarely change behaviour. Information may create awareness – of your product, your organization or some key issue. If such information is accepted and believed, then it may change knowledge. This is where many communications efforts end. Too many are involved in a one-way dissemination of information. Is this enough?

Observers of the organization can shape its reputation

Respected business and political journalist Fiona Ross sometimes despairs at the behaviour of major organizations. In dealing with her enquiries, she might expect them to be working to win the understanding and support of key observers. These clearly include journalists, who can not only reach a broad audience of importance but also can be influential in shaping perceptions. 'Every journalist approaching an interview, news story or simply an evaluation of a possible news story, usually comes to the news issue with some idea of the reputation of those involved. Whilst we should have an open mind – and be open to persuasion – the response of some organizations, who should know better, tends to confirm the perceptions we may already have.'

She quotes the all too frequent appalling public relations departments. 'One organisation I dealt with had a supposed public relations professional who always disappeared at the first sign of trouble. This had two effects on the attitude of journalists. First, his disappearance confirmed it was serious. Second, it demonstrated that there was no control of information, so you could talk to anyone, and speculate like mad. Neither can be the best way for an organisation to manage the perceptions that will shape their immediate situation as well as the longer term reputation.'

Ross, who has built a reputation in recent years for some astute and effective media training strategies, adds that some organizations get unhelpful adjectives attached to their names. 'A company, organisation, individual goes from being, for example, the BBC, to the "beleaguered BBC"... or from being David Blunkett to becoming "the disgraced Home Secretary". Such adjectives become part of the title and are used constantly by hacks, thereby underlining what the journalist thinks – and undermining the reputation of whoever/whatever is involved. Such descriptions tend to stick long after the crisis/scandal has passed.'

While reputation management and public relations should be about much more than just the media, she believes, her experience confirms that not only do journalists wield powerful influence, they often reflect, sometimes shape, the broader perceptions of an organization. 'When you see such corporate mismanagement reflected in share price collapse, fading reputation, declining sales and even public ridicule, then it seems obvious that such poor policies and weak action have a painful impact on the bottom line.'

Information alone cannot change opinion

A study of commercial communications programmes by the Public Relations Standards Council showed that more than half were predominantly information-based. These might have been effective at developing awareness, improving knowledge of the particular issues but would be unlikely to change opinions, attitudes and, most important, behaviour.

Not a penny should be spent on any communications programme unless you have a clear understanding of what changes you expect to achieve. Different techniques are needed to change, say, awareness and opinion.

Consider this simple example. You are in a bar enjoying a debate with a business colleague. She votes for one political party and you vote for another. You ask her why she votes the way she does. She expands on some of the philosophies of the party she supports and explains that they are aligned with her own feelings.

You do the same from your perspective. Before this moment, you did not know about each other's party political affiliations. By now you both may have more knowledge and better awareness of the other party – possibly even a better understanding. However, there is not the slightest possibility that either of you would change your political affiliations.

You continue the discussion. She gives you more facts. You give her more facts. If you both believe these, then you continue to become better informed. But you still have no intention of changing your voting behaviour. Why? Because this decision – along with all others that matter – is shaped not just by knowledge but by opinion and attitude.

Your opinion may be that her party (let us call them the Bendies) discourages enterprise and encourages low standards of personal responsibility. *An opinion is a view or belief on an issue which may or may not be related to the facts.*

Your attitude may be that supporters of the Bendies are passengers in society. *An attitude is the stance or the position adopted on an issue. It could be deep-seated and may have taken some time to develop. We can imagine an 'instant' opinion but hardly an 'instant' attitude.*

What applies to a pub argument applies to business communications strategies. Directors need to understand these fundamentals, or ensure that they listen to someone who does. The chairman thinks a television campaign will improve the share price; the chief executive asserts that the facts will win the support of the shareholders in a takeover battle; the production director feels that more investment in jobs will ensure good local media coverage for the new plant; a cabinet minister berates the media for an obsession with trivia that makes managing the country almost impossible... all are demonstrating ignorance of some of the basics of communications. No one in management can afford to be in this position.

SOME OBSERVATIONS, IN SUMMARY

1. All decisions are affected by attitude – and sometimes (often) that can be the most important factor. Ask yourself, would you be happy to invest in a company that boosted profits by skimping on product quality?
2. How the organization views the public shapes how the public will view the organization – we all tend to like people who like us. Is it any wonder we warm to companies that make it clear they care about us?
3. A spontaneous reaction to your company name can be a measure of your reputation. There are more sophisticated tests,

but few surer than the instinctive appraisal of your credibility by someone relevant but with no axe to grind.

4. Build the corporate personality to which people can relate. Integrity and character are qualities we all respect and the well-managed company can develop these just as effectively through its style and business ethos.

5. Public relations should be viewed as the management of the corporate and the brand reputation. We expect the finances, production, marketing and workforce to be managed, so why not that precious asset, the company reputation?

6. Communications is only part of public relations. We tend to think that all problems can be solved by listening and talking, but how the organization behaves is the critical factor in its stance to its public.

7. Policy must be set at the top, even if it is implemented at operating levels. Indeed, public relations is one of those important management responsibilities which must be driven from the top.

8. The soundest policies are those in the best public interest. You win wide support through pursuing actions that are of maximum benefit to the audiences whose backing you need for your success.

9. Effective public relations needs planning, resources and commitment as the wise company does not leave such an important area to chance. It should be treated as a professional discipline with suitable resources and responsibilities.

10. You cannot *choose* to have public relations – you *have* them and company behaviour is constantly shaping attitudes towards the corporation, ideally in a positive coordinated way.

11. Management problems cannot be solved by public relations alone – particularly where communications may be called in to solve problems created by poor management decisions.

12. Communications must be a two-way process – otherwise, strictly speaking, it is not communications. Feedback is vitally important to check how well your messages are accepted by the audiences you are trying to influence.

13. All senior managers should be communicators. Therefore we must train those who are likely to move up through the corporation, as well as those who might have communications needs in their current work.

14. The best corporate behaviour is likely to be the most profitable. Behaving well usually turns out to be the best commercial

option because we all prefer to deal with people (and organizations) of integrity.

15. Information alone will not change opinions and attitudes. It can develop awareness but where negative attitudes exist, more information can actually reinforce these unhelpful perceptions.

16. The end result must be to achieve a change in behaviour. More goodwill and better understanding may be desirable aims, but the real measure is the change in actions among those targeted.

2

Board policy

Win a good reputation through action from the top

Key factors discussed
Key factors discussed ● The communications responsibilities. ● Boardroom programme control. ● Winning goodwill and support. ● Involving all stakeholders. ● Making reputation a policy issue. ● The insurance factor of public relations. ● Integrity as a corporate value. ● Planning, monitoring and control.

DETERMINING COMMUNICATIONS RESPONSIBILITIES

The chairman must take the final responsibility for the effectiveness of the company reputation and supporting public relations. Every member of the board owes it to the chairman and all stakeholders to share that responsibility – and to ensure that the necessary information is available to allow intelligent discussion of key communications issues at board meetings.

However, it has to be said that many companies are not giving these matters the fullest level of attention they deserve. Where the chairman or the chief executive does not get constant and regular independent advice from a public relations professional, preferably on the board, the need for board reviews becomes even more important.

Company management might reasonably ask when is it involved with public relations? Whenever you have contact with people or organizations you are, like it or not, in the public relations business. Few corporations question the need for a finance or personnel function; those who doubt the similar value of effective public relations are misleading themselves and missing an immense opportunity to win real competitive advantage.

REVIEW CORPORATE REPUTATION AT BOARD LEVEL

Any failure of the directors to be on top of communications and associated efforts to build reputation could be most damaging. Should the company experience difficult times, it is likely that shareholders or statutory bodies might become interested in how the public relations aspects of key issues were being considered at board level, as they unfolded.

A code published by the Public Relations Standards Council of the UK sets suggested parameters for an effective public relations function within the organization. Among its recommendations is the need for the senior professional public relations adviser – whether on the staff or a consultant – to say what has to be said rather than what might merely be acceptable. This candour should be a requirement of the role and such views should be advanced without fear of retribution. The aim of this and other clauses is to ensure that the organization is always getting the best advice at all times.

Critical questions on public relations are asked when problems arise; companies that do not review their reputation and corporate communications at board level are taking a risk. And too many companies still are taking that risk, as a check of most board agendas will confirm. Indeed, very few companies have agreed reputation policies and even fewer publish these objectives as the codes of most public relations professional bodies recommend.

Of course, many directors will protest that too much is being squeezed onto overcrowded agendas. But communications policy is not something that can be delegated. It can and does make headlines. It can and does close companies.

Yet with proper planning, the review of a responsibly run programme takes little time. Indeed, the fact that the board signs off policy may be one vital element in ensuring that the programme is run responsibly.

Initially Sir Adrian Cadbury, chairman of the UK Committee on the Financial Aspects of Corporate Governance, was reluctant to extend the debate, during the early deliberations of his group, through the inclusion of the Institute of Public Relations. However, as I was president of that body at that time, I advanced the view to him that corporate reputation and relationship communications, particularly investor public relations, were an essential and integral element within proper corporate governance. He agreed this point and the institute submitted evidence.

The resulting Code of Best Practice on the Financial Aspects of Corporate Governance specifically says that it is the board's duty to present a balanced and understandable assessment of the company's position, focused on financial communications.

This code, developed in the UK in the 1990s, has been echoed, improved and extended by similar moves in the area of corporate governance across the globe.

There are, however, many other aspects of company operations that can impact on its reputation, its financial control and overall business position; and in each of them public relations will tend to be one of the main communications links between the company, represented by the board, and the audiences whose goodwill and understanding are being sought.

There is no other company discipline that can give a broader overview of company operations than public relations, yet some directors have little idea what is being done in their names, across vital areas of operation, involving all the audiences of importance to the company.

The responsibility of directors for investor communications may be clear. These responsibilities are extending steadily to encompass all aspects of corporate and reputation communications. Increasingly, companies worldwide have written and published communications policies. Such policies can be an invaluable way to help define the responsibilities of the board and senior executives.

In this book, the emphasis is on commercial corporations, but the public relations principles that build reputation apply as effectively to all organizations. Experience of many in the non-profit sector, for example, is extremely positive.

COMPANIES GET THE SUPPORT THEY DESERVE

The ideal reputation for your organization will not be earned by accident. It will be won through application and direction. What the organization does and not just what it says matters most. Of course, there must be a commitment to ensure that the reputational implications of all company operations are considered in all appropriate plans.

Ideally, the mission statement (and the corporate objectives) will include an appropriate commitment to the development of the corporate reputation. This will also need to be reflected in all business and marketing plans.

As an illustration, marketing may be all about *satisfying customer needs profitably*... but it also has a responsibility to develop and reinforce the reputation of the organization. A suitable statement in the marketing plan about the reputation objective will help avoid the adoption of unacceptable sales techniques or promotional activities – for example, those that may be better for short-term results than they are for the longer term's perceptions among those who matter. It is a circular argument. Will you go to heaven because you are good or are you being good so that you will go to heaven?

Make the policy shape company behaviour

Many companies are choosing to publish their mission and vision plans. It is undeniably true that these may have a certain sameness in feel with quite a high level of usage of words like *excellence, responsibility, encouragement, efficiency, productivity* and so on. However, they do make a formal commitment against which individual managers and employees can measure their own performances or, indeed, direct their staffs, peers or even their bosses when standards appear to be in conflict with some of the points in the mission statement.

One of the weaknesses of some corporate mission statements is that companies write them to be broad enough to cover most eventualities, which means they do not have enough focus. One helpful recommendation might be to start with a general mission statement but to refine it over a period of time. Certainly, no company should be publishing the identical mission statement year after year, for example, in the annual report, unless they are convinced that this is the definitive version. It can always be improved and the sharper the focus of the mission statement, theoretically, the sharper the focus of the organization.

Leading international public relations strategist Goran Sjoberg believes it is essential that management controls the corporate public relations. Failure to do this can result in external factors shaping the reputation – and these can include bodies and individuals that may not be sympathetic to the company. In contrast, the actions of the company, its employees, its representatives and its business partners can have an influence on reputation that can be out of all proportion to that of such extenal bodies. To be effective, all such stakeholders must understand the values of their organization and what it is trying to achieve.

One company with a strong ethical policy that shapes employee behaviour in powerful and positive ways is GE, whose reputation is of paramount importance. The company also states its values in clear and simple terms. The standards are set and endorsed at board level. All employees on all occasions know how they are expected to behave and this is one factor in giving the company a consistent personality. In summary this statement of values says:

All of us… always, with unyielding integrity:
- are passionately focused on driving customer success
- live quality to accelerate growth and ensure the customer benefits
- insist on excellence and are intolerant of bureaucracy
- search for and apply the best ideas, regardless of source
- prize global intellectual capital and the people that provide it
- see change for the growth opportunities it brings
- create a clear, simple, customer-centred vision
- create an environment of excitement, informality and trust
- demonstrate GE leadership with enthusiasm for the customer:
    - the personal **energy** to welcome and deal with change;
    - the ability to create an atmosphere that **energizes** others;
    - the **edge** to make difficult decisions; and
    - the ability to consistently **execute**.

There may be a touch of US jargon about the language but the messages are sharp and real.

THE COMPANY'S REPUTATION IS *EVERYONE'S* RESPONSIBILITY

Whatever his or her role in the organization, each employee has some personal responsibility for its reputation. As the old saying about duty to employers goes: *you can't take the money and knock 'em*!

It is reasonable for the board and all management to expect all members of the company to do more than resist criticizing their employers in public; each should be an enthusiastic ambassador for the company. If employees are not, then something is seriously wrong. It would be wise to include some suitable reference to these reputation responsibilities in contracts of employment, staff booklets and induction programmes.

Obviously, such a positive, supportive environment allows (indeed, should encourage) constructive criticism, designed to help the company improve performance – though even that should be 'in the family'.

Clearly, the responsibility on those at the top is more demanding. Directors and managers have both their personal and the corporate responsibility for reputation. They will not be able to exercise this properly unless they know and understand how the organization's communications work.

This is important for all managers; it is essential for directors. Indeed, it could be argued that a director who does not understand the processes by which the reputation of the company is developed is as ill-equipped as one who does not know where the product is sold or how it is manufactured.

A leading politician said to me: 'There's something suspect about public relations. After all, if your product or your company is any good, then everyone will know.' He was not wrong; but nor was he quite right.

He was not wrong, for public relations can never be a substitute for doing the right thing. Reputation is dependent on far more than polished words and impressive visuals. What the company *does* matters as much as what it *says*. Its products and services create goodwill (or otherwise) as much as its communications. Its attitudes towards its publics also influence the attitudes those publics will have towards the company.

Nor was my political friend right. *Build a better mousetrap and the world will beat a path to your door.* Many great mousetrap designers have starved as a result of believing that. Good products, good services and good companies demand effective promotion. Your competitors will be presenting their case to the media, to your customers, to your employees and to your shareholders. If you do not vigorously project the values in which you believe and which shape your approach to these audiences, do not be surprised if they are more impressed with competitive offers. Clearly your corporate and product reputations compared with your competitors will be major factors in decisions all stakeholders make.

DIRECTORS AND THE COMMUNICATIONS POLICY

Recent tightening of company laws virtually worldwide means that all directors, effectively, are responsible for everything that the company does, or that they should have known it was doing, as the Worldcom fraud trial dramatically illustrated. The introduction of codes and best-practice guidelines, such as that on corporate governance, set standards of behaviour expected even where not statutorily compulsory. Such guidelines may not have the weight of the law behind them, but someone in trouble who has contravened the 'recommendations' will have some explaining to do. Equally, increasing concern about business ethics among the public at large and informed observers in particular (notably the business media), also exerts pressure for better behaviour.

Reputation is rightly seen by shareholders (and other stakeholders) as a serious board responsibility. Therefore, a company that has no related communications policy is unlikely to be able to carry out its responsibilities to all its stakeholders, for information will be one of their prime needs. Each director should be concerned that the communications policy is sound; that it ensures that all who have a right to know are properly informed; that effective feedback systems exist; that early warning of problems can be assured; that the processes exist to deal briskly and sensitively with any crisis; and that a senior director is personally responsible for reputation and related public relations, with proper, regular reporting procedures to the whole board. It is also vital that the company policies address the approach to all issues that could affect the corporate reputation.

PUT YOUR REPUTATION ON THE AGENDA

The only satisfactory reporting method must be for public relations to be a regular and *routine* board item. Directors should not just be concerning themselves with communications *when there is a problem*. Winning a good company reputation is, perhaps, a little like building a good marriage or personal relationship – it requires constant work, through the good times and the bad. When problems strike, it may be too late to apply remedial treatment. Prevention is better than cure. Effective relations between the organization and its various publics require constant attention.

Remember that reputation is about what the organization does and not just what it says. Everything that is done and every policy should be reviewed and monitored to check that it reinforces the reputation ambitions. It may not be necessary for the board to become involved in the detail but each director must be comfortable that he or she has a good overview. Public relations strategy might be reviewed in detail once or twice a year with progress reports in between. A strategy review paper presented to the board might cover the following areas:

1. *Objectives.* What is to be achieved over the coming period to support the mission statement and corporate objectives? Where is the reputation and how does it compare with competitors? Where could it be developed and protected?
2. *Strategy.* What *tone of voice* is being adopted to achieve these objectives? Do all the elements support this and how do they combine into an overall plan? Is each activity complementary? Can any be extended to reach broader audiences and improve cost-effectiveness?
3. *Perceptions.* How is the company seen? What are the attitudes of those whose goodwill we need for success? (Periodically these must be identified by research, but interim reviews should note the observations of public relations, marketing, sales, personnel and other professionals in contact with prime audiences.)
4. *Messages.* How do we wish the company to be seen? What gaps are there between reality and perception? Is the company communicating in the way that will win support – and *behaving* in the way that will win support? Are all the communications activities reinforcing these agreed messages?
5. *Tactics.* What communications methods are to be used? How

will these relate to other corporate activities? Who is directing and implementing the programme? What company contingency plans have been proposed to deal with the unexpected?

6. *Initiatives*. Are there special events of which we should be aware, such as the preview of the new corporate video or the launch of the new sponsorship? Are these *on strategy* and, if so, how can they best be tied in to the broader company business timetable?

7. *Calendar*. What are the major activities in the corporate calendar that have reputation and public relations implications such as new product introductions or the financial year end. What are the plans to support these? Is the programme scheduled realistically to coordinate such events with any communications initiatives?

8. *Concerns*. What issues might affect company activities today and tomorrow? How will the communications professionals propose to audit and analyse these? Are there areas of policy where the directors' views and support are essential? Will members of the board be expected to participate in functions? If not, might these be enhanced if they did?

9. *Competition*. Are there public relations activities by competitors that should be evaluated? How is their public relations effectiveness, say, in the tone of media coverage, in comparison with ours? How are they managing their reputations?

10. *Appraisal*. How effective is the programme overall? What performance criteria are set so that the effectiveness can be appraised and the direction fine-tuned? What are the achievements to date, measured against the objectives that were set? How cost-effective is the level of performance achieved in each activity?

11. *Management*. How is the competence of those charged with managing the public relations function? Do directors have any commendations or concerns that should be voiced? How are consultants or other advisers performing? Are there any changes that need to be considered?

12. *Resources*. What is the total cost of the activity proposed, including staff time? Does anything require additional company resources, such as regional seminars, factory open days, wholesaler briefings? How well prepared is the communications team to handle any crisis that may arise?

REPUTATION MANAGEMENT IS MORE THAN INSURANCE

Some organizations spend money on public relations not just to protect and project reputation but because they see it as insurance, to protect them should things go wrong; some see it as a way of putting a gloss on their activities. Public relations can perform both functions, but these are negative approaches that will never create the real benefits that can come from wholehearted commitment to communicating properly.

Good public relations *does* have an insurance value. Crisis plans are an essential part of any company's proof of its preparedness. All organizations should know, in advance, how to react to a fire, a security alert, fraud, accident or other unwanted eventuality that may befall them. The public relations aspects of these may be critical and may even affect the survival of the company. The wise company will not only have developed a plan but it will take its responsibilities to its publics seriously. It will test this plan and ensure that all employees are familiar with their role and are trained to handle it.

But do people behave well or badly because of a plan? Do they communicate effectively because of this plan? In fact, it is almost the converse; those who believe in behaving well will insist on a plan; they will communicate effectively because they care about their responsibilities. Ultimately such positive attitudes prove to be central to building the credibility that wins the reputation.

Public relations that just exists as insurance against a disaster is passive and possibly just a little too cautious. Also it may not be the most effective. It may not even guarantee the expected benefits... less certain than giving to charity to secure your place in heaven!

Equally, public relations that exists only to put a gloss on the good news, but which disappears when there are problems, is simply not credible to those whose trust is essential. The best policy must be to tell the bad news as candidly as the good. Prepare for the impossible, then use that resource, continuously and positively, to listen to the views of your partners in business, your staff, customers, suppliers and others; and use that resource to inform these publics. Consistent, open, honest communications builds trust and goodwill. You can never have too many of those qualities.

Of course it is wise to have public relations plans to deal with problems. However, not all issues create potential problems. Some issues, as discussed in Chapter 4, can be positive to offer potential advantages, or neutral to allow opportunities to create 'competitive edge'.

Avoid the 'down the corridor' mentality

The reality is that public relations is something in which you do, or do not, believe. Try to impose it through an unwilling management or staff, and the public will soon see the artifice. This is the challenge that faces mass retailers like PC World or KFC: how do you make those who face the customers conform to and exceed the expectations detailed in the plan? Good public relations does not come just from the professionals; it comes from the chairman, the chief executive, and the directors, to whom it must be part of their thinking, not an afterthought or a bolt-on extra. If the chairman does not believe in these policies, how can you expect the counter staff to 'live' them?

In reality, the chief public relations officer is the chief executive. The professionals advise, manage and offer specialist skills. It is exactly comparable to other company disciplines, such as finance. In any company, the *chief* financial officer is, of course, the chief executive and the financial professionals advise, manage and offer specialist skills to their board colleagues.

Directors are constantly making decisions that have public relations implications. Indeed, there will be few senior decisions that do not have such implications. It is wise to have the most senior public relations professional very close at hand. Many companies such as GE, IBM, ICI, Microsoft, Virgin and Vodafone, have the public relations expert reporting directly to the chief executive or chairman.

When Simon Lewis was appointed group director of corporate affairs for Vodafone, he secured a place on the company's executive committee, unlike his predecessor. This was something he described as an important evolution in the head of communications role. 'It can be difficult to be as effective as you would want if you are not reporting to the very top.'

The industry journal *PR Week* regularly interviews top executives, and managing director Stephen Farish, observes a link at this level between personal relationships with the public relations professional and the effectiveness of company communications:

> Companies that achieve and maintain a good reputation are often led by chairmen or chief executives who clearly trust their public relations advisers. They enjoy a direct relationship that allows, even encourages,

the public relations person – staff or consultant – to say what needs to be said. The company profits from the integrity and independence of this comment. A good public relations adviser should be as concerned about how well company policies are accepted by those they affect, as by how well they are projected.

The chief executive with such candid but supportive advice can be confident that he or she is tuned into issues and concerns. Companies with good public reputations employ the best practitioners in the business. In truth, the best is always the cheapest option. Good people offer better advice and make fewer mistakes.

A regular topic of conversation among professional public relations people meeting socially is the misjudgements of those who should know better but who have not bothered to get public relations advice or, worse, have appointed a junior to do a senior's job. Mistakes in public relations can be desperately expensive. In choosing public relations professionals, the wisest solution is to choose the best. Anything cheaper can prove too expensive.

DO NOTHING TO COMPROMISE INTEGRITY

Transparency is the first requirement for any management policy for a company seeking a good reputation. It may be a cliché but it has to be the best way to describe the style of management that is as open and honest as possible, with no hidden agendas. Corporate life becomes simpler when decisions are made openly – and involve as many people as possible, as quickly as possible. Of course, there are decisions that have to be taken in private and which may not be revealed immediately – commercial needs, alone, may sometimes dictate confidentiality.

However, conspiracy management can become quite infectious and too much confidentiality can lead to paranoia about security of information. Taking secret decisions can be exciting, but any decision that matters will become known sooner or later and it may well be better to consider making it known sooner, rather than letting it be discovered later.

Journalists tend to smile when advised of a piece of information preceded by a 'this must be treated in the strictest confidence'. Often it turns out to be something already widely known, even common gossip up and down the corporate grapevine.

Transparency in the decision-making process is also much easier because it is a policy based on honesty. It takes no effort to remember the truth; subterfuge requires a totally reliable memory if the pretence is to continue in any consistent way.

Consider an example. The company needs to save costs and, say, the Birmingham factory is making losses. The commercial director outlines the facts to the board and it is discussed in detail. You agree that you have to close it at some date to be decided.

But when do you tell those people directly involved? At the earliest moment that wisdom and judgement will allow. Such actions need much consideration and planning, but the risk of a leak increases with every hour and with every person advised. As more people become involved in the decisions, the chances increase that someone will feel a certain loyalty towards the other workers and, so, a discreet word in the ear of a journalist might be an idea.

Try to get everything 100 per cent and you may delay too long. If so, when you are finally forced to make the announcement, all will know that you made the decision much earlier. Indeed, all will know that when you should have told the truth you did not. Even worse, circumstances may have required you to be more than economical with the truth in that extended limbo period.

If you follow this logic, you should therefore operate as if every-thing that you are doing is (or shortly will become) public knowl-edge. It is a good approach for personal integrity and so it works equally well for corporate integrity.

If you do not want your action to become public knowledge, then the simple rule is: don't do it!

Building a business of integrity with a strong reputation
Unite all the board behind a common, shared and uplifting philosophy

One the world's largest chemical companies with significant operations in virtually every industrialized nation had a problem. A public relations consul-tant had been called in because the company had been getting some disturbing negative media comment which was damaging the corporate repu-tation and related opinion leader comment. His brief was to improve media relations. After a little investigation, it seemed clear that not all the negative reporting was unfair. Some of the stories were reasonable reports of what the company was doing. The *real* problem was that some of the things it was doing were not winning the approval of the community nor of the journalists reporting on community affairs.

He pointed out to the chairman that negative comment was often justified. If a company, for example, polluted local rivers, suffered from works fires and site accidents, annoyed the neighbours with nasty smells and woke them up in the middle of the night with unexpected bangs, then declined to explain these occurrences, you could hardly criticize the journalists for reporting this. And the lack of balancing good news could be explained by the fact that nobody told the media about any good news – like major investments, important new products, community initiatives, VIP visits and trading successes.

Fortunately, the chairman laughed at this exaggeration, and invited the consultant to attend the next board meeting to outline such views to his assembled colleagues. Our hero readily agreed.

On that memorable occasion, he decided not to go into a detailed presentation on managing the media nor even to refer to the research that had been undertaken. The consultant decided to keep it simple and said something along these lines:

'In the main, companies get the media that they deserve. We have very little to complain about in the media coverage that we have been getting. If any of us here around the table were the editor of the *Wall Street Journal,* or the CNN business correspondent, we might well produce similar stories. As a company, what we are doing is of great interest to their viewers and readers. We do not complain about good news, but sometimes we make mistakes. These range from irritating to potentially dangerous. And we have to accept that it is the job of the journalist to report such matters.'

'Outrageous,' responded one director. 'I would never write such irresponsible, trivalized stories!'

'You would, if you were a responsible, popular journalist,' the consultant replied as calmly as he could manage. 'Because the behaviour of big companies when they ignore their responsibility to the neighbours and the community is of interest to their readers. If you did not, your editor would replace you with someone who did understand this fundamental of journalism.'

'But the stories are so unrepresentative,' complained the personnel director in a conciliatory tone. 'One tiny fire and a little smoke, entirely from cables and nothing to do with chemicals, does not deserve that sort of front page coverage.'

'It was only front page on the local paper and, in my view, it *did* deserve that treatment,' responded the consultant, equally calmly. 'If we were unable to provide the information that it was an electrical fire, then the journalist cannot be criticized for not divining this. Equally, if you lived next door to a chemical plant and had your house engulfed in clouds of billowing black smoke from the local chemical works, your first thought might not be… *I am sure that is only a little electrical fire and some harmless sooty smoke from cables burning.* We need to understand what is news. One fire in a chemical plant is news; 364 other days when there is not a fire is not news and nobody is interested.

'If one taxi driver sets fire to his cab, that is news, even if 10,000 others do not do such a thing on that day. News is not about balance and it is not the media's job to project the routine of our activities. But I do support their right to review the extraordinary and if we are sufficiently unprofessional not to know how to handle both good and bad news then we deserve everything we get.'

'Where does this lead us?' asked the canny chairman, keen to get back on the track.

'Well, chairman,' responded our bold adviser. 'As you know, many of the practices which they continue to discuss have long since been stopped. We are vigorously tackling safety. We have established an environmental policy and are about to publish this. I am happy to project this good news to the media. But I believe it is much more important that we are totally confident that, if we want a good reputation, we are not doing anything of which we are not proud.'

The chairman considered the point. 'I am proud of the company. We all are. We inherited some unhappy situations from generations of previous management working to the standards of their day; but I am convinced that we are doing it all right now and that things will be even better in the future. What are we doing, do you think, of which we cannot be proud? Why don't we go around the table and check?'

They duly did. After some vigorous and positive debate, the board instituted improved new safety procedures in all plants. It also agreed to pull out of the manufacture of a product responsible for severe pollution, even though it would lose some £50 million in sales. It also agreed to adopt an open-door policy at each of its plants – any member of the public could phone for any information at any convenient time. And, in addition, any professional group, any environmental or community association could come into the plant at any time to take any samples or make any tests of effluent, ground water or any other materials at any time they liked. Finally, the board recommended a more proactive approach to community and media communications.

These actions were eventually translated into a policy which was published. Because it was credible and backed by the open-door policy, this was positively and extensively reviewed by the media. Every incident thereafter, as had been warned, attracted even more negative coverage. There were very, very few.

And, at the end of the first 12 months at the plant which had experienced the most media problems, how many community bodies or pressure groups had asked for access? *None.* There was no necessity, for it was quite clear that the company no longer had anything to hide.

Pressure groups, the local community and the media all accepted the company had changed its ways, had learnt how to behave properly and to treat its stakeholders with integrity and respect.

The reckless public relations adviser was the author, the company Aventis.

The visionary chairman, at that time, was Dr Keith Humphreys, also a distinguished president of the Chemical Industries Association in the UK.

SOME OBSERVATIONS, IN SUMMARY

1. The chairman is ultimately responsible for the corporate reputation, and therefore how the company communicates. Effectively, everything is said in that person's name.
2. The chief reputation manager is the chief executive.
3. All board members must be happy with communications, for they have a duty to support good reputation initiatives.
4. Public relations policy must be decided at board level. Plans can be developed elsewhere but only the board can authorize the programme.
5. The board should regularly review issues that could affect future performance, usually as analysed by the public relations professional.
6. Make sure the public relations professional is close at hand, has regular access to directors, is up to date on developments and allowed to advise.
7. An experienced head of public relations can provide a useful perspective for the board, probably having the broadest view of the company.
8. Guidelines on corporate governance put a responsibility on directors to ensure that the company position is properly communicated.
9. Any mission statement should set public relations policy in terms of fair dealing with the publics on whom the organization depends for success.
10. Where possible, the mission statement should try to put levels of performance on each element and improve these, year on year.
11. All plans and proposals submitted to the board should include an analysis of the public relations implications and any effects on existing policy.
12. As every employee is responsible for the reputation of the organization, a requirement to support this should be written into contracts of employment.
13. What the company *does* is vitally important, not just what it *says*. Public relations must project positive and truthful messages.

14. The ideal starting point is a written communications policy which should be prepared by the professionals for board discussion and approval.

15. The time to concentrate on getting public relations policy right is when all is calm and going well. There will not be time when problems arise.

16. Do not try to keep information confidential for too long. Everything will soon be public, so issue the news as widely and as early as practical.

17. Those responsible for implementation should present the public relations programme and performance review to the board, say, quarterly.

18. Factors to be reviewed should be objectives, strategy, perceptions, messages, tactics, new initiatives, timetable, competitive position, performance, management capabilities, and resources.

19. The quality of the company reputation will be related to the personal relationship between the chief executive and the public relations adviser as this shapes the effectiveness of the reputation communications.

20. If you truly would not wish some considered action – personal or corporate – to be publicly exposed, then don't do it!

3

Managing the function
Manage your reputation investment

Key factors discussed

- Getting all personnel on message.
- How to identify the core elements.
- Converting ideas into a written plan.
- Try listening before speaking.
- The control of reputation standards.
- Finding a skilled reputation manager.
- Appointing external consultancies.
- The framework for performance.

DEVELOPING THE REPUTATION BRIEF

Some elements must be approved at board level. This is particularly true of initiatives to build and develop reputation. To achieve this, the public relations needs of the organization will be clear once the process of developing the objectives has been completed. However, what needs to be done to *achieve* these objectives will still need to be agreed.

The key to managing the function effectively is to agree the brief.

The chief executive needs to be certain that proper public relations management processes are established so that the board can be fully up to date on developments. While much of the public relations activity may need no more input from the board than an occasional review, some elements cannot be delegated. Policy *must* be approved by the board. Major issues must be reviewed at this level. Crisis strategy must be approved.

The level of detail in which the chief executive wishes to be involved will vary with the company and the individual concerned. These notes suggest areas that might be worth considering.

Getting the whole company heading in the same direction in the public relations effort to develop reputation is vital. For example, there will be confusion and frustration if the public relations professionals are vigorously concentrating on sales and marketing objectives while the personnel team are primarily concerned about staff turnover, local restrictions on night working and so on. In many cases, with thought and planning, such diverse aims can be managed compatibly. Some priority or weighting of the activity needs to be decided.

Agreement on these matters is fundamental. For example, Fiskars, the Finnish engineering group which owned the Wilkinson Sword brand in gardening and tools, brought in public relations professionals to support a major marketing drive. The advisers soon found that one director wanted all promotion to be built around this famous brand name, but another wanted the parent company identity to be more strongly featured.

The difference of view was significant and there were valid arguments both ways. At that time, the Fiskars name was not as well known as Wilkinson Sword; the ownership of this international brand name would be subject to review and renegotiation at some stage in the future. Should the short-term need take priority and the better-known name be promoted? Or should public relations be used to develop the awareness and, therefore, brand value of the parent name over a period of time?

It was perfectly reasonable that there might be differing points of view on how public relations should address this issue. However, if the consultancy had only had access to one point of view, they may well have been criticized later for undertaking a programme of action that was not achieving the aims that other members of the board considered to be a priority.

Such matters need to be resolved; the ideal solution is for the board to agree a written brief usually prepared by the senior public relations adviser.

The elements in any programme tend to be the same even when the aims and techniques are widely varied. The ideal brief may reflect these. Consider this simple Kipling-based *aide-mémoire* for these factors:

Who?	– audiences (*those we are trying to reach*)
What?	– messages (*what we want them to understand*)
Why?	– objectives (*what we are trying to achieve*)
Where?	– reach (*where these audiences are located*)
When?	– timetable (*the schedule of activity*)
… and …	
How?	– techniques (*the methods we propose*)
+ how much?	– resources (*budget and personnel*)
+ how effective? –	appraisal (*how performance will be measured*)

DEVELOP A WRITTEN PLAN

Misunderstandings can be eliminated by insisting on a written plan for reputation development and all company initiatives to achieve this. This needs to be to the board's brief and approved at board level. Normally, as noted, this is prepared by the senior public relations professional; he or she should participate in board discussions on strategy issues so that the background is fully understood.

A one- or two-page summary may be sufficient for the board to give approval, though the full plan will be a more substantial document covering issues, audiences, messages, objectives, timetable, resources, methods, appraisal and reporting back, as noted above.

The focus of the board should be on the strategies, polices and on the messages to be projected and to which groups, rather than on details of the techniques to be deployed. As suggested earlier, the plan should be related to the mission statement or the company credo to ensure that it is consistent and reinforcing the broader aims of the organization.

Confirm resources to be deployed

The company will be committing a team of people and a budget to the achievement of the objectives of the public relations reputation programme. The most important point is the confirmation of the person who has overall responsibility for the effectiveness of the work.

There will be diverse elements of public relations involved – for example, a customer-care team, internal communications staff, press office, marketing, public affairs and investor specialists. One executive needs to coordinate these efforts and take responsibility for reporting to the board.

Clearly, public relations activity should be undertaken within an agreed budget. Only rare contingency activity might be outside the confirmed budget. Public relations should be operating within the same disciplines that apply to any other business function. This control not only applies to those running the activity but to senior management. All must try to be objective and, for example, resist the temptation to adopt their favourite sport for company sponsorship or be wooed by the latest electronic technique, and adjust the budget accordingly. If the sponsorship is a cost-effective way of achieving the objectives, say, then it should be part of the programme recommendations.

Too many programmes have been hijacked and too many professionals demoralized by disproportionate resources being allocated to peripheral activity at the expense of the planned, strategic events. As Peter Ward, managing director at the time of the Electrolux speciality aluminium division in the UK, used to query every new marketing and promotional idea, 'Is it on strategy?'

Equally, some companies spend *too much* through resources not being properly directed. When a leading practitioner was brought into an international energy company as director of corporate affairs, he found what he believed was a classic case of a failure to communicate effectively at the strategic level. He explained that he inherited a large team spending millions but there was a complete lack of focus and much of the expenditure was counterproductive. His first step was to sort out the fundamentals and get the strategy agreed at board level – targets, messages, techniques and so on.

There are two vital stages before planning any programme: first, management must agree the reputation they want to achieve against a number of criteria; second, research must measure precisely the company's existing reputation among the target audiences. If the reputation does not match management aspirations, yet performance is good, then that sets a communications challenge; but if the research confirms low regard and this is because performance is below par, then management must improve this first. A company has only to fail to deliver the promise once for the reputation to be shattered.

Ensure that decision-makers are consulted

The managers of the public relations function will need to have access across all senior management to obtain their endorsement of key initiatives – and possibly participation in some of these. The new product launch may need to be fronted by the marketing director. The analyst meetings may require the financial director and the chief executive. The AGM and final results briefings demand the chairman. The regional workforce development policies may be best presented by the human resources director, and so on.

Such senior executives can reasonably make suggestions for improving the activity; the time for radical suggestions is at the planning stage. The public relations people, like their production or financial colleagues, thrive best in a stable environment where they know the ground rules, and these are not changed on a whim.

I once organized a European visit for the parent board of Air Products & Chemicals, the US corporation. The directors were booked to stay at the best national hotels in each of the capitals they were visiting on this goodwill mission. At these, they would meet senior company personnel, business leaders and the media.

The whole schedule was prepared, approved and developed into a printed booklet form for distribution in advance. Just a few days before the event, a US senior executive changed all venues to the Hilton in each city.

Whether it was the right or the wrong decision, the many executives who had spent time planning the event were not consulted. Their view was that the board lost an opportunity to gain local knowledge. Also, countless confused employees, customers and community leaders had to change their arrangements. But, above all, this change gave out the unintended message that the company was more American than European.

YOUR MANAGEMENT SHOULD BE TOUGH, BUT FAIR

As with all professionals, public relations people prefer to put their efforts where they will see success. The ability to shape reputation through public relations depends on getting the policies right. However, the public relations professionals should not be in constant battle with other managers to try to persuade them to undertake policies that they may believe are self-evidently in the best long-term interests of the public. Such efforts will prove exhausting and, sooner or later, lead to friction and a breakdown in the relationship.

Organizations that maintain a high profile in competitive markets usually have chief executives who take a personal interest in public relations strategy and the management of the function.

This hands-on approach can be even more important where the public expect stability and reliability. The chief executive should demand this of the public relations people. The rule is to expect a lot but do not expect them to jump through hoops. It is dispiriting and, ultimately, counterproductive to expect them to expend considerable energies in rectifying problems that might not have arisen if they had been involved in the decision at an earlier stage. Any decent professional will bear with management in resolving a problem; but if managers persistently ignore advice or, worse, do not even ask for it, then the enthusiasm will tend to fade after the second or third frustration.

Hap Wagner used to be chairman of Air Products & Chemicals Inc of the USA. In an earlier stage of his career, he came over from California to run the European operations of Air Products. Many of those on his team were a little nervous. He was young, and this was his first major management job – the first time he had ever worked outside California. Some felt they could take advantage of his lack of knowledge. Inexperienced he may have been, but naive he was not.

A typically pushy public relations person, I was through his door before he hardly got his feet under the desk, with a report on communications activity plus a presentation of the activities of my department. Politely (and patiently) he allowed me to run through my high-speed, whistle-stop tour around the company's public relations achievements and the amazing results that I claimed to be producing. When I had finished, he asked some perceptive questions and, sensing that the interviewing was coming to a close, I said to him, 'Well, now we've got that out of the way, I can forget that and get on with the job.'

'Not so,' said Hap, smiling. 'I expect you will be presenting your credentials, in one way or another, every day. We are all of us only as good as our achievements each day. It is true we work together as a team but we also challenge each other to achieve more and to set even higher standards. Whatever you may have done, you will not be able to rest on your laurels.'

I think that is a reasonably accurate recall of what he said, though it was not my laurels that he suspected I might be wanting to rest on. He was right.

He and members of his management team did challenge his public relations team. We produced some of our best ever work as a result of this. However, he was always a sympathetic, positive, enthusiastic as well as a demanding boss. I never felt I was fighting against him but, rather, fighting for him.

As most chief executives appreciate, good public relations people are very rare. Good writers there are aplenty. Good journalists (in or out of journalism) there are aplenty. Polished public relations salespeople, there are aplenty. Strategic advisers who want to philosophize (and do no work) there are aplenty. But the public relations professional that can be trusted for analytical skills, wisdom, judgement, solid advice and, very importantly, the practical follow-through are few and far between. They should be sought out, cherished... and challenged.

The personality mix can be important. Managing public relations sounds as if it ought to be easy, suggests Richard Carrick, chief executive officer of the leisure group of leading travel company, Airtours. 'It can backfire, for it is an art that cannot be entirely taught. Success will owe much to the personality of the public relations person.'

Whether you need your experts to work on your staff or to advise you through consultancy roles depends on the situation. It is probably less important whether they are in-house or not than whether they can win your confidence and deliver. Above all, can they tell you not only what you want to hear but, sometimes, what you need to hear... *and may not actually want to hear?*

Ensure the reputation manager is on the inside

Whatever other decisions may be taken, make sure that the senior manager of the public relations function is close at hand. Communications issues affect most company decisions and the chief executive will need regular public relations input. This will not happen if the public relations executive has to be 'called in' from some distant office.

Where this is the case, public relations becomes a publicity activity and not a strategic management function. Some time after the Hap Wagner experience, I turned down the position of public relations head of Air Products in the USA when I was head of the department in Europe. The main reason was that I found, on a visit to discuss the offer, that the public relations office in the US company was not even 'down the corridor' from the chief executive, but a half-mile drive away across the headquarters' campus in Pennsylvania. This told me more about the status and relevance of public relations, at that time, than the salary or any other factor.

Perhaps I could have taken the job and changed the attitude? Imagine a scene inside the executive suite, something like this:

'Hello Roger, what are you doing here?'
'Just hanging around in case any of you senior executives want to make a decision that has public relations implications.'
'I wouldn't waste your time. Don't worry, we'll give you a call when we need you – when we decide we need your input.'

BUY THE BEST PERSON YOU CAN AFFORD

Once an organization has established that it wishes to control the factors that shape reputation, then it has a public relations need. There may be a number of options on how this can be covered. The three main methods are:

- the nomination and training of an existing executive;
- the appointment of professional public relations staff;
- the appointment of a consultancy.

Sometimes the ideal solution may involve a combination of more than one of these three options.

A factor in deciding which route to pursue will be the level of commitment to public relations that the organization will need. A company operating in a competitive market, or under public scrutiny, possibly operating in a sensitive area, will find intensive public relations absolutely fundamental to trading success. Therefore, it is likely to have to use skilled, professional executives – whether staff or consultancy or a mixture of both.

Appoint a proven professional

Where the decision has been taken to put a professional public relations person on to the staff, the best option must be to appoint someone with proven capabilities – and in public relations, not in marketing, advertising or media. These may seem closely related but are actually distinct disciplines.

Mistakes in the public relations arena are regularly made by companies that choose to put a non-public relations person into the public relations slot.

Often this will be a journalist or media personality. Both will have some of the necessary skills to be a practical public relations tactician. Neither are likely to have the analytical or broader capabilities to be strategists. Both are likely to fail. The safer bet some companies feel is to move a loyal company servant into the role. This can be equally risky.

Imagine another *not-a-million-miles-from-reality* scenario. Bob has been a marvellous company servant for years. He knows the company inside out. He ran sales, later managed the national contracts office, set up the Australian subsidiary, won his seat on the board. The problem is, he has run out of steam and he can't go any higher.

> 'I know what,' cries the chairman. 'Bob can add up a bit. We'll make him financial director!'

Unlikely? I hope so. Why, then, are so many key company public relations jobs filled by people who do not have the skills and qualifications? Can public relations be left to enthusiastic amateurs, any more than finance or marketing could? It is daft... and dangerous. Bob is unlikely to become finance director, but there is a much better chance that he will be offered public relations – where his undoubted but irrelevant talents and hurt pride become a recipe for disaster.

In some of these companies Bob will have a professional reporting to him – nearly always because Bob has been imposed on this unhappy individual and seldom because he or she was recruited to work for Bob.

Surely that professional can give him the right input?

But when the chairman is discussing plant relocations, acquisitions, analyst briefings with the head of public relations (Bob), where is the professional? Will Bob resist giving instant advice or making his comment?

'Sorry, chairman, I need to talk to the professional before I give you an authoritative view.'

Not likely. So he gives the advice and the professional is saddled with working out a situation that could be already disastrously heading in the wrong direction.

'My view, chairman, is that if we keep quiet, there is little chance that anyone important will ever find out about that leak we had.'

Soon the professional gets frustrated and looks for a better job. And once he or she has gone, there is no one to understudy Bob discreetly, so he can go on making bigger and more damaging mistakes. And if you do not believe me ask the chairmen of xxxx or xxxx – or, I should say, the ex-chairmen.

As noted earlier, another less than intelligent option that some companies favour is to appoint a credible figure from within the media to the public relations position. That seems to make sense. That person will know the ladies and gentlemen of the media, and how they work.

But will he or she know public relations? And might not some former media contacts resent that person changing sides? In any case, what are a journalist's capabilities in strategic advice, or marketing? How proficient will he or she be at issues analysis, presentation training, planning, budgeting, managing, controlling resources, the consultancy and the research company?

These are not skills that are normally required by many journalists. So the newcomer may be credible in the media but unless and until someone offers training in the essential skills (also assuming he or she has the right aptitudes), then that person will not be credible in public relations. Who is going to do the training? Where is that individual to turn if, because of a prior media profile, he or she has been appointed to the top job and cannot afford to appear not to know what to do? Success in the media is no guarantee of competence in public relations.

As an example, Shaun Woodward was an intelligent and professional journalist. But from his position as an editor on *That's Life* he was recruited into the top job at the Conservative Central Office. He worked hard and effectively – but the fact that top television journalists considered him too young and not senior enough, while newspaper journalists resented anyone from television briefing them, made his position impossible. Eventually, he failed in the role, as was inevitable. Later, for reasons that may be related, he defected to the Labour party and, eventually, won a seat.

Why take the risk of putting an amateur into such a demanding role? Appoint a professional; appoint the best man or woman you can find and can afford. Someone moving over from the media should go into a subordinate role for a significant period – both to acquire the special skills and to avoid being a primary adviser before gaining the necessary experience.

Equally problematic, a seriously limited role for public relations also tends to be shown in those organizations where the function is defined by giving the executives such titles as press officer or, even more restricting, information officer. Clearly, a press officer is responsible for only part of a broad public relations function: press relations, however efficiently operated, can only be part of public relations.

Of course, many organizations have to rely on part-time or untrained assistance in public relations, because of the limits on their budget. This may be the case with voluntary groups, churches, schools, small charities, local arts societies and so on. However, even in such cases, there is usually a public relations professional within the group or community who will have an interest in the particular cause and who may be persuaded to lend his or her expertise in a voluntary capacity. Similarly, many consultancies will accept a 'good cause' client, often on a cost-only basis.

The least satisfactory option for handling public relations is to allocate the responsibility to a non-specialist executive. A limited budget is not always a legitimate reason for not tackling public relations properly. Sometimes, the reason why the budget is not available is that decision-makers do not rate the public relations function highly enough.

If the management does not need a significant public relations resource, then this may be acceptable. However, the contention that it cannot afford a proper resource is often questionable. Effective public relations, ultimately, costs no more than ineffective public relations; the returns from an investment in public relations are usually so significant that a company has to be spending a very substantial amount before it reaches the point of diminishing returns.

Identify the best candidate for the job

If a non-specialist executive has to be used to handle the public relations function, make sure that the candidate has the right temperament, the right commitment, the right brief and the right training.

- *Temperament* The candidate must be articulate, responsive, energetic and have plenty of initiative. Courage is one of the essential qualities; the practitioner will frequently have to make bold decisions and must be able to stand by them, sometimes even against management opposition.
- *Commitment* The nominated executive should be someone who is open, direct, prepared to put in the necessary effort, a believer in good communications, and must also support the aims of the organization. He or she will need to put time into asking, listening and analysing *before* making plans.
- *Brief* The writing of objectives is, perhaps, even more important where the public relations is being handled by non-professionals. Performance measures will be critical. The candidate must report in at the highest possible level and should not have to combine public relations with other responsibilities.
- *Training* The level of skill may not be the most important factor. The candidate must have the right attitudes and motivation, plus normal writing and language skills. He or she will need practical, operational training either in-house or through specialist external courses.

Buy a consultancy to meet the needs you identify

Consultancies can offer a range of expertise, with some offering special capabilities in the management of reputation. The company can choose the consultancy to suit the identified needs. The best way to handle the public relations activity may not be either staff personnel or a consultancy; it may be a combination of these resources.

Whether you decide to undertake the selection process yourself or rely on a trusted senior colleague, it is essential to follow a consistent procedure. The appointment needs to be right, for much will depend on it. Ideally, both sides will need to invest heavily and will be looking for a long-term relationship.

Above all, following a procedure reduces the likelihood of being influenced by attractive but irrelevant aspects that can affect the best of judgements.

A subsidiary of the Swedish giant Electrolux once asked me to select a market research company to conduct the programme of evaluation across Europe that I had recommended. We all agreed that this research should be run from the UK and I undertook the preliminary evaluations to a procedure very similar to the one noted below. We issued a brief to 12 candidate agencies and formed a shortlist of 3 from these responses.

The managing director at the time, Ulf Ahman, and his marketing director joined me for the final presentations by the three shortlisted companies. All were excellent, but it was clear to me which was the best and most appropriate to the client's needs.

The Swedes have their own special way of handling situations and they informed me that they were not too certain which company was most suitable. As I began to offer advice, Ulf started to discuss the terrible quality of coffee we seemed to accept in the UK. They agreed that the company that had served the best coffee was the one they wanted to work with – which, fortunately, happened to be the best agency, in my view. I sometimes wonder if I would have been able to persuade them to make the right choice (regardless of the coffee quality) if their 'selection' had been different! This was an unexpected selection method and, though it worked, it is not one to be recommended.

Public relations consultancies range from one-person outfits to international organizations with officers across dozens of business capitals. Happily, I chaired one such body myself with 120 offices.

The first decision is to determine the resources required; for example:

1. Do you need special experience of your industry?
2. Do you require national or international representation?
3. Do you need specialization, eg in parliamentary, industrial, environmental areas, or general public relations?
4. Do you want advice or advice *and* implementation, with or without an internal public relations operation?

THE SELECTION PROCESS

Produce a list of public relations consultancies with reputation experience which appear to be able to offer the services required. To produce a shortlist you may:

- talk to companies whose work you admire;
- ask editors which consultancies offer an effective service;
- talk to relevant professional communications bodies;
- check websites, registers and directories.

Time and money will be spent by both your organization and the consultancies before the final choice is made. Therefore, it is advisable to reduce your long list of possible consultancies to perhaps half a dozen before approaching them. Eventually you will want no more than three to make presentations.

Look at their existing clients lists. In Britain, these might be published in *PR Week*, the *PRCA Year Book*, *Hollis* or *Advertisers' Annual*. Check on the ownership of your prospective public relations advisers. It may be to your advantage (or disadvantage) if they are members of an international group, or subsidiaries of an advertising agency. It may be important to know whether the directors have been in business for 2 or 20 years, or whether the consultancy has 2 or 20 directors. You may also be able to eliminate one or two from your shortlist at this stage.

Put the first enquiry in writing

Approach the prospective consultancies. Adopt a consistent approach – with the first contact in writing. Give the consultancies the basics of the business sectors where you anticipate needing support. This preliminary introduction should invite each consultancy to reply, in confidence, with written details of its relevant expertise and services. Explain that the selection process must not be discussed with any third party.

You should ruthlessly eliminate all those whose letters or e-mails are not of an acceptable business standard. (If they cannot project themselves, they will hardly be able to project your organization.) Do not eliminate those whose experience or skills do not appear to match your needs, as this may not be a fair test at this stage.

From the responses, you will have perhaps two or, as suggested, the maximum of three consultancies you would wish to invite for further discussions. Suggest a date for a meeting and clarify your requirements, giving every consultancy the same information and the same opportunity. However, if one asks more perceptive questions, then this could be a critical factor. There is no need to provide this extra information to the others who are less enquiring.

With one prospective client, a small consultancy with special expertise spent days in research, including time on the road with the salesforce. From this, they revised the client's broad brief and produced a substantial and closer-focused document. They were astonished when the client gave copies of this to their competitors, all of whom realized they had been on the wrong track. Perhaps because of this embarrassment, the client appointed an international competitor with a name, but to whom the business was less critical – another nice name on the client list. Sadly, this consultancy was going through an unstable time and badly let them down within six months. The consultancy that had undertaken the substantial groundwork might reasonably have expected this to be a factor in the selection process.

So, what procedure should the client executive follow at the preliminary interview to be sure you are setting the correct course for the ultimate right choice? The interview should be conducted as seriously as any personal job interview. An appraisal form where you can note responses is helpful when it comes to comparing the strength of the cases presented to you. Avoid any lunch or drinks appointments unless you extend the same opportunity to every contender.

At the next stage, your selection team will visit the premises of the candidates – assuming that this preliminary interview will have eliminated one or two of your prospect consultancies. Give the consultancies you wish to visit a brief on what you wish to achieve – for example, meeting the team, assessing their facilities, looking at reputation, work for other clients and so on. Advise them of those members of your organization who will be attending this meeting. Again, only accept a meeting running over lunch or dinner if this opportunity is given to each public relations company.

Appraise the consultancy's home environment

If you have given the shortlisted consultancies a fair brief then you will be able to assess their response by direct comparison. Factors to be considered might include:

- their research into your organization;
- the physical resources available;
- the expertise of the team offered;
- the success of other client campaigns;
- their industry affiliations/credibility;

- their knowledge of your sector;
- their appreciation of key issues;
- their investigation of your claims;
- their understanding of your aims;
- their empathy/compatibility;
- the relevance of their observations;
- the way they set objectives;
- how they measure performance.

Do not expect the consultancy to present a programme to your team or field a particular account executive. It is more important to decide whether they have the skills to contribute to your organization's public relations aims than to be too concerned with details of staffing. Ideally, by now your shortlist should be down to two. Write to the consultancies you have visited. Those you have eliminated should be informed and politely told why. You should now be able to give the remaining consultancies a written brief expanding your aims. You should also clarify to whom they would report, when and how.

Ask for recommendations, not proposals

Those you have selected for further discussion should be invited to write a report on how they believe they could assist your organization in the management of its reputation. It is also fair to explain to them the position of your selection: 'You are now in our last three consultancies under consideration.'

Do not expect full proposals. These take considerable time to prepare and require a deeper knowledge of your organization than would be reasonable to expect at this stage.

Give each consultancy an opportunity to revisit your offices with the executives they wish to put on your account. Keep your own team constant.

Ask each consultancy to discuss their report and any recommendations they may have. Points to discuss should include creativity of their work, suitability of the executive, the back-up team, ancillary services (print, design, house journals, exhibitions, media monitoring, for example), calibre and reputation of existing clients, the reporting and control procedures, fee structure.

Ask for budget recommendations

Relate your company size and needs to their size. It may not be ideal for you to be either their largest or smallest client. If you are too big they may become nervous of jeopardizing the business and soft-pedal on their advice; equally, you may become wary of moving the account, if they do not perform, for fear of creating redundancies. Conversely, if your account is too small you may not get the level of service you wish – or feel able to assert authority when necessary.

Three main methods of fee charging are followed by most consultancies. All are based on hourly or daily charges for executive time. The most popular method of calculating fees is on a fixed monthly retainer (representing y hours at x per hour). The other common methods are fees billed monthly according to hours (or days); and a basic fee charged for an agreed programme plus increments for additional work.

Additional projects or costs above an agreed level should normally be quoted and approved in advance of commissioning. Consultancies also tackle projects on an ad hoc basis where they quote for an identified activity. This tends to be expensive and the least satisfactory way to build relationships between consultancy and staff personnel. It can be helpful, however, to support staff public relations departments at times of particular need for additional personnel or when special expertise is needed.

Do not judge solely on the hourly rate; an average executive at x may be a poorer buy than a senior man at $2 \times x$. Alternatively, you may not want $2 \times x$ an hour charges for writing a simple appointment story.

Ask the consultancies to prepare a budget or give recommendations on the breakdown of your own suggested budget. This may cover fee, operating costs, communications or issues audits, media conferences, presentation/interview training, print, photography and any other items that will involve significant work and expenditure.

Avoid an open-ended fee system and agree a level of expenditure you would allow without prior consultation. Clarify how you expect their invoices to relate to the activity reporting procedure. Where you are comfortable, it is best to accept their established processes rather than impose your own ideas.

Check the consultancy relations record

You should talk to their clients. Ask each consultancy to give you three or four senior client executives with whom you can discuss their public relations service. Talk to key journalists or members of other key audiences to check their experience of your preferred consultancies.

Should you need more detailed proposals, then agree some nominal fee with your final shortlist of consultancies. This will also help to avoid problems should more than one candidate consultancy suggest similar ideas; the fee can be negotiated to cover such an eventuality. If they want confirmation of your budget and the names of their competitor consultancies, at this stage both are fair requests which should be answered.

Finally, make your decision. Write to the chosen consultancy and ask them to attend a final meeting to confirm working arrangements and financial matters. At this stage, you could agree a fee for a limited period, say three months, to enable them to prepare full recommendations. Alternatively, you could pay them to prepare full proposals and costings; or you can agree an estimate of the workload for the first year, perhaps with an option to review at six months.

Some consultancies will offer a contract rather than simply letters of agreement. Check these carefully. Write to the unsuccessful consultancies, thanking them for their efforts and explaining the reasons for your choice. The PRCA has developed a sample contract.

BEGIN WITH A COOPERATIVE TEAM SPIRIT

Part of the skill in getting the maximum from the client/consultancy relationship is for the director responsible to manage this, as they say, firmly but fairly.

Some organizations talk about their consultancy as if they were in opposition – and not a vital part of their resource to help them succeed in a tough, competitive world. Equally, some consultancies talk about their clients as if the relationship was a constant battle of wits. And, perhaps, if that is their attitude, it is!

Here are a few suggestions for both consultancy staff and clients on how to get the best out of the cooperation. Both parties usually have a team, but, nonetheless, the relationship *does* depend on goodwill and understanding between individuals:

1. *Let your consultant act as a consultant.* Listen to advice; the consultant has expertise. Always try to tell your consultant what might be happening *before* it happens. He or she will appreciate having an input into the policy-making. Also create opportunities in which the consultant's views can be presented.

2. *Play fair and keep to the rules.* It is supposed to be a partnership, so treat your consultant as a colleague and not as a disposable 'supplier'. Hold regular meetings and supply copies of all relevant reports and documents. Remember to invite them into key meetings such as sales conferences, marketing reviews and brainstormers.

3. *Praise and criticize first-hand – and with equal candour.* If the consultant does a good job, have the sense to acknowledge that, preferably in writing. Such a letter gets circulated within the consultancy, pinned on notice boards and mentioned at internal meetings. All the best people in the consultancy will want to work on an account where the client is appreciative. Equally, if you have a criticism, make it plain, direct to the senior consultancy executive and verbal.

4. *Allow creative scope and a fair deal.* Allow your consultant the scope for creativity. You should ask him or her to solve problems and take advantage of opportunities, not simply to handle communications activity you have already decided. Otherwise you might as well do it yourself.

5. *Keep it worthwhile.* Make sure your account is profitable to the consultancy. Enter a long-term relationship so that both sides can develop the activity. Expect value for money but do not expect miracles for pennies.

Reputation is a vital element in building professional relationships

Organizations must plan reputation management, says Denplan

A decent person may earn a good reputation simply through behaving well. But with a corporation's reputation potentially influenced and shaped by many people within and without the organization, such a process may not be wise for the corporate reputation. And where the reputation is a central element in building and maintaining relationships, a more structured approach to winning the reputation that management feels the organization deserves is essential, believes Stephen Gates, managing director of Denplan.

His company offers the dental profession services that allow dentists to plan their workloads, the quality of service they are able to offer to their patients and the continuity of their income. A major benefit to the professionals is that the schemes allow the dentist to spend the time that is necessary with each patient – and, therefore the dentist can focus on advice and preventive care, not just invasive remedial treatments.

The company was originally formed in the UK by dentists for dentists, and has since grown to become a major force in the profession, holding close to 90 per cent of an open competitive market. This means developing and maintaining relationships with the 6000-plus dentists using the Denplan approach, as well as those practices that will continue to sign on to build the company growth.

The current roster of dentists is around a third of those practising in the UK. Gates claims this means that over 1.3 million dental patients on their registers are able to budget the costs of their dental care – and be confident they will get best advice, prompt attention when required and a global accident and emergency service. The costings to the patient are typically the equivalent of a daily newspaper; the only extras that most patients will face are laboratory costs for any crowns, bridges or similar work. Even there, the time of the dentist in specifying, checking and fitting these is fully covered.

The quality of service levels will be judged by the customers

Steve Gates believes that a good reputation is not a helpful option; it is essential to building professional relationships. Also, he feels, no sensible company can rely on chance, and it must have in place policies that ensure everything the organization does will enhance that precious reputation.

'If dozens, hundreds, even thousands of people are involved in running a company and delivering service to the customers, you need to be sure they buy into the values and reflect these in everything that they do,' he explains. 'In our case – and it is true of many businesses – our customers have their own professional reputations to maintain and they will only deal with those that they trust. Word of mouth across the dental profession is immensely powerful. One measure of how effective we are in delivering a reliable service at all times is what our clients say to each other… not just when with us, but when we are not there. Our research has also shown us the important part that peer comments play in our signing up new practices to our service.'

In dentistry, and indeed most areas of business, practitioners meet socially as well as through their trade, regulatory, business and professional bodies. Nothing is more impressive than a recommendation from someone who has enjoyed a good and lasting experience with a company wishing to expand its operations in their sector.

Denplan knows that to hold the confidence of the dental profession, it must understand current dentistry issues and have empathy with those in practice management. Gates believes that a consistent and honest approach is vital.

'We involve our clients in all the changes that a progressive company will consider it needs to make to keep its service up to date and relevant,' he comments. 'If we get something wrong, which we clearly try to avoid, it is always critical to put it right and to be open about how it happened and what we have done to avoid any such future occurrences.'

Good relations help in the process of change

An example of this level of client involvement is the introduction of new services. As an illustration, Denplan believed there was a market need for a cosmetic dental service that would move the service beyond the area of regular oral health and care. In all cases, the company plans all its developments with great care and uses research to test concepts.

'At the very earliest stages we involved dentists in our planning so we could get their views and make sure any new product we might introduce would be right and would be accepted,' Gates observes. 'We designed the concept and developed the brand "Denplan Enhance" with the input of our clients, and then ran a test with over 70 key dentists, before rolling it out. We needed to check how it might work in practice, how it would fit into their portfolio of services and how patients might respond to the new offer.'

This approach of keeping close to clients and involving them in planning works is vital, he argues. Indeed, it is confirmed by the fact that far bigger companies with much larger budgets have either entered (or tried to enter) the market without any serious impact on the relationships and the retention levels that Denplan has earned with dentists within its schemes.

Set policies for managing reputation

In summary, Steve Gates believes that the management of reputation must be part of company strategy. Companies should engage closely with their clients or customers; keep in touch with their needs and expectations; check their perceptions; and measure their satisfaction with the services that are actually being delivered. He recalls the wise advice that companies that were good in their time have sometimes failed because they concentrated on how good they were – and not how much better they could become.

Gates has advice for managers trying to build an operation where customer relations and reputation matter:

> Look 'em in the eyes. Understand and experience the taste and the smell of the market. Keep your management hands-on, open and close to all your colleagues. Never allow management ivory towers to be built. Make sure your internal communications are effective, constant and honest. Your team must be able to say what they want to say, not just what you want to hear. They must buy into and own the vision. If the company 'god' is cost cutting or shaving off the quality, these attitudes permeate across the organization. But, if top management worships customer care, then everyone in the team knows that this is what makes the company excellent, and they will support and create better service initiatives.

This case study is based upon the work the author undertook under contract as part of the advisory professionals that leading marketing communications agency Fox Murphy put together to advise Denplan, and is reproduced through the kind permission of the public relations team of Denplan, led by Brian Davenport.

SOME OBSERVATIONS, IN SUMMARY

1. The starting point for managing reputation is to agree what public relations must achieve in support of corporate and commercial objectives.
2. Public relations policy should be developed by the professionals but, before the programme is commissioned, this must be endorsed by the board.
3. Involve the head of each major company division and business function in the planning process, for example, by asking for reactions to the brief.
4. Coordinate objectives across all disciplines, particularly where different communications activities need to be targeted at different audiences.
5. Use formal or informal research, appropriate to the needs, to identify clearly where the organization stands at present.
6. Use an issues audit to ensure the minimum risk of crises disrupting operations and to win the maximum benefit from opportunities.
7. Ensure that the strategy and the programme are in a detailed report and that a summary of this is presented to the board.
8. The implementation and development of the action plan should be undertaken by the professionals but it must support the corporate aims, as defined by the chairman or chief executive.
9. Ensure that all external agencies and consultancies with company knowledge and special expertise are involved in the development of the plan.
10. Relate the budget to the importance of the work and the value of the expected results, and not to any historical allocation.
11. To develop the strategy and run the programme, the public relations professional leading the team needs open access to the board.
12. To gain the best from the programme, do not change the objectives in mid-stream and try to keep stable all those factors that you can control.

13. Make *all* information activities part of the broader public relations plan, and all campaigns part of the broader, long-term programme.
14. When you ask for advice, be prepared to listen and take action – and expect advice even when you have not asked for it!
15. Do not judge on your own what may have public relations implications but ensure that your adviser is aware of all decisions so that the best advice can be offered.
16. If you use staff personnel, make sure that someone has been given overall responsibility and is readily accessible – ideally in the next office.
17. Appoint the best person you can afford and avoid someone from an allied discipline unless you are sure you have the training resources necessary.
18. When selecting your top executive, be certain that your choice will be acceptable to those with whom he or she will have to deal – your colleagues, the media and other key audiences.
19. If you decide to use a consultancy, select one according to an agreed plan.
20. Try to keep the same selection team throughout and keep all stages consistent for all candidate consultancies.
21. Remember that, inevitably, selection is an artificial, arm's length process, so choose the team you can work with... not the programme.
22. As you can easily change the suggested activity but not the people, it is wiser at the early stages to ask for recommendations and not a definitive proposal.
23. The least satisfactory selection criterion is price, so state your thoughts on the proposed budget and do not expect the consultancy to guess.
24. Whether you appoint in-house staff or consultancy personnel or both, you will get the best from them if you treat them as team members and colleagues.

4

Objectives

*Plan public relations that will achieve
real advances in reputation*

Key factors discussed

- Agreeing the aims of the programme.
- Converting these to objectives.
- Using objectives to set the budget.
- Setting the measurement criteria.
- Encouraging open discussion.
- Evaluating evidence and intelligence.
- Applying creativity to the activity.
- Building plans on research.

SETTING OBJECTIVES

As noted, all corporate, brand, marketing and other company activities will shape its reputation. If management has agreed that the public relations director should be charged with the responsibility of managing reputation, he or she will need to monitor and advise on all activities. The aims of the reputation, management strategies and the allied public relations need to be linked.

Setting objectives can ensure that the public relations activity is under control. The bigger the organization, potentially the further the directors are from the sharp end – customers, shop-floor employees, new recruits, individual investors and so on. One of the helpful side-benefits of setting and approving the corporate public relations objectives is that the communications specialists, when presenting their recommendations to the board, must demonstrate where the company stands at present.

Many programmes set out *aims* even if they are called objectives. Such aims are better than no targets but should be used as starting points to develop something more focused.

An objective is a point to reach, not just a direction in which to head. This cannot begin to be defined unless it is quite clear where the organization stands at present. Indeed, an analysis of the current position relative to all stakeholders is essential. From this information, the objectives can be drafted related to improving relationships with all the publics the organization depends on for success. Directors must be as close as possible to the thinking of the respective publics with whom they are expected to manage relations.

In his introduction to *The Company Chairman* by Sir Adrian Cadbury, one-time chairman of ICI Sir John Harvey-Jones said:

> While the responsibilities of the chairman do not alter, the role varies with the changing social, economic and political environments in which we operate. Moreover, it behoves the chairman not only to be aware of the massive changes occurring in his own company and his own country but also those in many other parts of the world. There is no company that is immune to the changes which are occurring all around us.

Objectives can help decide the budget

The allocation of the appropriate level of resource to reputation management and, later, the calculation of the cost-effectiveness of supporting public relations can only be certain if meaningful objectives are agreed. Some measures of the public relations programme are simple to quantify if these original objectives have been well drafted.

As detailed in Chapter 5, these objectives can help in the calculation of a realistic budget and supporting resources. Clearly, the drafting of the objectives must be related to the methods that are proposed to measure effectiveness.

If it cannot be measured, how can you tell if it is worth doing? Or how much should you spend to achieve the result? Too few public relations programmes have such specific objectives. Many have some vague aims. Consequently, comments on performance have little validity as they cannot be related to any target levels that should have been set before the activity was approved by the board.

Setting specific performance measures

Subjective judgements of performance are no real measure. Differences of opinion on the effectiveness of the programme prove one of the biggest areas of complaint, research confirms, when relationships break down between consultant and client. This was quoted by 60 per cent of consultants and 70 per cent of clients questioned about areas of disappointment, according to an informal study carried out by Issues Managers, my independent communications audit consultancy.

It is not unreasonable to imagine that the same confusion might apply where problems arise in the area of relationships between in-house professionals and chief executives within companies.

Anecdotal evidence confirms many cases of senior public relations people being puzzled to find resources cut back by managements for whom they felt they were running effective programmes. Interestingly, in the study, some 70 per cent of the consultancy programmes where such problems had arisen had no agreed measures of performance.

Disagreement over levels of performance should not create problems. If the targeted level has been defined, these can be discussed and resolved.

The managing director of one consultancy was surprised to get notice from a company where he had handled two plant closures, one product recall and the firing of the marketing director – all with minimal negative media comment. On asking the reason for cancelling the contract, the client's chairman said he had expected to be quoted more often. 'Once a week or so in the *Financial Times* or *Wall Street Journal* with some good story would have been reasonable.'

The wishes of the chairman may have been ambitious, even for a company going places, but for one in crisis they were unrealistic. However, whether it was reasonable or not, they had the conversation after the problem, not before. Coverage in senior business media had never been identified as a requirement of the activity.

Public relations professionals (in-house or consultancy) may admit in private that they feel safer without the exposure of measurable objectives. Clients may think they are not necessary or are not prepared to pay the small budget percentage to appraise performance. Both are wrong.

There are four simple steps:

- Agree what is to be achieved.
- Plan a programme to achieve this.
- Run it, with any fine-tuning that may be necessary.
- Measure the effectiveness of the efforts.

The best objectives will set targets to be met relating to such factors as audiences, messages delivered, awareness developed, opinions changed, goodwill built, reputation enhanced, action taken by these publics and so on. *PR Week* has suggested that 10 per cent of the budget is a sensible figure to allocate to research and performance evaluation. But remember that, initially, any measure, however simple, is better than none as long as both sides agree to it. You can refine and develop the criteria in each succeeding year.

Build on specific targets, not assumptions

It is easy to waste money on communications. Some organizations run major campaigns based on assumptions about the perceptions of the target audiences. If these assumptions are wrong, then such efforts can be wasteful and, sometimes, even counterproductive.

Equally, some organizations do not coordinate all their communications effectively. One of Europe's largest banks, Barclays, found itself in trouble when its left hand did not appear to know what its right hand was doing. At the same time as it was detailing the newly approved customer-care policies, the company also announced the closure of many branches in rural areas where local communities saw the bank as a vital part of their life. Public relations is a lot more than information and news releases. Yet, even at this level, some companies manage to issue statements that could not have been designed better to make the organization look ridiculous. There are many journalists only too happy to point out the clash of policies to their readers, listeners and viewers.

Changing perceptions of a company in trouble

Some organizations, like Shell, do not seem to apply the lessons that should be learnt from problems; some observers feel this is because public relations, and therefore reputation management, are not truly corporate functions.

In some publicly quoted companies, the management thinking is that performance is all; certainly without a level of performance, problems can prove disastrous. Even with good trading results, operating problems do not help; yet to wise management, setbacks can provide opportunities to move forward. As an example, Barclays put in place serious processes to improve the company's corporate social responsibility (CSR) and associated initiatives. In the company annual report, Chris Lendrum, the bank's vice chairman, explained, 'We have fundamentally reviewed our CSR strategy against an agenda that is becoming more challenging and increasingly complex. With a clear mandate from the board, we have strengthened our determination that Barclays should be a leader in this field.'

As an illustration of the reality that real vision can only work if driven from the top, Lendrum says he has been charged with the responsibility of leading Barclay's efforts worldwide in pursuit of this goal. The company intends to embed CSR values into every aspect of decision-making, following the structure used by the Business in the Community Corporate Responsibility Index. This groups CSR activities under four main headings: marketplace, workplace, community and environment.

This has backed the bank's membership of both the Dow Jones Sustainability Index and FTSE4Good share listings. Additionally, the company received public recognition for its work on financial inclusion and for progressive human resources policies in areas such as employee pensions and diversity in the workplace.

Although reputation is managed from the top, equally the company will not win genuine support unless the initiatives are backed right across the staff. Barclays has developed policies that back over 20,000 employees in their volunteering and fundraising activities. The total investment in local communities in just one year amounted to over £32 million, making the Barclays Community Programme one of the largest of its kind in the UK. The scope of the company's programmes is spreading to match its global role. In Africa, for example, Barclays is regarded as a role model for the work among the disadvantaged, particularly in the field of HIV/AIDS prevention and support.

A key CSR priority, says the company, is to enhance trust and reputation. Setting up a brand and reputation group composed of the most senior business line executives not only confirms the link between these central business factors but suggests the company is serious in its intentions.

UNDERSTAND THE OTHER POINT OF VIEW

Experienced managers know the dangers of basing decisions only upon personal observation: we tend to see what we want to see, and hear what we want to hear. It is almost a truism, as an illustration, that every company thinks it is better known, better understood, better supported than it actually is. Keeping in touch is central to public relations and the chief executive may often have to accept that he or she is not closest to the key audiences.

As a general rule, the higher up the company executives move, the more remote they can get from many of the stakeholders. Often, managers of vision recognize this and set up procedures to ensure they get a full feedback of views. Others may prefer this isolation from the daily world of those who produce or buy their products.

The chairman of a large quoted company – now a shadow of its former self – was asked by a national press photographer to talk to a lathe operator during a board visit to its largest regional manufacturing site. Desperately searching for a topic of conversation, he remembered he was in the country and asked the bemused man: 'What's the hunting and shooting like round here?'

Fortunately, the journalists did not hear the reply above the machine-room noise – but the chairman did, and reddened. Later in private, he commented on worker hostility and their failure to appreciate their jobs. In touch? Understanding the other's point of view? Wise to trust subjective perspectives?

One-time cabinet minister Stephen Byers defended his press chief when she issued an e-mail to staff immediately after the terrorist attack in the United States in September 2001. She advised this was a good time to bury bad news. He described this as an isolated mistake but 94 per cent of a sample that the Public Relations Standards Council tested saw this as cynical and calculated manipulation, not an error of judgement.

Understanding the perceptions of your audience is critical

We have all experienced the impact of a speaker who understands – or does not understand – what his or her audience may believe. Consider two startling 'historic' examples, one a moment of glory and the other a moment of tragedy.

The funeral of Diana, Princess of Wales in 1997 was broadcast to a vast crowd assembled in a nearby park outside Westminster Abbey. The Earl Spencer was supposed to give a eulogy for his sister, but he chose emotional and bold words about her fraught relationship with the Royal Family, all the members of which were in the congregation. These powerful thoughts struck a chord with a sympathetic public. They had such an impact that, when he had finished, those assembled in the park began to applaud.

The television audience witnessed the extraordinary spectacle of the service halting as the sound of distant but thunderous applause drifted in from outside, an eerie echo to the earl's words. Of course, no one ever applauds in church, but even some of the great and the good were also so moved they very nearly joined in with the handful who wanted to acknowledge the validity of the earl's break with protocol.

At the other end of the human emotional scale, consider the horror of Romania as the cruel Communist regime of Nicolae Ceauşescu came to a belated close in December 1989. His excesses had grown over his 25-year reign to a point that would have been absurd had they not been so wicked. Yet he believed that his people loved him. As had often happened before, he gave a public speech to an assembled crowd, carefully selected and orchestrated by his security forces. Their role was to be loyal, supportive and enthusiastic for the vision and the gifts of their glorious leader. A demonstration of anything less by any courageous member of his audience could be fatal.

But on this fateful night, booing broke out at the back of the assembly, clearly audible to those at the front – and judging by his confusion, a sound that Ceauşescu clearly had never imagined he would hear. It grew and even swept across those in the front; they realized that if everyone expressed their true feelings for the oppressive dictator, no security forces could do anything about it. The floodgates were open, and he stumbled from the rostrum towards the ignoble end he might have expected, if he had known the real feelings of the Romanian public. Within a couple of days he and his wife had been tried and executed and the country was on its way to recovery.

CHOOSE YOUR WORDS CAREFULLY

Sensible reputation objectives will include some method of measuring feedback from important groups. All communications must be based on a two-way flow of information. A lack of knowledge of an issue among an important public should not be mistakenly interpreted as resistance. As noted earlier, you cannot be certain you will change opinion or influence attitude in the way you intend *unless* you know what these were in the first place.

Yet, many make assumptions about knowledge, opinion and attitude and do not put these assumptions to the test. At best, this might be a considerable waste of money; at worst, it may actually produce hostility in the audiences being wooed.

Even the language acceptable to the audiences you wish to influence can be a factor. For example, the owner of a large nursery garden in an attractive valley, lined with a handful of quality country homes on the edges of an English county town, decided to use part of his spare land to build a small development of expensive houses. He believed this would enhance the value of all properties in the valley and wrote to his neighbours telling them of his plans. He concluded that he felt sure that he would get their support.

His assumption was wrong.

While he was wise to write to them in advance, he should have done a little more homework. This could have helped him to put a more persuasive argument. To most of the readers of the letter the one word that stuck with them was 'estate'. That county town had been blighted, many felt, by 'estates' of housing and they wanted to see no more. Whatever he might have said after that, he had already lost their vote. The outcome was that the objection at planning stage was so strong that the project had to be abandoned.

If he had undertaken an investigation into their views, then he might have found a way of presenting his proposals that would have made an attractive scheme more acceptable.

An ill-chosen word can lose the argument

The Worldcom communications group partner in North Carolina, Epley Associates, uses a sophisticated computer-based response system for focus group research called Continuous Attitudinal Response Technology (CART). This allows selected representatives of any audience to show instant reactions to any promotional material being presented to them. Even the reaction to individual words can be analysed.

The company was asked to check one proposed television commercial for a new imported car. This was achieving very high acceptance scores with a target group of professional women – until the voice-over reached the phrase 'The ultimate driving experience'. Audience approval scoring instantly dropped drastically, never to recover.

Explains Epley Associates president, Michael Herman: 'Interviews with members of that audience showed that they consciously rejected that phrase as over-the-top. The ultimate driving experience for most people might be a Ferrari, a classic racing car or a vintage Rolls-Royce, not a popular sedan.' Their rejection of the remainder of the commercial followed because they felt that if the company could misunderstand that, then perhaps all the other claims were exaggerated. Once credibility is lost, it is almost impossible to regain.

A study of awareness of the logo of a major US insurance group failed to produce any intelligent result because so few could recognize the recently changed company name, including some 50 per cent of its existing clients! One German banking group was shocked to find that only 6 per cent of its customers across other markets recognized a logo that had been in use for 100 years.

Reputation may be vital but it can be lost (or destroyed) by one foolish or thoughtless action. Gerald Ratner, chief executive officer of the major jewellery group that bore his name, certainly was not thinking of his customers when he made cheap remarks about the 'crap' he sold; this was intended to win a laugh from his peers at an Institute of Directors' conference. He may have got his laugh but he lost any goodwill among his customers. Did he really despise those who controlled the future of his company through their spending decisions? Had he really lost such touch with 'the other half' that he could joyfully disparage his target market, those who could only afford a few pounds on a gift? In denigrating his product in such crude terms, he made it impossible for his brand, Ratner, ever to be respected again. His gift sales collapsed and soon after, so did his company.

Top directors may not need constant, day-to-day contact with, say, customers; but if this is so, then they should not be deciding the advertising, the store design or the packaging. These decisions need to be managed by professionals who can give sound, credible and confident advice. One certain rule for top executives is to be sure to appoint those with the courage to say what needs to be said.

Mike Beard, a distinguished past-president of the Institute of Public Relations, believes that every chairman and chief executive needs one or two senior staff people who will have the courage to give frank and fearless advice at any time and in any circumstance. He feels this advice can be most important when the top executive has lost touch with the feelings of, say, shareholders or the business market in which the company operates. On occasion, there may be speculation or rumour that could be potentially threatening and needs tackling. At these times, the need is for someone inside and, as he says, *onside* who is prepared to speak out.

Beard, through his earlier work as director of corporate communications for Taylor Woodrow, has many years' experience in top-level corporate advice. He argues that the corporate relations director must take this detached view; he or she probably also has the best internal and external grapevine of anyone in the organization. Get the personal chemistry right and that person will be uniquely equipped to handle sensitive and critical areas.

Indeed, this relationship of trust is essential if the board is to agree the correct objectives for the company public relations programme and to cope with contingencies that threaten to drive the organization *off strategy*. Management pays for advice; to get value, it must create the atmosphere in which honest and objective advice can be offered.

Consider the impact of your words

The more senior the executive, the more important it is that he or she retains the capability of understanding the other person's situation. The communications programme is not directed at the chairman, chief executive or other directors. This must be remembered when drafting objectives.

The managing director of a company making popular home computers objected to the inclusion of local radio on an advertising schedule, presented to her as part of an overall public relations programme for a new product launch. She told me she only ever listened to Radio Four during the week and Radio Three at the weekend. Radio One was bad enough but local radio was awful, she opined. The consultancy adviser resisted asking how she knew that if she never listened but went back to the objectives to remind her of the profile of prospective purchasers identified and agreed. Local radio would best reach these people; when reminded of the earlier discussion, and the thinking behind the decision, she agreed.

Without agreed objectives the consultancy client might have lost track. Indeed, in preparing objectives, a powerful client personality can push them off course if the advisers are not sufficiently confident or firm.

ENCOURAGE ADVICE YOU DO NOT WANT TO HEAR

Overpowering management may intimidate advisers into submission. Perhaps some advisers consider that there is more profit in being diplomatic to the point of compliance. The failure to agree objectives for public relations can also mean that different elements within the communications mix can be working to different agendas.

When Philips was struggling through yet another of its marketing crises, we were advisers to one of its business divisions. This was being merged with two others in allied sectors. It was an eminently sensible plan, which all fully endorsed. The company was going through a difficult phase but as it had excellent managers, fine products and a determined customer philosophy, the consultancy felt the company demanded our best possible support.

The public relations team could not, however, accept the proposed, euphoric, launch advertising; this, they felt, was naive and misleading. It suggested that all customers' electronic business problems could be solved by the new merged operation. They pointed out to the chief executive that three salesforces were still operating, not cooperating and, worse, competing. Each would exhaust the possibilities of selling their product lines, however poor the chance, before putting any business lead to another division where a more realistic sale might be likely. This problem needed tackling before such advertising could be run.

The marketing directors and advisers to the three divisions discussed this and related issues which lasted an exhausting morning. During this, one of the public relations advisers to another division said virtually nothing. After the meeting, his colleagues asked him why. 'There's no bonus in risking being wrong,' he explained. 'But we are paid to advise,' one objected. 'Wait and see,' he murmured. 'Will you benefit from disturbing the client?'

He was right. Later, part of the rationalization reduced the consultancies from three to two, then, one – and the diplomat retained his role as 'adviser'. It is no satisfaction to say that the directors who made that decision got the advice they deserved.

Public relations people will tell you that this is not a rare occurrence. Good advice can be right but it can be very unpopular. It takes good management to ask advice from a good public relations professional. Weak managements sometimes fire strong consultancies rather than face the issues.

Sir Michael Pickard, then chairman of the London Docklands Development Corporation, confirmed this point. Public relations is sometimes seen as a substitute for performance, he felt. Firing the public relations team is rarely the solution to a company's problems. It must be a team effort, working to clear objectives. The communicators and the executive team, working well together and closely with the chairman, will give you an outstanding success, he added. One without the other will underperform.

Of course, this need to cooperate within a framework of agreed aims is not peculiar to the public relations arena. Management should appoint, across all areas, only good advisers who have integrity, skill and vision. The management needs to be certain that the proffered advice is considered, independent, honest and presented with the best interests of the company at heart.

That is not always the case unless extreme care is taken in the selection of advisers.

The US chief executive of a group of European subsidiaries with major employee relations problems was getting his advice from a cynical and disillusioned human resources director; unknown to his boss, he was in the midst of a nasty divorce. He had not spoken to his son for two years and confessed to journalists that he hated the 'pathetic' workers.

Is this common? It may or may not be a truism that many personnel people don't like people. On the other hand, many teachers cannot stand children. Make sure you do not appoint a public relations adviser who does not like business or hates journalists; they exist! One highly qualified junior executive only left my team because 'she could not justify profit'. She joined an advertising agency!

LEARN HOW TO GET TRUE RESPONSES

Most people in senior positions underestimate the impact of their position on those with whom they work. They forget they have the power to hire and fire. They may see themselves as agreeable egalitarians yet forget that others may see them as ruthless or domineering.

When I was chairman of the Chartered Institute of Marketing and hosting a meeting of some of the most senior business leaders of many of the biggest businesses operating in the UK, leading industrialist Sir Alistair Grant, demolished a proposal with the comment, 'With the greatest respect – which means with absolutely no respect at all – this is complete nonsense.' I was about to respond in the same vein, when the president of the institute, Colin Marshall (now Lord Marshall), who was sitting beside me, wisely restrained me with the quiet, good-natured comment, 'Roger, do not respond. Let him finish.'

Of course, Sir Alistair was right and his comments needed to be said. My irritation was what I saw as a humiliation in the way it was said. For interest, later I checked this little incident with Sir Alistair. Had he appreciated the impact of his words? He commented: 'I was irritated by what I saw as a defeatist approach to a positive opportunity. Anyone could have responded to what I said in any way they liked, but I would not have much patience for anyone arguing something that should have been dropped.'

If I had responded equally as assertively to Sir Alistair, would I have won a small point but lost his support for our mission? As he is a generous, open person, then probably not; but such confrontations can easily escalate, and, of course, the skill is to ensure a good balance.

Try to listen as openly as you speak

If the chief executive truly wants to create an atmosphere in which colleagues can be outspoken, then he or she has to listen. Equally, those offering views or advice when the programme is being planned should not take advantage. All are equal, but the boss is the boss, and in that position he or she is more equal than the others!

One president of an international oil group regularly told his team: 'I'm a Texan. That means I'm blunt and say things as I see them.' Sadly, he did not hear things in the same way. His senior colleagues soon learnt what the boss found unacceptable. Those who cared about the company found this censorship impossible and were either fired for their 'independence' or moved on. Of course, he was soon surrounded by people in constant agreement; the company ran on the rocks, and he was eventually fired. What a tragic waste of all his talents. How sad that no one had the courage to tell him what he needed to do; build a cooperative team spirit; persuade him to listen as boldly as he spoke.

Again, in Brussels I was presenting a strategy and set of objectives for a proposed programme to a commissioner with a dozen of his team in the room. Discussing the proposed aims, I pointed out an important flaw in one of his assumptions, the result of some research that we had undertaken. He listened and accepted the point and later commented, mildly, that no one on his staff had made any observation about such a curious anomoly. He also failed to notice that none of his senior, experienced colleagues had made any comment of any sort during the whole of the presentation. They had learnt not to debate issues with commissioners. There had only been nods and words of approval at the end from them, but only once he had made it quite clear that he was happy with the proposition.

CHECK OBSERVATIONS AGAINST EVIDENCE

Good public relations is dependent on accurate intelligence. As noted earlier, it is impossible to change attitudes effectively unless the organization has identified what attitudes already exist. The views of senior executives may be helpful but rarely provide enough information on which to make decisions. In such cases, the only sound base should be research.

In Britain, it has been estimated that over 95 per cent of *The Times* top 1,000 companies regularly use research to find out more on subjects about which (it might be supposed) they already know enough. Such research is often aimed at understanding perceptions of key publics and how they have developed. But what factors create such perceptions, and how do they affect our reputation? Certainly directors use research mainly because they realize that while subjective views may be important, they do not always reflect the reality. Even where the research confirms the original views, it is still valid, as decisions about the corporate reputation can be made with greater confidence. As Epictus said; 'Perceptions are facts because people believe them.'

CREATIVITY REQUIRES DISCIPLINE

Public relations should be flexible, organic, responsible and creative if it is to help the organization develop the best reputation. It should be handled effectively by talented people – but the need for creativity must never be used as an excuse for a lack of discipline. It is essential that public relations is as well planned as any other activity of the organization. It must be working to agreed objectives that relate to a measurable change in reputation.

Though reputation is very specific, clear and tangible, it can be difficult to quantify. How good is a good reputation? Does the company have a good reputation in all areas – products, financial performance, environmental responsibility, overall quality of management, and so on? In reality, it is the value of the reputation that matters as well as whether it is improving or deteriorating.

Although it is difficult to measure, reputation is not impossible to quantify. The effort is worth it. A proper measure gives a benchmark against which to calculate the improvements achieved by the company activities, including reputation management initiatives.

Both formal and informal research methods can be used to establish this benchmark position. For example, a study could be run to identify the rating of the organization's reputation among those publics under investigation. Representatives of such publics could be interviewed to identify how they rated the organization in terms of its reputation. This might be on a scale from excellent through to poor – or might be classified by reputation in certain sectors from products to financial performance. For example, an analysis of the interview results will show the proportion of each of these key publics that rated the company reputation in each sector. This provides a very simple benchmark against which any changes in the reputation can be measured at the end of any period that the management chooses. From this, revised objectives can be developed for future years.

Alternatively, how such publics rate the organization's reputation in comparison with other organizations can be appraised. It can be helpful to check performance against competitors in the same sector and/or companies that are viewed as leaders in other industries.

Of course, in such studies, it is important to remember that what is being measured are perceptions, not realities. Any anomalies between the perceptions and the reality give a clear focus for management attention.

The setting of the objectives should be undertaken with a clear view of how any improvement will be measured. You can realistically set an objective to make a corporate presentation to x per cent of analysts that you have identified as important. This is easy to measure, simply by counting how many on your target list attended such presentations by the end of the year. However, an objective to get y per cent of these same analysts to rate the company as well managed in, say, its sector can be more difficult; it only has validity if you agree on what they would consider *well managed*. To do this you must set up some procedure to test how many have that view, at the start, and how many have been persuaded to that view over the period of the campaign. (See Chapter 5 on appraisal of public relations performance, which should be read in conjunction with these notes on setting objectives.)

AIMS AND OBJECTIVES ARE NOT THE SAME

In the draft plan, start with aims...

As briefly discussed earlier, it is important to differentiate between aims and objectives. Frequently in public relations these are used interchangeably. An aim is a direction in which progress is to be made. However, an objective is a *specific* point that is to be reached. Where possible, the public relations activity should be working to quantified objectives rather than broad aims, particularly in those initiatives aimed at shaping and projecting the reputation.

As an illustration, an aim for a corporate public relations programme could be to improve awareness of company community strategies; this would not be an objective, as it stands. This does not mean that it has no value. Aims may not always need to be refined into objectives; but this is likely to become necessary as the sophistication of the public relations activity develops, perhaps year on year.

A smaller company introducing a new product may be quite happy to have simple public relations aims. If, for example, there is no awareness of the brand in the marketplace then *any* effort that will increase the profile of the brand is likely to be of *some* value. It is also going to be relatively easy to see whether an improvement has been achieved. If at the beginning of the campaign no one is aware of the brand and at the end quite a number of people in the trade are talking about it; editorial enquiries are coming through; the product is being asked for at the point of purchase, and so on; then it is reasonable to conclude that some valuable improvement has been achieved.

... and move to objectives

On the other hand, how do you develop from that position? How do you assess the cost-effectiveness of the activity? How will you calculate how much you should improve in future? What budget will you allocate for what level of improvement?

In the second or subsequent years, the company is likely to find that its public relations is far more effective if it is working to objectives rather than aims. The essential factor in writing an objective is to put in elements that can be measured. These might not be a complete measure but must be something that would give some indication of satisfactory performance. As noted earlier, some firmly established base is necessary and this can best be set by formal or informal research.

If we continue with the brand reputation example, then it would require quantified research, before the campaign, to measure the level of awareness, and a similar study, at the end of the activity, to check the change. Such an awareness study would need to measure 'approval' or a similar quality related to reputation.

In practice, of course, this could be expensive and take a significant proportion of the total promotional budget. It could also be unnecessary: a fair indicator of the effectiveness of the public relations effort in meeting this objective often can be identified without going to the extent of a statistically validated answer.

A modest high street test may show that only 1 in 10 purchasers of a particular product could spontaneously mention your brand. The objective might be agreed to raise this to, say, 3 in 10 – or whatever seems necessary for the company to achieve the commercial targets it is setting. The advice of a professional researcher in putting together an acceptable measure for these objectives is necessary. However, the principles should be understood by those planning the campaign.

Obviously, care must be taken to eliminate any biasing factors. A well-known soft drink company once developed a disappointing campaign, based upon limited research carried out in the home town where their head office was located. They had forgotten that virtually everyone they were likely to interview would have a friend or relative who worked at the company. Public awareness was substantially higher than would have been the case in a city at the other side of the country.

Investigate the real problem

As well as personal interviews, this type of basic research can sometimes be undertaken through telephone interviews and post.

However, researchers will tell you that it is important to avoid assumptions. As an illustration, it is invaluable for a supplier to know which companies come first to mind when a buyer is looking for a particular product. One established way to evaluate this is to place a key question in the centre of a broader questionnaire and phrase the question along the lines of: 'Name five companies that manufacture this product from which you would consider requesting a quotation.' The answer to this question will not only indicate how many people are *aware* of the company in this market sector, but also how they rate it in comparison with competitors.

The importance of working to quantified objectives is that they can be used as the yardstick for measure at the end of each campaign to assess the success in performance. Where public relations is a new activity, it is sometimes acceptable for the initial aims to be expressed in terms of 'opportunities'. As mentioned earlier, these can be refined and developed into quantified objectives, step by step, over a period of years.

To quote an example, consider the aims for a public relations campaign specifically designed to support the marketing efforts of a manufacturer of home improvement products. Several key components of the company reputation had been identified. From these, aims had been developed, to:

1. project the professionalism of the company;
2. explain the company's fair-trading policies;
3. improve brand awareness at national and local levels;
4. attract high-calibre job applicants to the company;
5. promote a team spirit of customer care;
6. demonstrate the company's social responsibility.

These may be fine for year one of a campaign. Something more focused and measurable would be an improvement in year two.

Involve management in the objectives

The public relations professional presenting aims to the chief executive or the board should be expected to detail how management support for these will be obtained. Each aim should then be converted into an objective with some agreed measure that will give an indication of how it is being achieved.

Take the fourth aim above, related to recruitment. This might be converted into an objective by redrafting as, to:

4. raise the response to recruitment advertisements by 30 per cent over the year.

This may appear a little steep, presented so bluntly. Adding some element of strategy can make this more practical. For example, to:

4. raise the response to recruitment advertisements by 30 per cent over the year, through projecting to potential applicants the rewards and opportunities enjoyed by present personnel.

Or consider a more complex position. It may well be a *marketing* objective to increase distribution of the product from 20 per cent of retail outlets to 35 per cent. However, this would not be a fair *public relations* objective. Converting this commercial objective into public relations terms *is* practical, however. Depending on the industry, it might become, to:

1. raise awareness of our brand among trade buyers from A per cent to B per cent;
2. ensure that positive editorial coverage of our products is seen and noted by 55 per cent;
3. ensure that 45 per cent of potential stockists attend regional product presentations;
4. present the campaign video to 75 per cent of all potential retailers above a certain size; and
5. achieve a 60 per cent acceptance that the company is a credible and reputable organization.

Let us suppose that, in 1 above, the awareness levels to be improved at the trade level are among key retailers. If the objective is carefully crafted then, initially, the current levels can be assessed. Later, it will become possible to record the increase in the number of retail outlets where the awareness had been improved to some prior agreed level. An objective for the public relations along these lines might be, to:

1. raise awareness of our brand x among the managers of retail outlets, above y turnover or z shop size, from current 25 per cent to 35 per cent.

Before an integrated and comprehensive public relations programme can be developed, objectives have to be prepared relating to all key audiences, and not just to the area used in this example. These draft objectives must then be discussed across all operating divisions within the organization.

It is not sufficient for the head of human resources to approve objectives relating *only* to his or her personnel activities. If this were the case, it would be impossible to balance the proportion of the effort dedicated to personnel support with the other requirements of the programme. Therefore, it is important that the human resources chief is aware of the objectives that relate to production, finance, marketing and all the other aspects of the organization's activities – and, as regards cross-discipline understanding, vice versa.

Relate ethical aims to commercial objectives

It is advisable that the proposed objectives should be approved at a board meeting and endorsed at the very highest level by the chief executive officer of the company. This board approval might be necessary once a year, or whenever a major change in direction of the public relations activity is necessitated.

Part of the aim of getting public relations objectives endorsed at the senior level is to make all operating divisional directors or managers appreciate their own responsibilities in this area. Public relations must be seen to be closely related to the realities of commercial life – public relations can improve the calibre of recruits, help to reduce absenteeism, support the share price, see the company through a difficult phrase, help to cope with consumer criticisms, influence proposed legislation affecting the organization and, above all, establish a reputation for fair dealing, quality, customer care and corporate values. Indeed, such activity has sometimes proved strong enough to be used as evidence in legal proceedings.

ISSUES ANALYSIS AND REPUTATION

Issues analysis has direct relevance to reputation planning and gives valuable indicators on how to plan for the future. The idea is to look at all those issues that might have an impact on the organization. They will usually be external forces operating in the trading or community environment.

With the issues analysis approach, attention is focused on the external and internal issues that may have an impact on the company and, therefore, the way the company will need to accommodate or counter these issues:

1. What are the issues we should be considering?
2. How might these affect the organization?
3. What are our stances on these issues?
4. How likely are these to rise up the public agenda?
5. What organizations or other pressure might be behind them?
6. Do we have current policies to manage such issues?
7. If not, how will we develop such strategies?
8. What options we should consider for managing issues?
9. How do the effectiveness and costings of these compare?
10. Where do we need to develop support for our new policies?
11. How can we achieve this attitude change?
12. What are the messages we need to project?
13. When will these changes be produced?
14. How will they be monitored and measured?
15. What corporate contribution would an enhanced reputation make?

This audit should be run parallel to the periodic review of the crisis planning procedures. There can be some logic in this as certain issues – such as safety, industrial relations, new or planned legislation, shifts in public opinion and the actions of pressure groups – can potentially produce crises which create special communications demands. However, it is important to consider not just the negative issues (which may create problems) but also those that offer opportunities. Issues can be positive (an increasing public awareness of an environmental matter which gives your product an advantage), neutral (new EU packaging requirements) or negative (an environmental factor where your product case is weakened). *See the fuller analysis of issues in Chapter 10.*

The agreed objectives for the organization must take account of the public relations needs over, say, the next three years. The current activity needs to have objectives that are specific: at this stage, successive years may only require these to be drafted as broader aims. This longer strategy for the company can also look beyond the three-year period to try to identify trends that might prove significant to the organization. In particular, those issues that might develop over the next few years need to be discussed and evaluated, and possible action to cope with them needs to be discussed. Therefore, a schedule of the corporate public relations is likely to cover:

- quantified objectives for year 1 and, possibly, year 2;
- detailed aims for years 2 and 3;
- outline aims to cover those issues predicted to arise during, say, years 2 to 5;
- broad aims to cover alternative issues that might arise beyond year 5.

As everywhere in this book, although some of the examples quoted relate to commercial organizations, similar principles apply to non-profit bodies. If attitudes matter to the organization, then activity and communications must be managed to create the most favourable attitudes possible, and, through this, the goodwill that comes from an improved reputation.

THE ROLE OF RESEARCH

Informal research is better than no research

Earlier in this chapter, the relevance of research was outlined, particularly in developing objectives that will provide a real measure of effectiveness when the performance comes to be appraised. Quantified opinion research may be the ultimate, but less formal studies can still be appropriate in some circumstances.

Normally, there is considerable information that can be gathered by your public relations team through informal research. Even talking to people can be valuable. The head of public relations might put together a committee to represent the various operating sectors of the company; plenty of opportunity should be allowed for colleagues to raise issues affecting their own area. The chief executive should attend one of these meetings occasionally or, periodically, check the agenda and any debrief notes.

Make sure this panel meets regularly so that it performs a continuous monitoring operation. After a period of time, each member of this discussion group will be having discussions within the company and the group will be getting representative views from a much wider spread than could ever be achieved by one manager.

Organizations have available a large number of sources of useful information about the attitudes of important publics that can impact on reputation. Many of these sources are seldom tapped, yet can offer useful information. This can be, for example, from professional advisers and trading partners who observe reactions to the organization – or from confidential discussions with such specialists as banks, accountants, solicitors, union leaders, the advertising agency, suppliers, professional bodies, financial analysts, trade editors, stockbrokers, careers officers, even the government and civil servants. All these can put a fresh perspective on many aspects of the organization's operations.

Your public relations adviser should be getting a view of how competitors and other peer organizations are performing in comparison with your organization. Get members of the public relations team to develop the habit of asking and listening. Make sure they regularly read reports, literature and brochures. Get them to check on complaints received by customer services and talk to personnel about the reasons people give for leaving the company. Ask them to collate all such information into an informal perceptions report, say, quarterly.

The object of this research will be to establish the difference between how the organization is seen and how it would like to be seen – the public relations credibility. This will determine the gap to be closed and indicate where a carefully written objective will help focus the effort.

Start with existing published information...

In every sector of human activity there is a wealth of published material. This can include textbooks, publications, government statistics, journals, academic reports and so on. Many organizations maintain an information library while public or trade association libraries can be an additional source of information. Basic statistical information is available through web pages from public, industry and professional sources. For example, in most industrialized nations, it is possible to check on the owners of companies, the acreage of grain grown, the number of radios per household, how much per head is spent on packaging, the average number of TV hours watched by women over 55, etc.

Your marketing department may coordinate this effort, if it has a research executive. Where necessary, use professionals but try asking them to work in *your* offices so that members of your marketing or public relations team can develop an appreciation of the techniques involved in gathering desk research. Make sure you build up your own electronic library of statistical industry information, company data, trends and product information, available for media and company use. Internet information sources should also be filed electronically.

... before initiating new research

Broadly, research breaks down into those areas that give guidance and those that are statistically valid. The guidance information should not be used to make substantial decisions.

One widely used research method is the in-depth interview. This can give helpful guidance on awareness, perception and attitudes. Discussion or focus groups extend this idea by giving a selected group the opportunity to explore an area in some depth, under discreet guidance from the research leader. Though the findings are not statistically valid, discussion groups can give useful indications of where more substantial research might be undertaken. They can also help the researchers in drafting questionnaires to be used in any proposed subsequent survey. Focus groups can also sometimes identify attitudes and possible solutions to problems.

INVESTIGATION: FORMAL AND INFORMAL

Statistically valid research results are obtained where the size of the sample and the method of sampling give a response that is within an acceptable level of accuracy of the predictable response from the whole audience. This requires the sample to be selected to represent the larger universe being investigated, in terms of age, gender, occupation, income or other relevant factors.

Management should turn to a professional market research organization to assist in these areas. Even in modest surveys, the professional can often produce the results at no greater cost than an in-house effort. In some cases, the professional can draft the questionnaire, advising on the method of sampling and analysing the results.

Formal investigations of these matters can be undertaken professionally by one of the excellent market research companies that will not only run such studies but will offer advice on the best way to undertake the research. Good public relations professionals should also be able to guide management through the processes. In many organizations, such research is directed by the public relations adviser.

Informal evaluations of reputation

However, although formal studies may be essential, and certainly provide a useful benchmark, every so often informal evaluations of reputation can be very helpful in shaping both company and public relations policies. For example, simple questionnaires can be circulated to staff or management, put in salary notices, made an element in annual performance reviews, featured in the company newsletter, raised among attendants at the annual general meeting or the national marketing conference, and so on.

Respondents do not need to be representative of the larger universe but they can still give a general indication of areas that might be studied in more depth. At the very least, these initiatives demonstrate that a company cares about its reputation enough to want to find out what people think – and take the necessary steps to make any appropriate improvements.

Professional researchers rightly warn against putting too much weight on such evaluations. Remember that those who are most unhappy may not respond – or may even throw the questionnaire away. Be wary of putting too much trust in any findings from a study where the respondents are self-selecting.

Sometimes, a most modest appraisal can be a starting point. Before commissioning a deeper study, a leading insurance broker headquartered in the City of London sent a simple single sheet questionnaire to just 25 existing clients and 25 prospectives. It proved pretty clearly that work needed to be undertaken on name awareness; the fuller study could then be undertaken with a sharper focus.

Nothing beats asking good questions

The views of those you respect most can be highly valuable. I remember once being invited to fly to Allentown, Pennsylvania, to interview the late Leonard Pool, the founder and chairman of the world-leading industrial gas company, Air Products, for whom I worked at the time. It was a fascinating interview which confirmed in my mind why he had achieved so much in such a short lifetime. He asked almost as many questions at the interview as I did. The one I remember best was very simple: 'Tell me, Roger, what companies do you admire most and why?'

In a similar vein, earlier in my career I worked at Dexion, the international materials handling company. Some time after I had joined the company, I was introduced at a meeting to the founder, Demetrius Comino, who had built an international empire on the basis of the slotted angle concept that he had invented. His first question to me was very simple but, felt, subtle and wise: 'Why did you choose to come and work with us here at Dexion?'

The boss of such a large and successful organization might have been forgiven for concentrating on what his new employees were going to contribute to the empire. His perspective was different, more original and much more intriguing. He wanted to know what his company had done right that might have attracted someone to want to further his or her career by joining them. It made me think deeply and explore views that had certainly been neither foremost in my mind nor raised at the various interviews prior to my appointment. But then, perhaps that was why he was where he was.

Research can identify management and communications problems

Focus on the correct solution for each problem

Cargill, the major international food and commodities group, had encountered difficulties within local communities at key UK process operations. Before deciding on a solution, the company commissioned an issues and communications audit. This showed that many members of the community did not feel the company cared about its role as a neighbour. Some employees were getting worn down by the continual criticism from community members, even to the extent of being reluctant to identify where they worked when they met new people outside work.

The reality was that the company had spent considerable sums in improving its own operations to reduce noise, smells, traffic and other potential irritants to members of the community. This investment had used the best experience from similar plants around the world. One factor that made this situation especially difficult was that the company had bought the plant some years before; at the time it had been built, local government allowed it to be located far closer to residential areas than would be normal practice today.

Clearly, this identification of the company and its poor reputation in the community was a public relations problem. The issues also had an impact on company human resources policies: most employees actually lived in the communities where the concerns were being expressed. They had a highly personal involvement. Messages regarding investment policies and the level of care that the company took in these matters had not been effectively communicated.

However, the same study revealed that some operating procedures might need improving. For example, open doors and windows at the plant on hot days were understandable but could aggravate noise or smell disturbance. In addition, some employees and contractors were uncertain of procedures in a variety of potential emergency situations. Both these areas were problems for the management team to address.

Although there was clearly a communication element in this, no amount of communication, alone, would have solved some of the fundamental problems.

The procedural problems were most effectively tackled by publishing new guidelines for staff, and by training and running a series of emergency drills. Some aspects of the investment programme were also brought forward to minimize production levels of odour emission.

Public relations advisers, working closely with the Cargill in-house management team, focused on explaining these moves to the community. Activities included presentations to key bodies, site visits by representatives of the local authorities, open days and improved relations with local media. The company also decided that better awareness and understanding required greater involvement in the community within which it worked. As a result, support and assistance to local voluntary groups was offered and an imaginative educational scheme was started. This provided teaching packs on industry and the specialized milling operations at this site. These were available for class study in local schools, whose pupils could also visit the plant in groups to get a better understanding of its work.

The result? A more confident workforce, improved positive news coverage, and minimal complaints – down by over 90 per cent. Also, the educational scheme was so well received that the management was asked by the local education authority to extend it to schools across a broader area. The campaign demonstrated the power of continuing sensitive, responsive policies within two-way communications initiatives.

SOME OBSERVATIONS, IN SUMMARY

1. Use the presentation of public relations plans as a means of checking how in touch you are with perceptions of the company among key audiences.
2. A central responsibility for an effective chairman or chief executive is to understand and respond to the business environment within which the company operates.
3. The public relations professional should be one of the key people inputting information and observations from inside and outside.
4. The relationship between the public relations adviser, the chief executive and the board will be important if the advice is to have any value.
5. Carefully check the integrity and commitment of your public relations adviser and, at all times, allow that person to say what he or she feels must be said.
6. A true picture of where the company stands is essential before any objectives to change opinions, attitudes and responses can be planned.
7. Use research to determine current perceptions. Informal evaluations are better than nothing but use a professional researcher to guide such studies.
8. Realistic objectives will help define the plan of action, the timetable, the budget and resources that need to be allocated to the programme.
9. Objectives can only be of value if they are written with meaningful measures of performance and the methods of appraisal already agreed.
10. Aims can be developed into objectives. An aim is the direction in which you wish to move. An objective is where you want to be by an agreed time.
11. There is a rough ascending scale of achievement for the objectives that build reputation, from awareness through goodwill, positive opinion, acceptance and understanding to supportive action.
12. Be certain that you include the generation of some form of active feedback from key audiences within all your objectives.
13. Objectives that support broad and continuous communications are likely to be more productive than those that suggest short-term blitz action on problems.

14. Be sure that the corporate public relations objectives are applied to all communications activities and that each discipline behaves in ways consistent with these.

15. Before presenting the objectives to all employees, present them first in draft form internally to line managers so that they can have input and relate them to their responsibilities.

16. If the publics you target cannot understand what you are trying to achieve they may raise unnecessary resistance. Make your aims open and clear.

17. Use an issues audit to identify factors that could affect your business and to help develop the company stance towards each of these.

18. Issues are internal or (more usually) external elements that shape the environment within which you do business and they can be positive, neutral or negative.

19. Every crisis the organization might ever face will arise from an issue and all should be identified by the issues audit.

20. When objectives and the response to the issues audit have been agreed by the board, consider a review committee to coordinate activities across divisions and regions.

5

Appraisal

Measure the effectiveness of reputation management

> **Key factors discussed**
> - Performance measured against objectives.
> - Looking at change and not just effort.
> - Evaluating media relations.
> - Processes to prevent reputation damage.
> - Measuring cost effectiveness.
> - Using evaluation for forward planning.
> - Checking competitor performance.
> - Reporting back on success.

SET SOME APPRAISAL PARAMETERS

There are established techniques for measuring the effectiveness of public relations, the simplest being to compare the performance with the quantified and timed objectives set at the start.

But how do you evaluate the effectiveness of the processes adopted to manage the reputation? Often the first step is to manage the effectiveness of the key business function charged with this responsibility – the public relations function. This should be seen as a business discipline that must deliver a return, as any other investment should.

From this evaluation, management can move to appraise the performance of the steps taken to develop and promote the reputation. Although there is not yet a definitive technique, effective processes are being developed. Effective opinion research can give a good understanding of the perceptions of reputation, as noted by MORI, later in this chapter.

If it cannot be measured, is it worth undertaking? In business, that must be the rule. Of course, we can all argue that some things are so self-evident that they do not need measuring. How can you rate courtesy, for example? The staff in your retail operations, as an obvious case, must be polite to the customers because that is the proper way to be. We must treat people the way we would like to be treated: *Do unto others as you would they do unto you.*

Ah, we add logically, being polite is good business. But is it? Always? To an unlimited extent? Does that mean the customer is always right?

In business, we set standards of behaviour towards, say, our customers. They make us feel good but do they do us good? Certainly, we can measure the contribution of these policies to our commercial objectives. In much the same way, informing people may seem logical and good business. But we need to set the standards (as identified in setting the objectives Chapter 4), then measure the contribution these make.

Compare this with the appraisal we might make of courtesy or customer-care schemes. For example, Goodyear was among companies which introduced a *no-quibble* replacement service for its products. But no-quibble does not mean no question, otherwise your car could wear its tyres for 12 months and you could return them for refund or replacement.

American Express has an excellent guarantee on its travellers' cheques for a refund, if lost. But if there were *no questions asked*, might not some unscrupulous customers pass their cheques to friends to forge their signature to cash them, then claim they had lost them and ask for a refund? Is that not just conceivable?

So what are the guidelines? Where does management draw the line? What will it invest to get a return in goodwill to justify this expenditure?

The customer, clearly, is not always right. It costs nothing to smile when talking to customers, but it can cost millions to set up and operate a customer-care scheme with guarantees, refunds, replacements, repairs, and information with its attendant professional operating staff and support systems. Who would authorize such costs unless the benefits can be assured? How can they be assured unless they can be measured?

Similarly, public relations can often seem obvious, sensible, the proper thing to do and, on many occasions, can make you feel good. None of these factors will obviate the need for these efforts to be measured.

How can we measure the achievements of such a supposedly 'subjective' craft? But maybe it is not so subjective to those who understand its operations. The key elements in any effective public relations programme, as noted elsewhere in this book, are: issues, objectives, audiences, perceptions, messages, resources, tactics, timetable, performance and programme refinement. Each can be described and evaluated. The success in, say, getting a message over to an audience by a certain time at a certain cost can be relatively simple to assess. The skill is in writing the original objectives in such a way that the factors of importance can be measured.

Indeed, where a specific campaign has been planned and run using public relations as the only or primary communications technique, the measurement of performance can often be very direct. The voluntary accident and emergency service St John Ambulance ran a campaign with very clear aims: to encourage members of the public to learn resuscitation skills and to persuade the government to subsidize courses. This campaign was so effective it won a *PR Week* award.

In total, 1.7 million people asked St John Ambulance for information and over 180,000 were trained in the resuscitation techniques. Not only are such achievements directly measurable, they help to set a yardstick for future activity.

Measure 'change', not just output

Such results are not often reported publicly, particularly in the commercial sector where confidentiality can inhibit openness. In consequence, some business leaders feel that – through this inability to predict and measure results – public relations has not developed as effectively as it could as a communications discipline. They feel it is not always practical to separate its effects from other elements such as marketing, promotion and advertising.

Input is important but not the real key to success. Input is the effort, output is what this effort produces. But, most important, outcome is what the output *achieves*.

A number of organizations have been developing valid methods of measuring reputation. An interesting study in Finland identified Nokia as the company with the best reputation. The results came from a survey carried out by reputation management consultancy, Pohjoisranta Porter Novelli. The research was conducted using a specially designed tool for the measurement of corporate reputation. The media partner in the survey was *Arvopaperi*, the leading investor magazine in Finland. Nearly 3,500 respondents took part in the survey carried out via an internet panel. The respondents were asked to evaluate on a scale from 0–15 how well each attribute of reputation related to each company in the survey.

Such techniques, if based on large enough and accurately selected samples, can be robust and good indicators of the reality that is perception. And they can help take the step towards measuring the processes taken to build and project reputation.

FACTORS IN REPUTATION AND MEASURING THEM

We all know what reputation is, but many may not be so certain what factors make up this important quality, or indeed why some people and organizations have a good reputation and some do not. American and UK studies referred to in the introduction to this book suggest that the corporate reputation is composed of a number of factors on which most business analysts generally agree. Charles Fombrun, in the late 1990s, ranked US corporations on three reputation drivers: the share value, whether they could recruit readily and whether they could command premium prices for their products and services.

Such studies are interesting but the parameters are hardly definitive. Many dotcoms had high share values but no reputation. The airlines and offshore oil companies have queues for employees in some highly paid jobs but the number of applicants seems to relate more to the pay rate than their corporate reputations. And Tesco has highly competitive prices yet has a good reputation.

Other factors have since been suggested, such as the quality of stewardship of the organization, the sustainability of its operations, the levels of attention, and association – defined as the link between its corporate and product brands and the values it promotes and which shape its activities.

The UK-based research company MORI has earned an enviable reputation for trying to pin down the 'intangibles' that increasingly play a role in the success of the organization. The quality of this work (and that by business schools and universities) steadily establishes that many of these 'intangibles' are actually quite tangible. And the key to understanding such factors may be, sometimes, not to try to measure performance directly but to measure the perceptions of stakeholders. Even those who might be hard pressed to define reputation have a very clear idea about the difference in their feelings towards, say, one airline, one retailer, even one country and another – for example, Shell and BP, Asda and Tesco, Oxfam and Save the Children.

Stewart Lewis, head of the MORI Reputation Centre, believes that the essence of reputation is the sum of all those qualities that different stakeholders admire and feel strongly about. This naturally means that reputation varies according to the perspective of the observer or commentator. A customer may rate product quality more highly than the value of the shares, whilst the financial analyst may set other priorities. However, this is consistent with the observations made by many commentators that reputation is not something owned by the directors, let alone the company, but exists in the minds of the stakeholders and other observers.

THE IMPORTANCE OF STAKEHOLDER TRUST

Lewis adds that many MORI studies suggest that central to corporate reputation is trust. No organization can have a positive reputation – and the influence that it brings – if it is not trusted, and conversely, organizations that are trusted tend to have good reputations. In his view, trust is shaped by six main factors, although others may play a role. These are: the quality of the products; the business performance; the treatment of employees; environmental and social responsibilities; and the quality of the leadership. Factors such as ethics, integrity, vision are also of relevance, though these can be considered subsets of the main factors.

In a study that asked some 25,000 adults what factors were most important in forming an impression of a particular company, the most highly rated, at 56 per cent, was responsibility, with the brand qualities trailing a little at 40 per cent.

Things are changing. The corporation and the brand are increasingly being seen as closely linked, and by some as the same. Many of the values stakeholders respect are now seen by a growing proportion to be incorporated in the brand. This applies where there is a corporate brand as well as product brands – ICI and its paint brand, Dulux, for example. This view of business tends to be stronger where the corporate brand is the same as the product or service brand – the BBC, McDonald's and Mercedes are examples. MORI cites a *Business Week* article: 'Companies see the power of a strong brand. At a time when battered investors, customers and employees are questioning whom they can trust, the ability of a familiar brand to deliver proven value flows straight to the bottom line.'

The bottom-line value of the brand (and the links to corporate standards that match or exceed stakeholder expectations), would seem to be reinforced by the finding in another study, that social responsibility (as one indicator) influences the customer's decision about buying a product or service from a particular organization. MORI tracks such perceptions, and the level of those claiming this linkage has risen from some 28 per cent in 1998 to 44 per cent in 2002.

A parallel finding also suggests that good performance perceived by stakeholders in one aspect of company operations may reflect on other areas. Certainly it is difficult for observers to separate them; probably the public would find the concept of a company that was highly responsible but poorly managed difficult to accept. And common sense would suggest that good management shows its influence across all the reputation drivers.

Stewart Lewis believes that a company that stakeholders see as having a good reputation may be able to look to some direct benefits, many of which will show on the bottom line. These include higher customer loyalty; employee pride; investor confidence; better relations at the public affairs level; and improved media receptiveness.

THE REPUTATION IMPACT ON THE BOTTOM LINE

The value of the reputation of an organization may as yet be difficult to quantify in the ways that the accounting profession has learnt to value brands; however, it is clear from many studies undertaken by MORI and others that a good reputation is recognized by stakeholders and has a positive influence on many of the decisions that they may make relating to the organization. One illustration of this is in one of the most directly market-sensitive areas, the stock market. A US study showed that for companies with an enhanced reputation this resulted in a 16 per cent increase in stock value, and a weakened reputation resulted in a 36 per cent decrease – a difference between a good and a bad reputation of some 52 per cent.

Stewart Lewis observes:

> Reputation is a relatively recent aspect of the organization to be systematically studied and managed. Its influence is clear and its impact on corporate performance highly significant. We would anticipate that the research approaches would be refined, as company managers recognize the importance of this facet of their operations. Also the accountancy profession will increasingly seek acceptable methods to value reputation. And, as we have seen, business best-practice guidelines, legislation (and books such as this) will give an increasing focus on the need for the board to monitor and manage all factors that can shape the corporate reputation.

Certainly, it is wise to evaluate all those contributory factors that often shape perceptions of the organization.

EVALUATING THE IMPACT OF MEDIA COVERAGE

Too often, techniques for measuring effectiveness have really only been measuring the output, such as media coverage. But one of the most important aspects of measuring the effectiveness of a public relations programme is to gain intelligence to improve the activities.

A number of companies are now offering methods for appraising public relations effectiveness. Some systems can balance a complex range of factors to give weighting to media coverage, but this still remains a measure of output and not of the true impact upon the target audience.

Happily, evaluation companies are now combining coverage measurement with opinion/perception research techniques to give measures of greater value.

Keep comparative records of coverage and its tone

In addition, it is important to remember that media relations is nearly always only one element of a broader public relations programme. For example, lectures, seminars, briefings, mailings, exhibitions and similar activities cannot be appraised by these methods. Even with this measure, it is important to separate out the impact of other activities, such as the effects of the salesforce efforts or advertising.

Output measures of media coverage can be calculated relatively simply by monitoring the following factors:

- press space or radio/television time;
- the length of the stories;
- the number of times company or product name is used;
- the use of agreed corporate messages;
- a by-line or use of company quotation;
- the tone and news value of the headline;
- the use of photograph or illustration;
- the position of the item in the publication or the news programme;
- the credibility of the publication/programme;
- readership/viewership levels;
- total opportunities to see (OTS) or audience reach;
- the positive or otherwise tone of coverage.

However, of greater value will be an understanding of:

- the percentage of the defined target audience reached;
- the levels of awareness/knowledge that have been developed;
- how audience opinion/attitude may have been moved;
- above all, the change in behaviour that has been created.

Those computer-based systems which evaluate such elements and produce some comparative measure (normally given a title such as *media influence* or *audience impact*), have some value in comparing elements of each programme, or even the media coverage of one company with another.

Though useful, not too much weight should be put upon this; the computer is simply doing some complex calculations using a predetermined formula that might be carried out by the professional communicator. It may be more independent, but it remains mechanical. For example, could such a system truly measure the impact on journalists of the simple phrase 'I, too, am a friend of the earth', used by the then managing director of a major division of Aventis? It was not used in the news release, but, in the media briefing, positively changed the attitude of reporters who had been following company environmental issues.

Many of the better companies in evaluation have moved beyond media coverage 'measurement' to deeper appraisals of the shifts in awareness, understanding, goodwill and reputation on which effective public relations should be focused. Many techniques may be used in programmes to build reputation, of which media relations may just be a part.

Good public relations sometimes stops a negative story

Even in the area of media relations, such techniques have limited relevance on those occasions when the public relations professional has prevented the appearance of a damaging story, say, through convincing the journalists that their proposed approach was neither accurate nor fair.

Barratts, then Britain's leading house builder, had its reputation severely damaged (and tens of millions knocked off the share price), through one damaging – and misleading – television programme criticizing its methods of timber frame construction. How would you measure the media relations of its competitors? Did they use superior media relations to avoid such damage or were these companies simply of less media relevance and interest?

I was once concerned about the ethics of diverting a potentially damaging review from my client, Cadbury Schweppes, to a less alert competitor. This was looking at the dangers to children's teeth of soft drinks, and was planned by TV programme *Public Eye*.

Both examples are in media relations and yet not subject to any sort of measurement relating to quality or quantity of exposure.

Public relations is the management of reputation; therefore, the ultimate measure of the effectiveness of public relations must be the change in the company's reputation. It is reasonable to deduce that a good reputation is achieved to some extent through the planned and sustained delivery of positive messages about an organization, to the publics upon whom it depends for success. These messages will have been developed as a result of the organization's study of practices and policies acceptable to the public. A measurement of the acceptance of such messages by the publics exposed to them will complete the circle. Only good policies can win goodwill.

PUBLIC RELATIONS AND MANAGEMENT

The delivery of negative messages, or the weakness of the positive messages that are delivered, will both suggest that the company needs to change its policies. The CEO should recognize this as a good indication that the company is not behaving in a way that is acceptable to these key publics. You cannot properly appraise public relations performance when it is being used to compensate for management inefficiencies.

Public relations played an important role in changing perceptions of Jaguar, the UK car maker now owned by Ford. But this could only be achieved by projecting real changes in the quality of the product offered to the market. Communications cannot be an alternative to good management.

'Truly effective communications efforts are those which are based on real achievements,' says Sir John Egan, one-time chief executive of Jaguar himself, then chairman of BA and Inchcape. 'In my experience it is a lot easier when I can point at a business success and say, *that's how we did it.*'

Some executives fall into the trap of imagining that the veneer of a good story is a substitute for the hard slog of achieving significant improvements. Public relations can provide some of the sizzle but you must start with a real sausage, as Sir John tellingly puts it.

Equally, the public relations professional needs to have the confidence and authority to be able to advise management that while the delivery systems may be effective, what is being said is not meeting with approval. This is one point where public relations shifts from communications into the area of policy: not just what the company says but what it does.

The shareholders of Chrysler, as it faded away, did not want more information, they wanted more action; the customers of Nike did not want more information, they wanted more respect; the marine staff of Exxon did not want more information, they wanted better shipping policies; investors in Enron did not want more information, they wanted more company integrity.

Appraise the elements in communications

Output measures of media relations coverage can only represent part of an appraisal – sometimes a minor part. There are many other factors relating to the public relations performance where measurement can be made before and after the campaign to quantify the results. These measures can also indicate the cost-effectiveness of the activity undertaken. Some of the more frequent measures include:

- *Budget*. The completion of activity within the agreed budget and timescale.
- *Issues*. The success in identifying and addressing incipient issues *before* they rise up the agenda.
- *Awareness*. An increase in the knowledge of the organization among the defined audience.
- *Attitude*. A shift in opinion or attitude towards the organization.
- *Position*. The placing of the organization in the market among competitors.
- *Response*. The number of enquiries and/or leads generated by the campaign.
- *Share price*. The value that the investor puts upon the company.
- *Sales*. Any change in sales volumes or prices that can be related to public relations alone.
- *Cost-effectiveness*. The level of performance per Euro, pound or dollar spent.

Advertising agencies and many other professional advisers are expected to quantify the effectiveness of their work. This is becoming the norm within public relations. Some consultancies use sophisticated methods to calculate their audiences.

Both public relations directors and consultancies are increasingly using formal attitude research for pre- and post-campaign measurement. Founder of Countrywide Communications, and director of Porter Novelli, Peter Hehir, said, 'Public relations professionals who complain about the low status accorded them but don't try to give their proposals a scientific platform, continue to bite the hand that starves them.'

The position identified by research will be an important part of the appraisal. Any change in awareness, or shift in opinion, needs to be related to the resources deployed to achieve it… to appraise its effectiveness and, indeed, its cost-effectiveness.

Formal research of a substantial sample audience into perceptions of reputation, awareness, opinion and attitude, remains the best measure of the true effect of the public relations programme.

MEASURING THE EFFECTIVENESS OF PUBLIC RELATIONS

Consider informal reviews of cost-effectiveness

Although a quantified measure must always be best, almost any measure is better than none. Broadly, such practical assessments will fall into the subjective or objective categories. Certainly, if the goals for the public relations performance were originally set only as aims, then there is not much point in taking the assessment beyond the subjective stage.

One well-established subjective measure is to hold a performance review towards the end of a programme of activity and before the detailed planning of the next stage. This needs to involve all the people who contributed to the original discussions and helped to prepare the aims. These might include personnel, production, marketing and international directors. Each representative invited to attend this meeting should be given ample advance warning and asked to obtain some assessment in the change of attitude in any sectors for which they are responsible.

The meeting should then look at each of the aims originally defined and discuss whether there is evidence to support any improvement related to the targets. As an example, the marketing director might have prepared for the meeting by talking to distributors and asking them for their views of the company's approach to the market. (He or she will find it is better not to ask directly about, say, news coverage, but rather about the influence that the coverage might have had on the targeted audience. An increase in coverage would not necessarily be recognized by the trade as 'better media relations'.)

The marketing director should select a representative range of distributors with whom to discuss this change in awareness. This might cover, for example, larger and smaller wholesalers – northern and southern – or some appropriate balance.

The performance review has no real quantifiable validity. However, if the campaign has been working effectively, there should emerge a clear consistency of opinion. This should be helpful in giving guidance on how to adjust the programme – and perhaps, in future years, how to improve the objectives. These views might also suggest a better method of measurement, such as a more formal audit of wholesaler attitudes.

Certainly, informal reviews or small pilot studies are always a wise investment before undertaking major research. They enable you to refine the approach at an earlier stage to get the maximum from the efforts that will be expended in the later formal research.

Use formal attitude research for major campaigns

Market research specialists will confirm that monitoring the effectiveness of a public relations campaign is not as difficult as many imagine; nor need it be an expensive activity.

It is essential that the measure is of the public relations effectiveness and that the influence of other parallel activities is not inadvertently monitored; for example, other influences could include an increase in the salesforce, the effectiveness of a new sales manager, the impact of an advertising campaign, the introduction of half a dozen new products and so on. Therefore, as the original objectives should have been phrased in relation to some form of quantifiable awareness or attitude factor, it is *this* that needs to be measured.

Attitude surveys are probably the most valuable method of assessing the effectiveness of many campaigns. On an annual basis, it is probably sufficient to monitor the section of the market at which the public relations is specifically aimed. However, periodically, it is valuable to look at overall public attitudes towards the organization. This is certainly useful before the start of a major campaign or at least every year or two. If it is properly constructed, the attitude survey will be of invaluable help to the public relations advisers in their planning.

Attitude research also should provide the benchmark against which future effectiveness can be measured. Therefore, it is important that it is structured to enable it to be repeated at a later stage. This will enable the results to be compared and any advances or declines identified. It may be of less value to research attitudes among retailers then, five years later, to research attitudes among wholesalers... and try to draw any comparisons between them. Similarly, the same research format and, ideally, the same research specialists should be used.

On some occasions, the research will reveal information about other aspects of the company's operations that have an effect on public opinion: counter staff behaviour, complexity of paperwork, telephone attitudes, salesforce structure, corporate identity and so on.

A study we undertook for one engineering company showed that one of the groups that had the most influence on repeat orders were the delivery drivers. If they were helpful, punctual and reliable, the salesperson stood a better chance of obtaining the next order. Yet the drivers had not featured in any part of the marketing or public relations programme. Indeed, the recruitment policies did not reflect the need for drivers to have this 'customer care' temperament. These findings enabled the company to develop suitable policies to bring them into the planning.

Relate the measure to the quantified objectives

Some proposed measurement of the effectiveness of the public relations programme can be simpler to quantify if the original objectives have been well drafted. Both these objectives and the appraisal methods to be used can help indicate the level of resources that might be allocated to the effort.

It cannot be emphasized too firmly that the drafting of the objectives must be related to the methods that are proposed to measure effectiveness. There is little point in working to an improvement in an area where no method has been agreed to check this movement.

Suppose one objective has been to improve awareness of the products at retailer level, in order to help the salesforce improve distribution; it would be possible to record the increase in the number of retail outlets where the awareness had been improved to some prior agreed level. This would separate the awareness and sales objectives. In other words, sales management would be expected to take advantage of the improvement in awareness by increasing the number of stockists holding the product, say, by a comparable percentage.

An objective for the public relations along these lines might be to:

- raise awareness of product x among the managers of retail outlets, above y turnover, from current 25 per cent to 35 per cent. Awareness to be defined as unprompted identification of x as one of the top three products in its sector.

Let us assume that public relations had developed such product awareness among retailers from this 25 per cent to 35 per cent. Then, let us suppose this additional awareness could be converted by the salesforce into actual distribution. If this potential increase in distribution were to represent sales of, say, £500,000 at ex-factory prices, then we are beginning to have a figure against which to compare the effectiveness of the public relations spend.

Alternatively, we could begin to calculate how much might be expended to achieve this goal. For example, the marketing manager might feel it reasonable to expend 10 per cent of the value of the potential ex-factory sales on the promotional effort. It might be worth spending a *bigger* proportion if it is a one-off activity; for example, this might be valid if it means that once distribution has been achieved, sales will automatically follow year-on-year. If, however, the nature of the product is such that it needs *continuous* trade support, then a lower percentage but spent regularly might be necessary.

Or, as a further example, consider the public relations activity undertaken to reduce staff turnover in a fast-growing, high-technology company. In an actual US example, such a campaign was undertaken under a brief from the human resources vice-president. At the end of the first complete 12 months during which this new scheme had been in operation, staff turnover had declined from an annual equivalent of 30 per cent to 18 per cent and continued its downward trend.

The direct costs that appeared to have been saved in cutting down this turnover – in terms of recruitment, training, the effect of limited performance during the induction and so on – were estimated at $250,000 per annum. The total cost of the public relations campaign (not including the time of the executives, as it was run parallel with other activities) was less than $25,000. Even if the time had been considered, it would still have totalled less than $35,000. This investment produced a substantial saving that would be continued year-on-year. The percentage of the savings that was spent on the efforts to reduce this turnover would seem to be reasonable.

USE THE APPRAISAL FOR FUTURE PLANNING

Whatever our limited ability to see into the future, many of us have stunning powers of seeing into the past. But hindsight can be invaluable in public relations. It can help develop alternative tactics and improve the strategy. At the end of every campaign, the analysis must identify those techniques that have worked most effectively.

Let us consider a practical example. A new public relations campaign supporting a branded package food included a series of presentations to housewives through tasting evenings organized across the country. These had been successful in improving awareness and directly stimulating sales. The level of sales could be positively measured in each of the towns after each of the events.

A success, you might think? Not exactly, for both the public relations consultant and the client were aware that this success had taken a very substantial investment to achieve the results – and the sales improvements were only achieved in those areas where the demonstrations had taken place. As less than 5 per cent of the market could be covered in any one year, it would take 20 years to cover the total market. To gear up the operation would create a budget out of all proportion. Yet, all were agreed that the technique had worked. A little bit of hindsight – plus a dash of lateral thinking – made the public relations advisers question whether it was necessary for the company to be carrying *all* of the costs and logistics of these demonstrations.

An investigation showed that several other manufacturers were undertaking similar exercises. One, in particular, was handling a product that was not only non-competitive but complementary to the client's brand. A little negotiation followed and the result was a modest financial contribution to the other company's costs, plus an unlimited supply of the product, supporting literature, recipe leaflets, trained presentation staff and so on. The agreement covered how the product should be presented under this cooperative promotion plan.

The end result was a far broader coverage than could possibly be undertaken by a solo effort. Awareness and sales levels were monitored and found to be comparable with earlier results, but the final costs in the second year were only 25 per cent of those in the first.

And both companies benefited from this synergy.

The same analysis can be applied to other presentation activities such as exhibitions, mobile showrooms and roadshows. These events often create a considerable buzz but the actual impact can be very local and limited. Check that the excitement is not outweighing the effectiveness.

ANALYSE COMPETITIVE PUBLIC RELATIONS ACTIVITY

When undertaking any public relations activity, look at how other organizations are performing. Ensure that your media monitoring service is covering competitive companies so that you can get some indication of their coverage. Try to calculate their promotional budget – by finding out what staff they have deployed on the activity, what the fees to their consultancy might be and so on. Try to establish if there are any industry norms.

This research does not need to be solely related to your industry. It might be interesting to know how much it costs to support the sales of €100 million of sports shoes every year in comparison with the sales of €100 million of gardening tools. If there are substantial differences, why? What methods are being used by these other manufacturers? Are they better than your own?

Try talking to trade associations to discover if any statistics exist on promotional activities, budgets, relevant market shares and so on. If your company is number one in a market with a dominant position, should you be spending more or less pro rata to hold this situation? Perhaps, you cannot compare yourself with other companies in the same market, but find a parallel sector where there is also a dominant supplier.

Talk to the public relations professionals involved in this area. They may be as interested in your observations as you are in theirs. Some may even be prepared to exchange budget figures and market data where there is no direct conflict of interest and where this may be to mutual benefit – for example, the sports shoes versus gardening tools comparison.

Consider a communications audit

One technique that can help establish clearly the present position of company communications and their effectiveness is to undertake a communications audit. This surveys the important audiences, methods of communications with them, the effectiveness of these communications channels and where they can be improved or gaps filled. An effective approach is to combine this communications audit with the compilation of a corporate reputation 'balance sheet'; this can often be combined with the issues audit described in more detail on pages 233–248.

The aim is to establish those factors that have an influence on the reputation of the organization among the target audiences. For example, good products, excellent service and major investment in research may be positive factors upon which you can build. An unstable management, poor environmental record or recent safety issues may be negative factors to be counteracted.

Remember that all activity undertaken in the public relations programme is designed to build and develop the reputation of the organization, its management and the brands or products and services it offers – in other words, to build, promote and manage the corporate reputation.

REPORT TO ALL INVOLVED IN THE PROGRAMME

Whatever the results of your research and analysis, always ensure that a proper report is prepared and circulated to all executives who have contributed to the original planning.

Colleagues will wish to know if company money has been spent effectively. They will be interested to see how well the intended results have been achieved. It can be even more important if the results are not encouraging. The problems that will arise from pursuing the wrong course can be worse than ignoring a difficulty that has been diagnosed at an early stage. As with all communications, remember to ask for a response to this report.

If you have been instructing other colleagues to work on this subject, be certain that you have the opportunity for a full debriefing and an appraisal of their performance related to the overall programme success. These colleagues may be members of your own team or they may be the consultancy that you are retaining. Measured success must be one of the factors that contributes to their motivation and their rewards.

With an outside consultancy, this may form part of the renegotiation. If the consultancy has not performed to satisfactory standards, then you need to decide whether this requires a change in direction of the programme or a change in the consultancy. In either case, you will be able to base these decisions on a more substantial level of information. At the very least, the data provide a sound base for an intelligent and rational discussion.

Success demands as much praise as failure would demand criticism. Where the public relations work of colleagues is successful, recognize it. Praise can be the most motivating aspect of work. It does not cost a lot, but it pays dividends. The public relations adviser will gain far more satisfaction from performing to objectives. The value of his or her contribution to the development of the organization can only be assessed if it is measured. Good public relations demands such effective measurement and due recognition of achievement.

Managing communications to improve credibility

Camelot measures the effectiveness of revised reputation policies

A good reputation will not prevent a challenge to corporate policies or even criticism from any quarter, not least the media. However, if the organization is respected and has earned its credibility, comment may be more balanced – and critics may even give the management a chance to comment on a crisis.

Sadly, public relations history is littered with examples of organizations retreating into the bunker when subjected to intense media scrutiny. The in-house communications teams of many companies in the public eye often develop a 'reactive-defensive' media relations culture in the vain hope of avoiding further media attention. Nine times out of ten this policy fails to avert those unwelcome press calls and – by definition – does nothing to improve public reputation.

It would be fair to say that the national lottery operator Camelot has inhabited that bunker. Following a hugely successful launch, which catapulted the National Lottery to the very top of Britain's league table of consumer brands, the company soon hit controversy. A noxious combination of 'tall poppy syndrome' in the media ('we've built 'em up, now let's cut 'em down') and a very public row with the newly elected Labour government about 'fat cat' pay forced the company back onto the front pages for all the wrong reasons. And Camelot retreated.

The company briefly went 'proactive' in 2000 when it was essentially ruled out of the bidding process for the second lottery licence by its own regulator. A counter-challenge by a consortium backed by Sir Richard Branson seemed to making all the running at that time and gained much media backing. Camelot came out fighting and its robust campaign – fronted by the then chief executive designate, Dianne Thompson – transformed the company's image to that of ballsy underdog, which in turn helped secure it a second term.

But old habits die hard. Later, in the face of further difficult media attention the company retreated. The criticisms had been about such factors as the rebranding of the main game to 'Lotto' and falling sales – let alone controversial lottery grants that hit the headlines but were outside Camelot's immediate control.

New policies often need new thinking

In January 2003, Thompson – now the chief executive proper – recruited former ITV and ITN communications director Mark Gallagher to Camelot. His brief was to rebuild the proactive culture that had served the company so well two years previously.

Within eight weeks, the old company newsroom was repopulated on the principle of 'fewer and better', reducing overall headcount from 17 to 12, but simultaneously doubling the aggregate years of public relations experience in the in-house team. The new press office was organized around three core teams. The media relations unit delivered issues management 24/7, vigorously rebutting any ill-informed enquiries and correcting all hostile or inaccurate media coverage as a matter of policy.

This unit also provided cover for two publicity teams, one covering the unique area of lottery winners' public relations and the other dealing with core publicity for the company, including game launches and important events in the life of the lottery. These included the triple rollover in May 2004 and the lottery's 10th birthday. This latter team also developed better working relationships with the lottery distributors. And crucially, the media relations team allowed both publicity teams to work exclusively on positive stories, regardless of how tricky things got in issues management.

Internal and external professionals with a single focus

The new in-house professionals were relocated from Camelot's headquarters in Watford to join the government relations team in London, so individual PROs could develop eyeball-to-eyeball relationships with journalists. Finally, four external advisers were retained to provide ad hoc advice on difficult issues and extra resource for big projects. They also met quarterly with Gallagher and Thompson to provide a sanity check and an independent assessment of progress. To complement this check, Gallagher introduced monthly and annual targets for positive coverage as a proportion of total media coverage, and quarterly audits of the financial value of such positive coverage.

Gallagher comments, 'Nearly two years later, the proportion of positive coverage has risen from 28% to well above 70%. And in the financial year 2004, the team generated £49 million worth of positive media coverage on an investment of just over £2 million. There is a clear link between our public relations, the reputation of our brand and our bottom line.'

Camelot has discovered that a public relations team in 'permanent campaign' mode delivers significant dividends and that life outside the bunker can be really quite enjoyable. Reputation can be enhanced and understanding developed.

Dianne Thompson sums it up: 'For a company like Camelot there is a clear link between media coverage and sales. The radical changes to the press office and our media relations – coupled with our new marketing campaigns – have had a direct impact in improving the reputation of the lottery and the returns to the good causes.'

SOME OBSERVATIONS, IN SUMMARY

1. If it cannot be measured, how can you be certain it is worth doing?
2. The most effective methods of appraisal start with the way in which the original objectives were written, making them specific and targeted.
3. True communciations is two-way and will focus on listening to the market as well as the projection of acceptable messages that relate to real achievements.
4. The best appraisal should be of changes achieved (the *outcome*) and not just the *output* of the public relations programme, though that will be a start.
5. One central aim to justify any expenditure on appraisal is to gain the intelligence to improve future activity and cost-effectiveness.
6. *Input* measures are the level of activity and effort.
7. *Output* measures include for example the number of events held, stories issued, journalists briefed, media briefings and level of coverage achieved.
8. Where you need to measure output, try to make this relevant to the objectives such as the use of agreed messages, the tone of coverage and the percentage of the audience reached.
9. *Outcome* measures are the most valuable as they record the achievements of the activity – for example, the shaping of opinion, development of favourable attitudes and, above all, change of behaviour.
10. Review the control of difficult public relations situations that may have occurred in the year, including any reduction in or prevention of negative coverage.
11. Information alone may not make good communications, however thoroughly disseminated; for example, it may not be able to change poor opinions.
12. Informal reviews of effectiveness can be helpful in low-priority areas, or as the first stage in creating definitive measures.

13. Where possible, use professionals to plan the measurement of the performance, either to run the studies or, at least, to plan the approaches.
14. The appraisal of the effectiveness of the communications should become a benchmark for future performance if it is properly structured.
15. Try to use the same team or company on such studies to get the best year-on-year perspective and ask them to help modify future objectives, based on this experience.
16. Compare performance with competitors – or with companies in other industries where an exchange of information will not compromise commercial confidentiality.
17. Consider appraisal and issues analysis as part of a communications audit to review all public relations efforts, identifying any gaps or overlaps in reaching key audiences.
18. Make sure your public relations professionals prepare a written report on any agreed appraisal and ensure that they present this to the board.
19. Report back these findings to all who contributed to the development of the original objectives and ask for their views on next year's activity.
20. Use the appraisal to adjust resources and activity for the coming year, putting budget where it is effective and needed.

6

Marketing

Make public relations work closely with marketing

Key factors discussed

- The influence of brand on reputation.
- How marketing shapes perceptions.
- Building brand asset value...
- ... while creating the corporate brand.
- Marketing impact on corporate publics.
- The products and corporate values.
- Getting communications coordinated.
- Managing marketers and creatives.

THE BOARD'S KEY DECISION

There is a difference and a close link between the corporate and the brand reputations. The aim of reputation management must be to get these two both consistent and working to the best advantage of the company. As marketing can be one of the highest profile activities of the organization, often with significant budgets, it is important that reputation is a key factor in all marketing activities, particularly marketing public relations. Ideally this should be closely linked to the corporate public relations.

Public relations as a marketing-support technique is well understood. Indeed, the craft has come of age over recent years. This success has sometimes overshadowed even more important areas of influence. For example, public relations is less often seen as a strategic approach to undertaking business – in effect, creating the environment within which the marketing efforts can be most successful.

Yet the growth of CNN, General Electric, Microsoft, Virgin, Vodafone and Wal-Mart, or the decline of Boots, Marconi, Marks and Spencer, Olivetti and many technology companies, all owe much to the use, misuse or non-use of public relations – though other factors were clearly at work.

Major business successes have been built on the strength of effective public relations. Brand awareness and loyalty can be more credibly developed through communications channels.

In an earlier edition of this book, published just a few years ago, the author quoted the then UK managing director of McDonald's on the company's success. It had built a new market largely on its reputations for being in touch with consumers and following through on the quality of its products and service. It won major market share through reputation. At the time, he said:

> Some people think that the company has achieved its success by serving great food quickly, in a clean environment and at reasonable prices. It has, of course, but it was Ray Kroc's policy of making a huge commitment to local community relations, consistently, year after year, market by market that built a deep consumer trust in the business.

In its early growth stage, the company followed the quality concepts of its founder, Ray Kroc. He died, management changed and times moved on. By then, a big and profitable venture, it felt it was invulnerable. But it lost touch. Its reputation faded, then collapsed, and the business ran into serious trouble through not understanding market needs. The lesson is that reputation is not for ever. It depends on maintaining policies that reflect needs and win stakeholder support.

Get the corporate projection right and your company will have the business environment in which to thrive... with the right products, service, prices and people. Get it wrong and, whatever the quality of the rest, your company may not survive.

So where does public relations fit in... and how does it relate to marketing? Marketing is defined by the Chartered Institute of Marketing as the management process responsible for identifying, anticipating and satisfying customer requirements profitably. Implicit in this definition is the need to create the best business environment within which these products or services can be sold and supported. It is reasonable to extend this to the creation of goodwill between the organization offering the products and services and the purchasers of these.

REPUTATION: A CENTRAL AIM OF MARKETING

Public relations is an essential element in the building of goodwill. Any marketing plan that does not consider public relations will have a dangerous deficit. One MORI survey confirmed that goodwill towards the company is closely linked to public perceptions of product quality – a central element in marketing. Some 70 per cent of a sample of the general public believed that reputable companies do not sell poor-quality products.

Also, shoppers are more likely to try something new from a trusted name. Such an advantage, built through marketing techniques (including relevant public relations and advertising), can be very significant in sales and market share terms.

Other studies have demonstrated the direct relationship between familiarity and high regard. All such evidence confirms the importance of the brands as well as the company behind the brands. The credibility of public relations as a communications technique which tends to be trusted by consumers can be important in the marketing mix – and certainly able to justify its own significant proportion of the spend.

However, does that mean that public relations is part of marketing? Certainly not. Is finance part of human resources or production part of sales? However closely they need to relate, each has separate responsibilities. Of course, public relations has a crucial role to play in supporting (and, sometimes, leading) marketing, but these are different disciplines with distinct responsibilities. The critical decision that management must make is, *where should public relations report?*

PUBLIC RELATIONS LINKS TO MARKETING

With companies that have a major presence in consumer sectors, the most substantial expenditure on public relations may well be in marketing support. The logical decision may seem to be to make public relations report to marketing. But that can be a mistake. Public relations is involved with many company audiences that are not the responsibility of marketing. These can include employees, shareholders, trade and professional bodies, educationalists, suppliers, national government, local authorities, factory neighbours and pressure groups. Make public relations report to marketing and you risk neglecting these important audiences – or creating friction when marketing management finds its resources are being deployed into areas that will not affect its success.

Most major and successful companies, such as Dell, Disney, IBM and Sony, will have solved this by establishing a corporate public relations function at head office. These units advise the chairman and handle investor relations *and* public affairs. 'Marketing public relations' is the responsibility of the operating divisions or companies. The corporate specialist often offers an advisory service on the recruitment of public relations professionals or the buying of appropriate consultancy services and, of course, on corporate strategy.

Such companies view an investment in marketing as an investment in building the capital value of their company.

USE MARKETING TO BUILD TANGIBLE ASSET VALUE

The reputation and the goodwill this generates will be one of the company's most valuable assets. With consumer goods companies, this goodwill is often represented as the value of the brands. In recent years, there has been a move to show these on the balance sheet.

Sectors of the accountancy profession are still concerned about intangible assets being given such a value. A football club cannot put its player onto the balance sheet; therefore, theoretically, a club operating from a leased stadium, yet with a team valued at £100 million or more, may have minimal book value. The argument behind this is that players can break a leg and drop from being worth millions to virtually nothing.

Perhaps this accountancy caution is understandable with football clubs but it seems less logical with national and international consumer and business brands. Putting the value on the balance sheet strengthens the position of the company and significantly reduces the risk of unwanted takeovers.

In the UK, the Accounting Standards Committee suggested that brand value should be written off against profits over an agreed period of 20 or more years. Of course, this makes no sense as major brands like Apple, Boeing, Coca-Cola, Electrolux, Intel, Rolls-Royce and Turtle Wax may be of vastly increasing value and some of these have been around for many years. Of course, in some cases it becomes difficult to separate the brand value from the company, particularly where the same name is in use, such as Campbell's, Hoover, IBM or Kellogg's.

THE VALUE OF BRAND MARKETING

Consider the commercial value that brands can have and, therefore, the potential return on the marketing effort that can build those brands. Swiss company Nestlé bought Rowntree Macintosh of the UK for a sum in excess of £2.5 billion when the physical assets represented only 20 per cent of this price. The balance was to pay for marketing expertise, distribution capability and the range of brands. In other words, Nestlé were prepared to pay five times as much as the assets to acquire these brands and the mechanics that had been perfected for delivering the brands to the market. Similar deals have regularly valued companies at four or five times the asset value.

The lead in valuing brands was begun in the UK because of its open markets and the relative ease of agreed or hostile takeovers – the latter then unknown in many markets such as Germany and Japan. One company that led this move in the UK was Rank Hovis McDougal. It had a stock market capitalization in 1988 of £1.4 billion but net assets of £265 million. At that time, it had sales of £1.7 billion and owned some 50 or so leading brands, not just in the UK but across the United States, Asia Pacific and other markets. It seemed unrealistic that the value of these brands was not recognized on the balance sheet and that RHM might be compared unfavourably with other companies in similar sectors whose brands had little value.

The outcome was that the board decided to put a value on these commercial assets. RHM's brands were valued at £678 million, bringing the total net asset valuation of the company to a much more realistic figure of close to £1 billion.

Today, these brands, whoever owns them, will be valued at many times these levels, reflecting both the marketing investment in them and their enhanced brand reputation.

Keep brand valuations realistic

Of course, one argument against this practice is that there is no certain formula for valuing brands other than, perhaps, the price on the open market; no company wants to go through a takeover situation to work out what figure it should be putting down on its books for these assets!

An over-optimistic or even unscrupulous management could protect a difficult trading position by putting an inflated valuation in the books. This was one criticism of the now defunct Maxwell Corporation which revalued a number of its newspaper titles and then borrowed against these inflated values. Enron and WorldCom were also accused of having unrealistic brand values on their books. One sensible defence against any criticism of these valuations is to have these independently calculated.

Whether a formal evaluation of reputation (goodwill plus brand value) is put onto the balance sheet or not, some estimation of this can be helpful, particularly with non-quoted companies it will allow management to agree the budget to undertake the programme of issues management and marketing support to protect and enhance this asset.

Brand management and accountancy firms have developed formulae that are gaining increasing acceptance and, in some countries, may become accepted as 'best practice', possibly even moving into company law.

The value of the 'corporate' brand

In recent years, some companies with a strong marketing orientation have put all their public relations muscle behind their brands. The corporations behind these brands face possible risk through adopting a low-profile approach – such problems can arise in the areas of public goodwill, consumer pressure, industrial and parliamentary relations. Consistently, organizations with a recognized public personality are subjected to less criticism and tend to operate with greater public support.

The types of most valuable brands have changed over the couple of centuries since the earliest ones were established. Today the top brands are almost all retailers. Occasionally a brand such as Vodafone enters the top 10 by value. But it was not always like that. During the 1980s the top 10 advertisers were all product brands, yet to be overtaken by the retailers. The trend was logical: in early Victorian days agriculture and food production became the basis of wealth.

As explorers and adventurers opened the world, trading became a route to influence and affluence. With such major world markets, cheap labour and raw materials, the industrial revolution made manufacturing the business. As those world markets became independent and developed their own manufacturing, so competition grew and, in this century, marketing became the powerful discipline. Many companies believed that brands were everything.

Although all company assets contribute to corporate success, brands can be mighty powerful. As noted, accounting conventions across the world allow the brand to be shown on the balance sheet as a financial asset. That means money spent on protecting and promoting the brand can be seen as an investment in the capital growth of the value of the brand. This can be of great significance both to company reputation and to the public relations professionals. An investment of, say, 1 per cent of the capital value of the brand in its promotion, that achieves a 5 per cent increase in the value, can be seen as a 500 per cent return on investment in reputation management.

Although brands are immensely valuable, this does not always justify the accepted reverence that is sometimes shown them. The right strategies, the right marketing and promotion can turn the most unlikely names into brands with real equity. Who would call a chain of grocery stores Wal-Mart? What was Walt Disney before his name meant something other than son of Mr and Mrs Disney? Does Accenture really mean anything? And how much investment has it taken for it to reach the levels of credibility of the name that it replaced? Many of the great and famous names simply reflect the names of the founders and not a cent was spent in brand development. Consider Nestlé, Ford, Hewlett-Packard, Boeing and Rolls-Royce.

Does it really make much difference that Ford is the founding family, the corporate name and the product brand, compared to General Motors which is only the corporate name and barely even a brand itself? Probably not. Either can be made to work if there are real brand values behind the name, supported by proper marketing and promotion with the right emphasis on reputation.

Using the corporate brand to build confidence

The chief executive of Lever Brothers, at a conference of The Marketing Society some years ago, proclaimed that the company values were vested in the brands; it was a deliberate policy to maintain a low profile for the organization behind the products. For example, Persil told the purchasers all they needed to know about Lever.

It was ironic that he chose Persil to illustrate his point for it was the problems over a new development of Persil, perhaps with hindsight imperfectly launched, which focused much media attention on the company behind the brands. Journalists had little perception of the company, limited understanding, and it had little corporate reputation. So their probing was perhaps tougher and less sympathetic than if a company with an outstanding reputation and a credible profile had made one mistake.

Compare that to the media reaction to British Midland and of its one mistake when an airliner crashed on a motorway. The news reporting was probing and thorough, but nearly all focused on that flight. Any coverage of the company was reasonably positive. It had already established its credentials over the years.

Lever Brothers has since changed its policy. Of course, the company has an excellent record and much to be proud of in such areas as product development, consumer care, employee relations, safety and the environment, but had not felt this to be as important as brand promotion.

The moral of the story is make sure that the power of the promotion of your products does not overshadow the projection of the company, its values, its authority, integrity and quality of leadership.

The marketing emphasis has shifted in the past decade or so towards the retailers which, after all, are closer to the ultimate customer. However, even companies that do not supply products directly to consumers recognize the importance of their brands *and* their corporate reputation – Intel and Cisco would be good examples.

Parallel with this, supportive communications have become essential as we all demand to know more about the companies that influence our lives.

Linking core values at brand and corporate levels

Of course, while reputation is more often considered at the corporate level, brands themselves have a reputation, which ideally should share core aspects of the corporate stance. Certainly, these two must be mutually reinforcing.

Sometimes the corporate and the product reputations and identities are virtually the same – for example the BBC, Birds Eye, Boeing, Cadbury's, Electrolux, Kawasaki, Kellogg, Microsoft, Samsung, Xerox and many others. Some corporations prefer to keep their corporate and brand identities distinct: ICI, GlaxoSmithKline, Merck, Pearson Publishing, Procter & Gamble and Unilever are examples. There are arguments for both approaches; neither is right in all situations, for the wisdom is to consider the options and make a conscious decision on the best strategy to meet corporate ambitions.

Corporate and brand reputations are not static. Management can control how they present themselves, and therefore how they are perceived; reputations can be developed over time. For example Tesco, the supermarket group, grew from its modest origins as a simple market stall through its policy of 'pile them high and sell them cheap'. After the passing of the original founder, Jack Cohen, the competitive changes in the market meant management needed a new strategy; the cheap and cheerful end of the grocery trade, it decided, was not where it wanted to be.

Over time, the managers of the company moved Tesco steadily from that position to where the groceries the company sold were more than cheap: they aspired to quality and value. Indeed, research confirms that Tesco now has a quality reputation that has overtaken many of its competitors, some of which were once seen as quality leaders. This reputation is a key factor in shifting customers from one supermarket to another.

This example also illustrates the relationship between the company as a brand of reputation and the product as a brand of reputation. Consider Kellogg's or IBM, where the corporate name and the brand name are the same and therefore positive aspects should reflect well on each other. On the other hand, companies like Mars and Pepsi-Cola also own major brands that need to have their own identity in the marketplace. In the case of Pepsi-Cola, its sub-brand, Pizza Hut, needs to be promoted as a separate operation with its own quality reputation. At the very least, this pizza restaurant brand might appeal to people who are not necessarily Pepsi-Cola fans, so why limit the potential market by associating the two brands too closely? Mars, the chocolate bar giant, has a very significant pet food operation; clearly putting the Mars brand name onto these products would not relate well to the confectionery side of its business. Consider the relationship between say, ICI and Dulux, or Procter & Gamble and Ariel/Bold/Fairy/Flash.

The corporate reputation and the brand reputation – whether they are working under the same name or not – should be approached as different aspects of the whole reputation management business. Usually, consumers make decisions about the brand in terms of the added value it delivers, the promises it makes and keeps, their expectation of its performance, its value and any enhancement that it might give to the quality of their lives. However, when consumers look at the bigger picture, such factors as corporate social responsibility, environmental policies, the record in employee health and safety and so on, come into play. These are aspects at corporate reputation level, and sometimes at a distance from the brand reputation. Yet there are many examples where customer concern over corporate behaviour has a direct impact upon product sales – for example, Barclays Bank, Coca-Cola, Exxon, McDonald's, Shell and many others have seen corporate behaviour impact on product sales, without any change in price, quality, service or delivery.

Of course, brands can be new or old; they can be trendy and progressive or traditional and stable. The marketing professionals promoting them may use the whole range of communications techniques to establish the personality of the brand, and therefore its reputation in the marketplace.

Brands may not be what they seem. Aqua Libra, the very expensive bottled water with all sorts of added extras, is projected as being a product with a long and interesting heritage. It is described by its distributor, BritVic, as 'reflecting the natural balance proposition of the product, a healthy, refreshing drink made with fruit juices, natural herb extracts and no added sugar'. In reality, it is a development of the marketing people, of relatively recent vintage.

Crabtree & Evelyn, the epitome of old English style, is also in fact an American invention. Bombay Sapphire gin* recalls the glory days

---

*See separate case study.

of the Empire but is, again, a relatively recent US invention. These approaches clearly can work effectively: however, if the marketing is designed to deceive the consumer, this can be very damaging to the reputation when the truth comes out. In fact, there is no need to deceive consumers, as they accept newly created heritage if it is presented as being part of the quality of the product.

A good example of this is Bailey's Irish Cream. This drink was an invention to sell Irish cream and not Irish whisky, and in fact was so well developed and promoted that it carved out a new sector in the alcoholic drinks market and has built itself an enviable reputation, not matched by the efforts of many imitators. Most consumers are aware of the story behind its development. Although it is presented as being something traditional and worthy, the consumer is not misled and does not seem to be too worried about its relative newness on the market – indeed this is almost part of the fun of the product. Similarly, Vladivar Vodka is designed and presented as if it were a traditional brand, perhaps from Russia or Poland. Yet in its advertising and promotional materials, it made the bold and very clear claim that it is from Warrington, an unimpressive town in northern England! Again, this anomaly was part of the enjoyment and value that was offered to the consumer. Indeed, no brand should consider building a reputation on the basis of anything that is not true. Brand managers who try to disguise their made-up heritage are running the risk that the consumer will be disillusioned if he or she believes the deception, then finds out the truth. And of course, in all matters related to reputation, there are always plenty of people around happy to spill the beans.

Brands can also have a long history and can even change over time, yet still retain the loyalty of consumers through the quality of reputation that has been developed. A good example is Tide, which in the last couple of decades has been subject to over 70 measurable improvements and is now available in several different forms. The quality and reputation of the brand continues, and consumers move along happily with the changes as they enhance the perceived value that they get from purchasing and using the product.

In contrast, Marmite is a product that has had its ups and downs in terms of credibility. It has a very long tradition (and a name that originates from the French for a small casserole, a fact unknown by most of its purchasers). Although the brand has sometimes faded a little in the public mind, it has always had a place in the market. More recent efforts by the brand managers to rebuild the product reputation have been extremely successful. Research identified that while a proportion of the market was very keen on the product, a similar proportion were repelled by it! Rather than being embarrassed by the revelations of this research, the brand owners used this fact to develop a powerful campaign along the lines of 'you love it or hate it'. The end result was that what might have been seen as a negative was converted into a positive.

Indeed, to be a major brand, products often only need a small percentage of the market. Equally, it is possible for products to be liked and disliked by similar proportions and still be a great success. The rationale of this is that provided the like and dislike proportions are less than 50 per cent each, they can exist alongside each other in the same survey. As a point of comparison, when Mrs Thatcher was at the height of her powers in her premiership, she was voted both the most popular *and* the most unpopular prime minister ever. The reason for this was that she split popular opinion: the proportion of each vote was around 40 per cent, which could be comfortably accommodated within the overall 100 per cent maximum.

Many marketing directors are concerned not just about managing the profile of their brands and promoting these, but in looking at the deeper matter of reputation; such professionals are usually careful in analysing research on these lines. Failure to do this can be expensive. Some well-known brands – and indeed corporations – have discovered to their cost that a percentage of the marketplace is not happy with their policies. During normal trading this may not be of great significance, but when the company finds itself in the spotlight or under pressure from shareholders, competitors or the media, this proportion can become very vocal. Shell and McDonald's have both suffered from this factor.

Other organizations that might experience such problems at some time in the future include IKEA, PC World and Ryanair, all of which have appeared to be rather cavalier in their attitudes to their customers, and therefore have seemed not to give reputation the attention it might deserve. Increasingly, these factors will be monitored by business analysts, commentators, pressure groups and the media, and may well become important predictors of the likely success or otherwise of trading operations. Also, such companies are in a vulnerable competitive position. Someone planning to come into the furniture, technology retailing or low-cost airline business could research the market and see that such companies are not putting customer care and service at the top of the agenda. This not only identifies a weakness that a sharper competitor could exploit, but could suggest that customer loyalty is low and many might happily move to a rival that would treat them better.

As in all aspects of reputation, a good one is profitable today and insurance for the future.

TARGET CORPORATE AUDIENCES WITH BRAND MARKETING

The growth of consumerism has made marketing important. Brands were a natural development of the importance of customer loyalty. Inevitably, the retailers, being closest to the consumers, took the dominant position. All are also committed users of public relations both to support marketing and to project the corporate position; reputation management is central to their strategies. This must be an obvious approach for a major retailing company with its important investor and corporate audiences. However, the principles can be equally effectively applied to business-to-business, technology and service companies.

Corus Steel, IBM and Intel are just as much brands as consumer product and retailing names. In these cases, the company name may be the same as the individual products – as it is in consumer sectors with names like Braun, Gillette and Yardley.

The strength of this company/brand synergy is the mutual rein-forcement. Indeed, these brands can have such strength that their associations create difficulties in developing into other sectors. Yardley can cover male or female personal care products but might be less credible in small electrical domestic appliances, and so on.

Some companies choose to keep their corporate identity distinct from their brands, such as General Motors, Unilever or Procter & Gamble, as noted earlier. Another advantage of this policy, as major corporations have discovered, is that brands can be both bought and sold without changing the corporate umbrella brand.

MARKETING PROMOTION VERSUS CORPORATE PROJECTION

Whatever your company policy, it is still important that the public relations keeps the brand statements separate from the company values. Ideally there should be two public relations programmes: promoting the products and projecting the corporation – separate, but coordinated.

The marketing approach to the corporation can put a fresh perspective on the management of this important asset, the company name. Sometimes companies can create an aura around an organization. 'We try harder' was credible and worked hard for Avis – for a while. 'The Wonderful World of Woollies', to quote an old UK advertising theme, was ludicrously glitzy to anyone who knew the rundown stores, as they were then.

In the business-to-business sector, Scheering created an interesting example of creative thinking that added a potential reputational edge. The company operates in the agro-chemical world and recognized that many products were seen as damaging to the environment. Through a skilful mix of public relations, technology, new products, customer service and marketing, the company repositioned itself under a theme, 'Green Science'. The result was better credibility, an enhanced reputation – and an award for excellence from the Chartered Institute of Marketing. Even more important, it won for itself a stronger commercial competitive position.

USING BRANDS TO PROJECT CORPORATE VALUES

The corporate reputation is a little like your personal reputation. If you know its values and what it stands for, you can anticipate how it will react. You know this not just from what it says but from your experience, from observations of how the company behaves, and from personal contact.

Would you believe reports that Pepsi was reducing product quality without advising customers?; that BP was instructing tanker skippers to take more dangerous short routes to save shipping costs?; that Philips' electrical insulation standards were below standard?; that BMW was cutting safety protection for its workers? Such values do not remain constant, and companies need constantly to renew and promote them. In an earlier edition of this book, I asked whether you would expect Ford to make cars that could kill you! Whatever your feelings on these issues, you will be making judgements on your knowledge of their reputation and the corporate personality.

Though public relations has this prime corporate role it can be used to support marketing in many areas – by improving awareness, projecting credibility, combating competition, evaluating new markets, creating direct sales leads, reinforcing the effectiveness of sales promotion and advertising, motivating the salesforce, distributors/wholesalers/retailers, introducing new products or services, building brand loyalty, dealing with consumer issues and in many other ways. Good public relations can not only build brand loyalty it can reinforce customer relations efforts, backing both the salesforce and customer services operations.

Richard Yallop, international marketing consultant and business lecturer, speaking at a major marketing seminar in Dubai, observed that it seems nowadays that marketing is obsessed with 'new' and 'different' rather than 'better' and 'more effective'. Many major international companies, and their brands, seem frantic to get this point across in their promotional messages. The real value of reputation management may be more about subtly shifting this emphasis back to real corporate values and marketplace impact.

DEVELOP COMMUNICATIONS STRENGTHS AS INSURANCE

The best-laid marketing plans can sometimes be devastated by factors that are outside the control of marketing management. Confidence in products has been shaken by health, safety or pollution scares which often attract wide news coverage. A few angry shareholders at an AGM have been known to attract more attention than the announcement of a massive new production facility. A few neighbours have been influential in stopping planning permission for extensions to factories.

A historical problem with mercury pollution at one site created poor local media coverage for a division of chemical giant, Aventis. Under an enlightened management, the company developed possibly some of the finest environmental policies in the industry and called in professional public relations resources to improve community relations, measures designed to reinforce a reputation under threat.

These joint initiatives were so successful that, with the full cooperation of local communities, the company has since invested over £50 million on that site in new research and manufacturing facilities.

Community relations was essential to enable the products to be properly marketed; a poor community reputation can be equally damaging to sales.

Demonstrate corporate values locally

A chicken production facility jointly owned by UK food leaders, Spillers and Sainsbury, had such an odour problem that local residents successfully blocked planning permissions for extensions that would have created many new jobs. Again, the reputation of the company as a good employer and thoughtful neighbour had been damaged. The problems could not be solved by technical improvements alone. The goodwill and support of the local people had to be won through a public relations programme to show that the company listened and acted vigorously to end the nuisance and become a good neighbour.

A Cargill corn milling plant was threatened with closure through complaints from neighbours, also over smells. A Morton chemicals facility in a residential area also faced major problems through complaints over coloured but harmless emissions. At both locations, technical improvements were successfully introduced in parallel with effective communications to win community support and to rebuild their reputations.

In all cases, the product marketing could not solve the problem and sales were threatened by issues remote from the normal responsibilities of the marketing function. Clearly, corporate values override the promotional properties of marketing.

LEADING MARKETING WITH PUBLIC RELATIONS

Some marketing campaigns will be led by advertising. Everyday products of limited news value, which are frequently bought, may need the strength of advertising to lift them above competition, stress their special features and benefits, and remind the purchaser of their brand values. Examples might include soft drinks, coffee and most grocery products. Public relations may be used in support to reach both trade and consumer audiences. Coca-Cola has an active involvement in many youth sports, including soccer, for example: even a company as powerful and well resourced as this has learnt how the handling of issues, even unrelated to products, can impact on sales and affect the corporate reputation. Yet many products and services can best be supported with public relations, with this discipline taking the lead. This will be particularly relevant where the product or service has a broad interest, because it is new or affects the quality of our lives, for example.

Philips, the Netherlands' electronics leader, used public relations to launch a sophisticated energy management system for business premises; the UK mushroom industry developed a public relations approach – *make room for the mushrooms* – into which the advertising was designed to fit. First Direct, the world's first electronic home banking service, established its position of strength almost entirely through public relations.

Your marketing professionals will be making the decisions on which discipline will play which role. However, a useful exercise is to ask the advertising, sales, promotion and public relations professionals to identify the balance and the priorities for each craft. You may be surprised how often they will agree, as they did the approach in all the examples outlined above.

Product euphoria can result from uncontrolled competition between disciplines. This needs to be watched. For example, care must be taken to ensure that all claims made are sustainable. Richard Yallop, the international marketing consultant, points out the dangers of unrealistically boosting customer expectations about your offer. If these cannot be delivered, such actions will add cost (in dealing with complaints and problems) rather than customer value. This can seriously undermine the chance of achieving customer satisfaction and, therefore, weaken both customer retention and company reputation.

CONDITION THE MARKET THROUGH COMMUNICATIONS

Another area where public relations may be able to make an invaluable contribution is where the market needs to be educated to a new approach or concept. Communications targeted at the key influencers can often condition the market. This will allow more direct sales and marketing efforts to follow, to convert interest into sales leads.

Specialist US accountants, Howard Schultz Associates, found a good but limited market for their sophisticated, computer-aided accounts payable audit service. This could recover large sums for major retailers who had overpaid suppliers or not reclaimed discounts to which they were entitled. The service was too complex to explain through advertising. Direct mail was not an effective method of reaching the few dozen senior people who made the decisions, as they tended to be flooded with mail approaches. A public relations route based on editorial briefings, articles and features provided the solution.

Of course, advertising and public relations should not be viewed as competitive but should be run as complementary, reinforcing communciations techniques. Therefore, liaison between advertising and public relations must be close and effective.

GET PUBLIC RELATIONS AND ADVERTISING TOGETHER

Coordination will only be possible if marketing management brings the advertising and public relations people together and establishes mutual understanding and trust.

Both sides may resist the restrictions which the need to work together inevitably imposes. It is as important to establish areas of independence as it is to agree on the common ground between them – for example, it might be necessary to coordinate the timing of the advertising and public relations events around the launch of a new product, but it may *not* be necessary for both to work to the same creative approach. This flexibility can win the most from integrated communications.

Regular meetings between company marketing professionals and external advisers can be invaluable. Sun Valley, the leading international food company, is among those that successfully pursue a policy of integrating marketing disciplines. All agencies meet and share ideas, therefore developing campaigns which complement each other. This approach ensures that the company's advertising, public relations and direct marketing activities work in tandem, producing the maximum consumer awareness. The end result is not just improved marketing but an enhanced projection of the company reputation.

CONTROL THE MARKETING SPECIALISTS

It could be argued (and often has been) that the primary role of marketing is to shift product, not build reputation. This may be true, but intelligent marketing initiatives will often add 'reputation' values to the products.

It is essential to get all elements in the marketing mix working together. This puts a special onus on the client, for there are usually quite powerful personalities at work heading up the advertising agency, public relations consultancy, marketing, research house, design company, sales promotion specialists and so on. The loudest or most powerful should not dominate the others.

However, when these disciplines work together the effect can be quite extraordinary. Quite often the advertising can be news itself. The Gold Blend couple and their on/off romance was an accident where a television campaign began to generate news comment, rather than being planned to be of media interest.

QBO, the public relations consultancy, worked with ad agency HHCL to make their advertising proposition news. The agency had created a character who, when the ad was cast, became balding actor Jim Dunk. The proposition (hardly original but extremely originally treated in the advertising) was to try to put people off the product on the basis that there was not enough of it to go round.

The product was Molson lager, then a new beer from Canada, trying to squeeze into a highly competitive marketplace. Jim Dunk protested in press and television advertisements that beer drinkers would not like it. In one memorable press advertisement, he said, 'Don't ask for a Molson, as a refusal often offends.'

Editorial columns, chat shows and cartoonists took up this idea and the ensuing media coverage multiplied the effectiveness of the advertising by an estimated factor of five plus.

Creativity can give a new market edge and enhanced reputation

It is possible for companies to take existing identities and give them renewed currency through the use of creativity. A good example of building competitive edge and changed perceptions was the fresh thinking shown by one contender in the crowded insurance market. This innovation took place in 1986 but the impact continues today.

Scottish Widows, as its name suggests, is a long-established insurance company whose original aim was to allow the working Scotsman to provide for his widow and family should he die before his children had grown, a sadly frequent occurrence in the 19th century. Of course, the whole market has changed significantly over the past 100-plus years, and today the company is one of over 30 sophisticated firms competing for market share. The company recognized that clear, strong branding was critical in order to overcome the perceived lack of differentiation between both the various financial products and the companies that were offering these. Research suggested that the branding of Scottish Widows was not as high-profile as it could be, and the name associations, seen by many as rather dated, were not always working in its favour.

The idea was to create a living logo. The key driver was to use differentiation, not just across all its 30 competitors but to distinguish the company from the other six in the sector that also had the word 'Scottish' in their name. The vital need to build brand awareness within a limited budget required a creative execution that would make the spend seem bigger than it actually was. The aim was to build positive attitudes towards the brand while confirming the proposition that Scottish Widows is 'good with your money' in every aspect, from investment strategy to performance.

The result of a creative brainstorm was the concept for a relaunch campaign to be built around a proposed television commercial that would use some lateral thinking. This was planned to feature a young woman, attractive though a little mysterious, and dressed in a style that suggested that she was a widow. The approach was intended to counter all the negative factors associated with the word 'widow'; this proposed to present the company in a competitive position with positives such as strength, reliability, integrity, innovation and heritage.

The concept was approved and the commercial and all supporting promotional and public relations material was planned and produced. The impact of the first television commercial was immediate. Name awareness, which had hovered around 30 per cent as long as the company had subscribed to advertising research services, shot up to 86 per cent within six weeks of the launch of the campaign, and has stayed there or thereabouts over all the years since. Since then, the company has consistently used the idea of the living logo, and this continues, management believes, to give the brand both the currency and the related identity that helps separate and distinguish it from competitors.

Explaining the thinking that led to the brand updating initiative, Alan Whiting, head of brand development at Scottish Widows, said:

> Creative communications costs no more than a routine approach, yet can vastly increase the effectiveness. Our business is all about reputation and relationships, as our clients are often with us for a lifetime. Sometimes, companies attempt to change their identity to bring a new freshness to the approach: however, I think our example proves that a fresh approach to an existing property can add both new dimensions and build upon existing strengths.

ADVERTISING VERSUS PUBLIC RELATIONS PERSONNEL

Setting objectives for both advertising and public relations that relate to enhancing the brand reputation makes sense. Equally, it is important to be sure that no aspect of the promotion damages either corporate or brand reputation values. One way to build synergy and positive values is to get these professionals to cooperate.

The advertising and public relations elements of a campaign should each have their own distinct budget. Advertising is usually handled through external resources. Consequently, when an agency is working alongside an in-house public relations team, budgets may get disproportionate. Effective public relations requires adequate funding and this applies as much to an in-house programme as to a consultancy programme.

Once the budgets have been agreed, there should be no competition for expenditure between advertising and public relations. Although the approaches each might take may differ, both must project consistent messages that reinforce corporate *and* marketing objectives. The effective coordination of advertising and public relations could be assisted by following these 10 simple suggestions:

1. Involve both disciplines in the marketing planning.
2. Define complementary objectives.
3. Allocate separate and firm budgets to each.
4. Agree responsibilities and planned activities.
5. Establish practical routines for coordination.
6. Have regular joint planning sessions.
7. Get each to present their campaigns to the other.

8. Make a joint presentation to the organization's management.
9. Ensure regular exchange of all documents/information.
10. Insist that all parties work together this year, or they might not get the chance next year!

Celebrities and their relationship with brand reputation

Famous people use products and services in the same way as every other member of the public. Companies that have been able to identify those who are users have often found an opportunity to add the glitter and glamour of a celebrity to support their brand, enhance its reputation, build their customer base and create shareholder value.

Hamish Pringle is the director general of the Institute of Practitioners in Advertising, the trade body and professional institute representing advertising, media and marketing communications agencies. He has written *Celebrity Sells*, a marvellously helpful and comprehensive book on how to use stars. Sir Martin Sorrell, the leader of world-leading advertising group WPP, described the book as 'A rigorous analysis, solidly reinforced with case histories which will provide clients with invaluable insights and great comfort.'

In a chapter on how to use celebrities to support brands, Pringle discusses the various levels at which the star can provide brand endorsement, including participation in advertising or in interviews set up for public relations purposes. He observes that at another, much deeper level of engagement, the celebrity might be hired as an employee of the brand: for example as a sports team member, a named designer for an haute couture house, a star analyst in the financial services sector, a conductor of an orchestra, temporary guest editor of a magazine or even a chief executive.

In such work, the right celebrity with the right associations does not just promote the brand and the company, he argues. The star can also add considerably to the demonstration of the values that help to build the reputation, which in turn is the bedrock of the relationships on which the business depends. He stresses that the use of celebrities must be undertaken in a managed and planned way, with strong strategic thinking and adequate promotional muscle.

As an example he quotes the campaign that M & C Saatchi developed when it won the brief from the Home Office to improve police recruitment. This used carefully selected celebrities to drive home points about the importance of and the social benefit of the work of the police service. The people who starred in the 'I couldn't, could you?' campaign included Joan Bakewell, John Barnes, Bob Geldof, Lennox Lewis, Patsy Palmer and Simon Weston.

The result was a 73 per cent increase in recruits, reversing a seven-year decline. Although the campaign cost £15 million, he feels that should be compared with the cost of achieving a similar level of success through recruitment consultants, which would have been £43 million. Using the police themselves to recruit would have cost £124 million in lost police resources, while simply paying the police more to attract more recruits would have cost the taxpayer an initial £428 million, plus ongoing costs. So it was a big spend but big results, with a campaign that significantly enhanced the reputation of the police as a community service.

Bombay Sapphire builds worldwide sales

Marketing concepts that project and reinforce the brand reputation

The company produces the products, yet in truth, the brand and its perceptions exist in the minds of the customers and potential customers. Good marketing professionals must try to control all factors that could influence brand reputation.

Just as one measure of public relations might be what those who matter say about your organization when you are not there, so brand reputation could well be what influential observers say about the products, the services and the corporate back-up to these. When the Brand Council described one consumer brand as 'an iconic design with its own distinctive taste' this was a powerful testament to the strategies of those who managed all those factors that could shape public perceptions.

The brand is Bombay Sapphire London gin, a product in a highly competitive drinks market. How did it achieve its icon status and a recognition that many longer-established spirits respect and admire? With total worldwide sales well in excess of a million cases a year and rising, Bombay Sapphire has more than doubled in size since Bacardi acquired the premium spirit brand from Diageo (themselves no slouches in the marketing department) in 1998.

The brand owners believe that the rate of growth under Bacardi ownership is consistent with the company's policy of focusing on premium spirits. Bacardi explains that it has taken great care to protect and raise awareness of the special characteristics of Bombay Sapphire without endangering these through over-exposure. This strategy has paid off, ensuring that even in markets where gin sales are flat or in decline, Bombay Sapphire stands apart as a premium spirit brand, continuing to reach a growing number of enthusiastic consumers.

'After making a significant brand acquisition, a more conventional company might try to force growth through aggressive marketing but Bacardi has done the opposite,' says Bombay Sapphire global marketing director Marshall Dawson. 'Our highly targeted approach to marketing has allowed Bombay Sapphire to flourish. We've taken the time to create the right consumer experience; careful nurturing over the last six years has turned Bombay Sapphire into one of the most successful spirit brands in the world.'

The brand proposition shapes its reputation

Good brands, of course, are strongly positioned through good marketing. But great brands also have an additional attractive benefit, once called the unique selling proposition. Bacardi believe the USP is that the gin is actually manufactured in a distinctive (and, they claim, better) manner. Unlike most gins, which boil their botanicals directly in the spirit to achieve their taste, Bombay Sapphire Gin is distilled alone; the 10 uniquely combined botanicals from around the world are infused to achieve a greater subtlety of taste. Although it is a recent developed brand, the manufacturing formula is based on a recipe from 1761; Bombay Sapphire is produced by passing the spirit vapour through the botanicals, which are held separately from the spirit in a perforated copper basket. This process known as vapour infusion allows the gentle absorption of each of the aromatic flavours; this, they believe, results in what they describe as a balanced, crisp yet delicate finish.

'Bombay Sapphire has broken the mould of what people expect from a gin,' says Marshall Dawson. 'Its distinctive flavour and striking packaging set it apart from the crowd but, while the eye-catching bottle design successfully pulls in consumers, it's the quality of the spirit in the bottle which keeps them coming back.

'By talking about its 10 botanicals and vapour infusion production process, Bombay Sapphire has raised awareness of the great care taken in how it is made. There is a growing appreciation of quality food and drink; consumers understand the benefits of trading up to premium products which source the finest ingredients and have an element of craftsmanship in the way they are created.'

The marketing approach that helped position Bombay Sapphire in its premier position included a concept that allowed the marketing professionals to promote the brand, in a controlled manner, through advertising, public relations, events and sales promotion activity; this idea was originally developed in the Diageo days but has been developed internationally. All activities are designed and run to support and enhance the brand reputation.

Marketing concept built around design excellence

The Bombay Sapphire striking translucent blue glass bottle is instantly recognizable; this suggested to the marketing planners that the concept of innovative design could have a direct relevance to both the product and the interests of many of its current and potential consumers. From this thinking, the marketing team expanded and added new initiatives that created powerful links with the global design community. Today, Bombay Sapphire supports the inspirational designs of many international artists, designers and architects.

Bombay Sapphire began its association with the world of design in the 1990s, when internationally acclaimed designers first created their versions of the ultimate martini cocktail glass inspired by the brand. Since then glasses by design leaders, such as Karim Rashid and Dakota Jackson, have been show-cased in a global advertising campaign for the brand.

Today, the Bombay Sapphire-inspired world encompasses a broad range of design disciplines including ceramics, textiles and furniture. London-based artist/designer Dominic Crinson has created a stunning wall of Bombay Sapphire-inspired tiles by manipulating digital images to achieve a kaleido-scopic effect, and US designer Emma Gardner was inspired by the qualities of Bombay Sapphire to create a richly decorated textile design. Both designs are showcased in the latest evolution of the Bombay Sapphire global advertising campaign. Celebrated lighting designer Paul Cocksedge, short-listed for Designer of the Year, was similarly inspired to create the Bombay Sapphire Light, which glows blue despite having no visible source of electricity.

The Bombay Sapphire Foundation was established in 2001 to recognize, encourage and reward the very best in contemporary design and in particular glass design. The members of the Foundation include leading international designers and some of the world's most respected figures from the glass and design industry.

To support and reward excellence in glass design, the Bombay Sapphire Foundation launched an international glass design award, the Bombay Sapphire Prize. As the biggest international glass design award, this celebrates the achievements of international artists, designers and architects who work with this challenging material to create stunning results. The best entries for the Bombay Sapphire Prize are showcased in a touring glass exhibition called the Bombay Sapphire Blue Room. In 2004, the Bombay Sapphire Blue Room began its first international tour when it opened at the highly acclaimed Powerhouse Museum in Sydney.

Strategy meets aspirations of target market

Sales analysis confirms that Bombay Sapphire is particularly popular interna-tionally with the younger, 25- to 35-year-old consumers; these tend to reflect a strong interest in style and design. The brand's global advertising campaign – Bombay Sapphire Inspired – and global design initiatives such as the presti-gious Bombay Sapphire Prize (and the Bombay Sapphire Designer Glass Competition for up-and-coming designers) mean that Bombay Sapphire is more relevant to consumers worldwide.

Bombay Sapphire global marketing director Marshall Dawson believes that good marketing is closely linked to reputation management. 'The reputation of a company is dependent on the reputation of its brands; these absolutely affect the bottom line. After all, what you're selling is the brand not your company. A company which prides itself on delivering quality and service, must reflect this in its brands. At the end of the day, the consumer is buying into the brand not the brand owner.'

The results of these marketing initiatives can be measured in enhanced brand reputation and, equally important, on the bottom line. Even competitors would accept that Bombay Sapphire is now a global phenomenon, with sales growing in every one of its markets around the world. In the United States and the UK, for example, Bombay Sapphire is attracting increasing numbers of consumers, despite a raft of new entrants into these markets. Dawson adds that in one recent 12-month period, sales of Bombay Sapphire overtook Beefeater in both markets, making it the number one premium gin in the UK and the number two in the United States.

In the United States, sales of Bombay Sapphire have outperformed the market, increasing nearly 10 per cent,* and in the UK, where overall sales of gin are flat, Bombay Sapphire is bucking the trend with sales up over 23 per cent in the off-trade, according to the latest figures as this case study went to press.**

SOME OBSERVATIONS, IN SUMMARY

1. Use public relations, properly planned well in advance, to make a strategic input to marketing, helping to shape the total approach to customers and its reinforcement of reputation.
2. Consider the role of public relations in, say, market education, intelligence, countering competition, and not just its publicity function.
3. The overall brief for marketing public relations is usually (and valuably) to create the favourable environment within which the business operates.
4. The goodwill towards the company is directly linked, so research confirms, to public understanding and acceptance of product quality and...
5. ... of equal importance, research also shows that the more familiar the market is with the company, the higher will be the level of regard.
6. Public relations is essential in marketing but it is not *part* of marketing, as it has responsibilities for non-marketing audiences...
7. ... though these two areas must be coordinated – for a pollution incident, share speculation or plant closure can all have an impact on marketing initiatives; the issues audit will identify areas of risk and opportunity.

---

*IWSR 2004: average 9-litre case sales.
**AC Nielsen.

8. However large the function may need to be, make sure it is run by one person, reporting to the top and preferably in the 'next-door' office.

9. An investment in public relations should be considered and planned as an investment in the company capital value, particularly in the contribution it makes to strengthening relationships and reputation.

10. Make sure that separate promotional plans are prepared for each company brand, but work these consistently together.

11. Your most important brand is the corporate name so be certain that both the corporate communications and marketing reflect this in the corporate values that are projected.

12. Strong and well-organized public relations will help protect the company from damage when it encounters problems.

13. When planning marketing promotion, make sure the quality of company management is fully projected for they are custodians of the reputation.

14. Relate the marketing public relations to the customer-care programme so that both are working to harmonious objectives and projecting consistent messages.

15. Consider leading your marketing with public relations, say, when you are launching a newsworthy product or when the market needs educating.

16. Manage your public relations and advertising to work together, but to separate plans and budgets and with separate resources.

17. Develop advertising that has news impact, say, an intriguing storyline or characters, and use of personalities or topical approaches identified through research.

18. You, the client, must always keep control, particularly when the powerful personalities in agencies and consultancies might exceed their responsibilities.

7

Employees

Mobilize a vast volunteer army of goodwill ambassadors

Key factors discussed

- Generating positive staff attitudes.
- Listening before setting policy.
- Using internal messages externally.
- Monitoring employee needs.
- Making every employee a PRO.
- Winning support for reputation policies.
- The communications pyramid.
- The right technique for the right job.

EMPLOYEES AND PUBLIC RELATIONS

The company makes more than profits through the efforts of its employees; it makes good vibrations or bad. Employees perform some important functions to which most managements pay too little attention. As many of these services are totally unpaid and can make a big contribution to commercial success, this may not be the wisest approach.

What are these valuable, voluntary tasks that employees undertake for free? First, whether you ask them or not, they put out messages about your operations to *all* the audiences upon whom you depend for success. Second, if you ask them, they can tell you exactly what these audiences think about your organization.

With a little imagination and management skill, all this goodwill and powerful feedback can be a bonus on top of their *paid-for* efforts that build your success. However many listeners, viewers or readers the communications may reach, no audience is as important as your own staff. If company personnel are not briefed and, indeed, accept ownership of the corporate stance, then external communications will be undermined as soon as this credibility gap is exposed, as surely it will be.

Employees are a powerful part of the company marketing. They can project the messages about the company and embody the brand. In a service business it is vital not to underestimate the role that employees play in the brand – and hence their central role in creating and managing reputation.

Why brief the analysts, inform the shareholders, woo the institutions, persuade the customers, flatter the legislators, or court the journalists if you keep in the dark those who have committed their working lives to the company? The influence of employees (for good or bad) can be very significant. Poor employee relations can bring down the company, while a well-motived team can dramatically improve productivity.

Employees are the living face of the organization and must project the values that reinforce the reputation. Steve Gates, managing director of Denplan, runs a company that provides sophisticated services to the dental profession. 'As in any service sector, you depend upon good relationships and a strong reputation. Clients will only work with people and organizations that they can trust. This means that every employee must not only believe in the company values but also must project and demonstrate the reality of these in everything they do.'

Gates does not think it is sensible to allow this goodwill and understanding to develop on its own. Everyone on the team, he feels, reflects the values that the top managers project. If customer care or integrity are slogans on the walls and not part of management attitudes towards the business and the customers, then standards of service delivery can go astray. 'Good, consistent and continuous two-way communications across the whole team is the only way to make sure everyone owns and is committed to the qualities that make the company special,' he asserts.

In Denplan, as well as communications being part of everyone's job, the whole company regularly goes away from the office for real, in-depth and candid reviews of company policies, progress, new developments, issues, problems and solutions. 'Our colleagues know they can say what they want to say and not just what the bosses would like to hear. That way we are all always dealing with reality. Therefore our service is not some conceptual idea, it is real and relevant. And our client retention levels of close to 100 per cent seem to confirm that these policies work.'

Build favourable employee attitudes

The late Leonard Pool, chairman of Air Products, once told me that companies rarely have the 'wrong' people, more often the wrong management methods.

After all, Sir Iain Vallance and his team created the BT success with largely the same employees (slimmed down, true) that had made the nationalized organization an inefficient, work-to-rule, unresponsive megalith. But success is not permanent or guaranteed. Later, the *same* teams got complacent and turned one the world's largest telecoms operations into a sad shadow of itself.

How was ASDA changed from the *who-cares* to *the customer is king* style? This success profited managers and shareholders alike, as it attracted Wal-Mart to buy the company as an attractive springboard for its growth into Europe. The differences lay in the management, and the business environment in which they could work.

There are, however, other factors affecting success which are equally as important as good employee relations. Third party publics upon whom the organization depends are likely to form opinions based upon their observations. For example, their decisions to invest in the company, write favourably about it, lend to it, work for it, listen to it or buy from it will often be affected by the attitudes of those closest to the reality – the employees.

If a Sears' salesperson were unhelpful, would it affect your attitude as, say, a shareholder, if the management wanted your support to resist a hostile takeover? If the Mercedes sales or service staff criticized their dealership bosses would you be as keen to buy from them again, regardless of the fleet deal you are offered?

The famous John Cleese training film for Video Arts *Who Sold You*

That Then? demonstrated the damage that disaffected employees can cause. But real examples are even more telling than the fictional.

Focus on what employees feel and say

I was once part of an advisory group planning a computer installation for the Chartered Institute of Marketing which, eventually, cost over £5 million. An order worth having!

One company with whom I had some minor dealings approached me to see if I could get them on the tender list. As I was planning to pass their offices a few days later, I agreed to call in to discuss it. I was kept waiting in an untidy reception – not a good start, but time that proved not to be wasted. As always, I ask questions to find out as much as I possibly can. The receptionist was bright and chatty. So I launched into the standard start: 'Do you like working here?'

By chance I had hit upon a disenchanted employee, and they had let her loose on reception to wreak her revenge without inhibition! With a little coaxing she told me all.

> Not bad, I suppose. It pays the rent. But the way they treat you. Something chronic. They break all their promises. They told me I'd be getting a new switchboard, but they can't pay for it because they're still waiting for some big deal to be confirmed. They're just plain disorganized and unreliable. The boss is hardly ever here and, when he is, don't try talking to him after lunch because he's three parts to the wind and makes no sense to anyone.

I exaggerate a little (but not much) for effect.

In contrast, I was once picked up by the driver to Yutaka Harada, then the European managing director of Japanese steel and shipbuilding company, NKK. 'What is your boss like?' I asked, slipping into the familiar routine.

> Best person I have ever worked for. A true gentleman and highly professional. Reliable, polite and courteous. Everyone in the office has the highest respect for him. We'd do anything he asks. You'll like him.

And I did. The chauffeur gave his comments with such genuine warmth that there was absolutely no doubt about his real feelings. He had seen the man behind the business leader and he had liked what he had seen. There could be no better public relations officer for that company. And how many others had heard his positive message?

START BY LISTENING

At the top in the company, the human resources and the public relations functions need to cooperate closely to achieve the best results. In some organizations, internal communications policy is the responsibility of human resources, even if the delivery systems are operated by public relations. Coordination and consistent messages are essential to creating a well-informed and motivated workforce.

To some degree, the corporate reputation is dependent on listening and adopting, not just talking louder!

One of the best contributions that your employees can make is to act as the eyes and ears of the organization. You need to know what they see and hear when dealing with customers, competitors, factory neighbours and other groups. Everyone in the organization is a member of the public relations team. They should be listening to public comments and feeding them back, as well as putting out positive messages about the company, its aims and its performance.

Feedback systems play their part and there are many excellent books on how these work – as well as organizations, such as the Industrial Society, which advise on setting up team briefings and information feedback processes. These are beyond the scope of this book, but there are some communications principles that managers should consider.

Consider the *external* impact of internal messages

One benefit of planned internal communications systems, say the cascade type, is that core messages will be presented consistently. These can be reinforced at briefings by notes, newsletters or other handout material. Local, branch and department activities can also be discussed at such meetings as well as broader company developments.

Remember that the more open you are in briefing and providing information to employees, the closer the coordination that you will need between internal and external communications – and, indeed, this is one reason why these two aspects of public relations are better coordinated through one person.

From long experience at the top in business, Sir Edwin Nixon, when deputy chairman of National Westminster, offered a word of caution:

Spend as much time as you can on communications but, whenever you are communicating some important message internally, you must assume that what you say will be transmitted externally, sometimes to the press, sometimes in minutes, but certainly within 24 hours. Write nothing internally without considering its impact in the public domain.

Lead from the front, but listen to the others...

How can the company ensure that it understands what people really think so that communications are addressing the real issues and shaping the actual perceptions?

A listening philosophy starts at the top – and that means a real 'listening' style. Leaders must lead but it is no sign of weakness to listen before leading. Those who consider they know best, without input, risk making mistakes; good decisions depend upon the views of others who may be better informed or closer to the action. The listening chief can be truly decisive; he or she can participate in all policy discussions because the views of those affected are known. The listening chief *listens!*

Listening is an infectious habit. It can spread throughout the company. Indeed, it can be made part of the business culture. True listening – not the synthetic artifice – has kept such companies as Unilever, Cadbury Schweppes, Microsoft and Procter & Gamble consistently at the top. Listening proved a key factor, for example, in the recovery of Microsoft when the company underestimated the internet revolution; lesser organizations might have failed and missed this massive opportunity.

Dr Don Spencer, then managing director of Air Products where I once headed public relations, told me: 'I don't always like what you say; but I need you to say it.' He agreed to a new company newspaper without any external clearance procedures, editorial committee or supervision ('I'll tell you what I don't like when I've read it,' he said, but never did). This publication was important in building superb internal relations in that company. Managers were trusted, for they listened. They expressed their thoughts and encouraged all staff to speak out. The company achieved over 20 per cent year-on-year growth throughout that decade.

The chief executive will be working with a small team who know each other so well that candour should be routine. But ensure that a dominant personality on the team does not bully colleagues into compliance. This is likely to be far more of a problem at mid- and lower-level management. During and after the privatization of many state monopolies including, say, KPN the Netherlands telco, one of the obstacles to effective internal communications was the attitude of an important minority of middle managers. They acted as blocks in the communications chain for they believed that information was power and their role was strengthened if their staffs did not know as much as they did.

Make listening as much company policy as directing. Perhaps the key elements in developing the environment in which views that matter will be advanced might be:

1. *Practise listening at the top.* Ask for views *before* advancing your own. Hold listening sessions with representatives of key groups.
2. *Hold back on your judgements.* Acknowledge all views as constructive. Encourage further comment by refraining from criticizing those you do not like.
3. *Expect your managers to listen.* Encourage all members of your team to follow your example. If necessary, set up training sessions in listening. Run a stopwatch on talking and listening ratios.
4. *Ask executives to report back on views.* Set up some cascade information system or similar. Be sure that a central element is feeding back views gained from listening.
5. *Constantly monitor views.* Make an understanding of opinions a factor to be discussed constantly. Monitor these opinions in a way that allows comparison. Circulate interesting or challenging views.

USE INFORMATION TO ENLIGHTEN, NOT DROWN

Today's employees expect 'communications', as do all other audiences. But even in the most sophisticated companies, too many employees are communicated 'at' rather than 'with'. Often only lip-service is paid to the concept of two-way communications.

Management needs to question seriously whether one-way information activity is productive. Effective employee communications must create understanding and support among employees to enable the company to operate more efficiently. Again, some organizations produce too much information of the wrong kind.

With some companies, communication almost becomes easier than

management. This was a problem in the early stages of the spectac-
ular growth of companies like Cisco, Microsoft and Virgin, for
example, before management addressed the balance.

Involvement is no substitute for leadership. It is the responsibility
of management both to manage and communicate: these are insepa-
rable. Any employee misunderstandings, confusion or lack of
support must be the result of management failing to communicate
effectively. This responsibility cannot be delegated or abdicated.

Analyse the information needs of your employees

Checking the balance is simple. What would *you* want to know if you
were an employee? What would you *like* to know? What would you
accept that you should not know, for reasons of confidentiality,
commercial sensitivity or otherwise?

Employees of an organization have information rights, needs and
desires... and these are not all the same. For example, some information rights are detailed by law – contracts of employment, rights
relating to sickness, holidays, pension, safety at work and many
other factors. Some companies have negotiated agreements which
cover information requirements, and these soon become established
as 'rights'. Across the EU and in the United States there is a growing
level of legislation that is identifying and defining the information
rights of all employees. We are seeing some important changes; in
particular, European legislation affecting multinationals could
involve companies needing to consider changing policies in countries *outside* the European Community, where these have become a
requirement for employees in an EU country.

Different practices in different national divisions or subsidiaries of
multinational companies will increasingly become anomalous. For
example, workers in the United States have the right to more information on hazardous substances than those in the UK. Some factory
safety standards in Portugal are not as strict as in the Netherlands.
German safe working levels with chemicals and radioactive materials are tougher than most. Building workers in parts of the Far East
are not protected from asbestos risks that would not be allowed in
Europe. The pressure on achieving global best-practice standards is
slowly eliminating such anomalies.

Where major companies operate to different standards in different
markets (albeit as a result of different national requirements), the
information democracy will pressure these steadily up to the highest
standard. As one of the more pragmatic of the rules of public rela-

tions suggests, if you are going to have to do it sooner or later anyway, why not do it sooner and gain the brownie points for enlightened management?

However, the *needs* of employees in relation to information are rather different from their legal rights. At present there may be no statutory *right* for employees to know about the anticipated development of their company, but it might be a very *realistic* need; such information may ensure that they understand and support management plans. Equally, employees might want to know what new investments are likely to be made that will materially affect their jobs and so on. Where commercial factors or stock exchange regulations limit the information that can be provided, employees will appreciate this being explained.

The corporation needs trust and it should have the confidence to trust its own employees. And those who have tried will confirm how surprisingly loyal and confidential employees can be when they are trusted and brought onto the inside track. Pamela Taylor, then BBC director of corporate affairs, recalls how she encouraged the director general to brief the top 160 staff on confidential plans. This was at the time the BBC was going through controversial changes. These senior managers included journalists in the news business (some of whom were deeply concerned about the direction of the corporation's plans). Every single one respected the confidence and there was not the slightest leak.

All new business initiatives need the support of employees. Kwik-Fit's top public relations adviser, Robin Dunseath, spotted the potential in 'Operation Christmas Child', a project run by the charity Samaritan's Purse. This organization invites British youngsters to fill shoeboxes with toys which are subsequently distributed to children mainly in Eastern Europe, whose lives had been destroyed by poverty, disease or war. Kwik-Fit offered to open all their 700 centres in the UK as collection points for the shoeboxes, calling the campaign 'Operation Shoebox'. The addition of this national network helped persuade the national breakfast television channel, GMTV, to adopt the project as their Christmas campaign. The result was that over 1 million shoeboxes were donated.

For Kwik-Fit, the campaign brought several benefits. Through television and newspaper coverage, the company's caring culture was projected to the public. The scheme also attracted new people into Kwik-Fit centres. Above all, the Kwik-Fit people, who were fundamentally involved in the shoebox collection, were able to participate in a face-to-face relationship with those who brought in the boxes. 'The scheme was a major success for us,' said Sir Tom Farmer, Kwik-Fit's then chief executive. 'Operation Shoebox itself is a tremendous project, which enables us to involve our people, from fitters to customers, in helping others in a meaningful and sympathetic way. The support of a major television network projected our caring culture to the public and enabled our people to interact with them in a meaningful way'. Dunseath felt that Operation Shoebox reinforced the company's community approach, earning goodwill and an involvement across key audiences that helped to build reputation.

Of course great concepts depend on employees for success, and ideas work best if they capture their imagination. Indeed, creativity can be applied anywhere to any exercise and few areas have the potential offered by public relations, particularly when the concept can involve the whole team of employees.

Operation Shoebox was a simple, inexpensive but highly original concept that helped the disadvantaged, won much goodwill from all who participated and reinforced the community reputation of the company.

EMPLOYEES AS CORPORATE AMBASSADORS

Of course, directors will need to have a clear view of the information that has to be provided by statutory right, union negotiation or trade precedent; that should be provided in the interest of good understanding; and that is confidential and does not have to be freely available until the time the company decides it is appropriate.

To build a company-wide public relations force requires skill and dedication; it will not happen by accident. Even if employees are content and well motivated, they may not see it as part of their job to be positive in their discussions. A *good old moan* may be a diverting pastime but criticism of the company by one of its own employees can be devastatingly damaging.

There are a number of key steps to be taken to ensure that every employee is an ambassador for the company. These could be summarized by saying that staff need to:

● understand how the company stands, and its vision;
● support what it wishes to achieve;

- appreciate clearly their own role within these plans;
- become involved and contribute in their own areas;
- support management efforts to move the operations ahead;
- make a commitment to the aims of the organization.

Do not make the mistake of thinking that information alone is enough. Information is often not enough to change opinions or to create the right attitudes. It is quite possible for employees to know what the policies are but not understand why they have been adopted, or even resent them or disagree with the ambitions. In one study, 45 per cent of the workforce of a US high-technology company were not familiar with the corporate mission, widely published in literature and proudly displayed in receptions – but not presented properly internally. More seriously, even when shown this, almost 55 per cent either did not agree or felt the company was not operating in the way it professed.

Always brief your team first-hand

Communications should be organized so that employees are briefed directly and *ahead* of getting the information through other channels. This can present some practical difficulties, but they must be overcome.

To be told about developments one day and to read about them the next day in the national or local paper gives this news a special interest – and treats the employee as a trusted confidant. Reading that same news one day and being briefed on it the next is demeaning and can create massive resentment. Exactly the same news can be motivating or, handled badly, can be totally demotivating.

Stock exchange rules on insider trading may prevent a company from briefing employees in advance. However, with a little planning, the workforce can be briefed virtually simultaneously.

European engineering group Laurence Scott had constant industrial strife and problems with many of the workers. The management would brief national and trade media on information they refused to give to shop-floor employees. Some responded by buying shares so they would receive mailings and invitations to attend AGMs. At one infamous shareholder meeting, angry employees picketed the AGM and voted (in vain) against every motion. This created damaging and totally avoidable critical news reports. This was a company that offered newly recruited 18-year-old clerical staff better employment terms than shop-floor personnel who might have put in 40 years' service.

Sadly, but not surprisingly, this company is but a pale shadow of the firm that was once a global leader. This may not be a result solely of its personnel policies, but they could be indicative of poor management.

Support figures with the right information

Of course, shareholders and employees may want different information. Some staff may require additional explanation if they are to understand fully the significance of the developments. They will certainly want to know more about how business and financial performance affects their jobs and their positions within the organization.

UK entrepreneur Sir Richard Branson, maintains that in running a company the priority must be employees – even ahead of customers. If employees are well informed, supportive and well motivated, he suggests that they are more likely to provide the levels of customer service that keep clients coming back for more. And if customers are getting the levels of service they want, this is far more likely to generate the returns to shareholders. Many companies reverse this order and put little weight behind forming and motivating their employees – the people who actually generate the profits.

Whenever a major policy decision needs to be presented, employees should be treated as a priority group. They need to have the opportunity to understand and discuss such policies if they are to implement them effectively.

Employees should only be asked for their views where the directors are likely to take notice of these in formulating decisions. Where a policy has been decided, it is an insult to ask people for their views when they know that these will have no significance.

Clearly, it is perfectly legitimate for a company to say: *This is our policy, this is why we have developed it, we would like to discuss this with you so that you can explore any areas of confusion or uncertainty and, when we have done that, we will be asking you to support this.*

That's enlightened leadership, even effective communications, but it is not consultation.

MAKE INFORMATION BELIEVABLE AND CONSISTENT

The organization should be at the centre of its own communications network with information radiating out to the key audiences. At the same time, as noted earlier, information should also be flowing back into the organization. And, whether the company likes it or not, information will also be flowing between the various audiences, bypassing any official source; none of these is operating in a watertight compartment. For example, there will be communication between factory neighbours and company shareholders; customers and suppliers, prospective employees and environmental groups. Often these are the same people, for neighbours can be customers and so on.

This is one reason why all information must be consistent and that the corporate personality must be reflected in all communications. If the company personality is well established, then potentially damaging information, rumour or gossip will be rejected immediately.

This up-and-down (and sideways) communications network is particularly important to employees. The well-run organization will ensure that the communications responsibilities of each manager are fully understood and implemented. Indeed, these responsibilities should be part of each manager's job description.

It is essential that *all* communications at all levels are factual, accurate and consistent. As an illustration, it is damaging to management credibility if the chairman suddenly reveals policy changes in the foreword to the annual report; this may be picked up by shop-floor shareholders but may come as news to middle managers when asked to explain. Who is managing whom? A programme relating to a substantial expansion by one consumer giant was thrown out of gear when a member of the personnel department included one short but revealing sentence in the middle of an article on employment prospects in a local newspaper survey.

The public relations adviser may recommend to management that the communications capabilities of all managers should be regularly assessed and their performance monitored.

Do not disseminate information from the top and allow it to filter down without checking its progress. Equally important, make sure the information coming back up to management is of the quality necessary to make proper decisions. Some people believe that information is power. Therefore, they tend to be very careful about how much of this they give away. This covetous attitude towards information can create weak points in the communications network. Any information bottleneck must be identified. One manager may be reckless, while another may be miserly with information.

Some managers act as a *one-way* communications valve, constantly transmitting but never receiving; they are all mouth and no ears, the opposite to the ratio that nature gave us! Again, it is a relatively simple process to check each manager's ability to feed back information into the communications network. Special attention should be paid to any manager who is not providing any information or whose assessments are constantly adrift. Try a test: feed in information at an open level (perhaps through a story in a local paper) and see which managers react – and how they respond.

Training will help improve communications weaknesses but the most critical point is for each manager to realize that the company *requires* him or her to be an effective communicator. Include an appraisal of each manager's communications skills and motivation in annual performance reviews. Offer management communications training.

INTERNAL COMMUNICATIONS

One effective way to help establish the principles of two-way communications is to work with each department in creating an internal communications programme. One of the most effective ways of communications is face-to-face, and all managers should ensure that their communications programme includes an element of this. This need not always be on a one-to-one situation and can often be the manager talking to groups, but special attention needs to be paid to ensure that these do not simply develop into lectures or pep-talks.

Such face-to-face briefings by management need to be held regularly. Within a very large organization, *some* of these personal briefings may contain an element of prepared audio-visual or internet material, such as a video interview with the chief executive. Even this must be presented by a senior manager who is able to speak authoritatively and can handle the discussion.

Such briefings must be accepted by executives as part of their responsibility for good management. All personnel giving briefings must be equipped with briefing notes covering agreed answers to all possible questions. Of course, the manager can and should put comments and explanations in his or her own words, consistent with the brief. It is the manager's responsibility to stimulate, note and take action on audience reactions. Response has to be worked at and managers have to be trained to encourage input and response.

Every company publication should be written to encourage a response. It may mean that the reporters on the publication need to be recruited to represent the main employee groups. The editor should be one or two steps sideways from management; should have a duty to establish strong links at all points within the organization; and should report all feelings and attitudes. The publication might also carry readership surveys, letters, guest columns and other direct response features.

Use the technique most appropriate to the audience

Perhaps the communication should not be on paper at all but be on a video or audio tape or on a website. Many organizations are using video to put over management or policy information. Some companies prepare a simplified version of the annual results presented by the chairman or chief executive. A number of companies have taken this one stage further and organized a video recording of a studio discussion (sometimes chaired by an independent TV or radio commentator) where selected representatives of the employees question the chief executive. This can gain wide distribution through the website.

Some record the discussion sessions that follow the presentation of the video: in this way, the observations and comments from employees, often at distant locations, can be fed back to the chief executive. Where this had been done, it provides the opportunity for a second discussion on issues of concern. This creates far more acceptance of the concept of a *genuine* exchange of information and views. Many organizations now have their own radio and TV studios. Such techniques add the two-way dimension to an essentially one-way communications method.

PRESENT THE POLICY TO ENSURE COMMITMENT

The overall communications policy should be presented to the board for approval. At the next stage the public relations practitioner should present the agreed corporate public relations programme to the heads of department to give them the opportunity to observe and react. Eventually they will need to ensure that their own employee communications activities are consistent with this corporate public relations plan.

Each divisional or departmental head should have the opportunity of agreeing on his or her priority audiences, the communications policy, the messages and methods. It is also essential to identify the potential problem situations that might arise. The company should be prepared to handle the bad news situations as well as the good. (These contingency procedures are covered in more detail in Chapter 10.)

Of all areas of public relations responsibility, there are few that have more impact than employee relations. In virtually all organizations, the major resource is the people working in the enterprise. Above all, the people are the only *intelligent* resource... only people can think, plan, enthuse, dream, and make things happen. The organization is as big as the ambitions of the people who make it work.

David Ogilvy, the late advertising guru, said that if you recruit people smaller than yourself you build a team of pygmies, but if you recruit people bigger than yourself you become a team of giants. It is equally true that if you deprive people of information and treat them as insignificant, they will behave like pygmies. If you communicate properly, negotiate and treat them as important colleagues, they will behave like giants.

TRAIN EVERYONE IN COMMUNICATIONS SKILLS

Communications is part of life but that doesn't mean that we are all proficient, without effort. Communication skills can be learnt, can be developed, and can be focused.

Although we can all communicate to some extent, you would not expect anyone to give a major presentation like the prestigious BBC Reith lecture without a great deal of preparation. Similarly, we would not expect someone to handle a major sales negotiation unaided. We would not expect a novice to chair a broadcast debate. Yet all these areas require capabilities that are only extensions of the basic communications skills that most people possess. Therein lies the central point. Our everyday communications skills are rarely developed enough to cope with specialized business communications.

Everyone needs training in business communications if they are to be truly effective – even the most experienced. Training teaches the inexperienced the basic principles and allows them to practice new-found skills, and make mistakes, away from the attention of peers.

For the experienced, training sessions reinforce those fundamental principles we can all forget, while allowing executives to experiment, check, test, and revise approaches. This can be done in a way that would be difficult, if not impossible, in a real-life situation where penalties for a mistake tend to make the presenter extremely cautious.

Use your own personnel for training in communications wherever you possibly can, even if you initially employ outside expertise to help set up the systems. Your own people will understand the real issues as well as the culture and communications style of the company. This will help to ensure that such sessions are used as discussion opportunities and become of maximum value. Outside specialists can run training sessions but you need to be careful that lecturers do not give a lecture. An effective programme of such sessions on a regular basis for all employees can also become expensive.

However, you can use external specialists to design and help put together the programme of training courses and discussion sessions. This they will often do for a fixed fee plus some retainer to keep a watchful eye on progress, and they might also include an annual review of the effectiveness of the programme, giving suggestions for improvements and the maintenance of quality.

In addition, your trainers may wish to attend external courses to keep up to date with the latest thinking and to compare notes with peers from other organizations. There are many excellent courses on communications: the Public Relations Society of America, Public Relations Consultants Association, the Chartered Institute of Public Relations, the Institute of Directors and the Industrial Society are among those that can offer advice, as do their equivalents across all developed markets.

Monitor the communications capabilities of personnel

Before formal training sessions, it is useful to check the communications skills of all members of the team. Such appraisals should be available for those running the individual training so that they can structure sessions that will be of most assistance to employees and will generate the maximum results from their participation.

It is also useful if the trainers keep a note of participants and their capabilities and attitudes – as illustrated during the training and later discussion sessions – so that problem areas or progress could also be monitored. Such appraisals should form part of managers' personnel records and can be part of any appraisal process.

As with all areas of communications, it is always best to lead from the front. The chairman or chief executive should demonstrate his or her belief that effective communications at the personal level is an essential skill for all managers. Sometimes senior people will need some assistance to get rid of inappropriate ideas or habits and develop their positive skills. In addition, acceptance by the top team will demonstrate to all employees the seriousness with which the topic is being addressed.

- *Explain how staff can support company aims.* Employees need their communications responsibilities detailed. Members of the company will not communicate positively as an automatic procedure. They need to be advised that this is part of their role. They need to understand the impact that they can have on important audiences. They need to appreciate that they can help shape opinion and are therefore part of the company's public relations resource.
- *Make staff part of a feedback system.* Employees of an organization mix across a very wide range of audiences and are exposed to various types of comment, many of which may be more candid than those addressed to senior executives. Training must identify the ways in which they can feed back these reactions as part of the company's systems for monitoring public opinion.
- *Brief staff on the aims of the organization.* Employees can position their role within the broader ambition of the organization if they understand what the organization is trying to achieve. They will also be better equipped to explain to third parties how individual elements of the organization's stance on certain issues can form part of the larger picture.
- *Give staff suitable support materials.* Employees can quote articles from newspapers, notices, news stories and so on. New developments may be supported by briefing sheets or newsletters that

can be used externally. Employees also need to be advised what is confidential and what is available for public discussion. And why there might be a difference between the two!

Formal training in communications for all employees ought to take place at least once every year and, certainly, should form part of the induction for all new employees. Between the formal training sessions, employees need to be updated. This can be part of staff briefings.

Communications should be on the agenda for every such meeting, so that these sessions can discuss whether to present externally the implications of internal policy matters. Be assured that employees will be discussing these matters with friends, colleagues and family. You might as well brief them properly so that at least they are projecting something close to a consistent picture. This will be particularly true if your organization is one that is likely to be in the national or local news.

FACE-TO-FACE COMMUNICATIONS ARE BEST

The chief executive or other senior manager is unlikely to select the communications methods for the internal audiences. However, it is useful if they understand the main advantages and disadvantages of each. Specialist communications books will detail these but a brief overview may be helpful.

As noted, the best form of communication is one person talking as an equal to another, with question and answer, view and counter-view being debated. All other communications techniques are substitutes for this ideal. It is broadly true that the further you are from this personal situation, the less effective the communications, the more the emphasis on projecting messages and the less the emphasis on feedback.

On the other hand, the broader the communications technique, the greater its efficiency in terms of the numbers of people who can be reached and the speed with which they can be reached. While the ideal situation might be the chairman talking individually to each person with whom the company wants to communicate, it is hardly practical. Even if the chairman had the time, some messages must be transmitted to all simultaneously. Therefore, the right mix of techniques needs to be selected for each situation, and this mix will change according to the communications need. The appointment of a new managing director may require different techniques to a name change, or factory closure, or new acquisitions, or an environmental campaign, or product launch, or change in employment procedures, and so on.

This approach is sometimes called the (Haywood) communications pyramid: the power and effectiveness are stronger at the top, the breadth and reach are broader at the bottom; conversations and briefings will be nearer the top, while mailings and advertising are nearer the bottom.

Select organic communications for believability

It is important to appreciate the principal differences between printed communications and live/audio-visual. The arrival of popular radio, television, and later the internet were supposed to signal the death of newspapers – yet newspaper readership is still thriving, despite setbacks in some sectors.

The obvious appeal of radio is real people talking; much of the rest is imagination. With television you use less imagination but add colour and movement. However, television and radio are taken at the pace and in the order decided by the editor. At a reading speed of, say, 120 words per minute, the *Daily Mirror* contains several times as much 'news-volume' as the *The 10 O'Clock News* or *ITV News*. A 'long' news item on radio or television will be 500 words or less. There will be dozens of stories of that length in most newspapers. There will be up to 10 major news stories or features of 1,000 words or more in any serious newspaper.

A single edition of *The Times*, for example, might contain 4 hours of editorial reading matter. A paper like the *New York Times* may have the equivalent of 20 hours of reading in each edition. The average person reads twice as quickly as he or she talks and, therefore, can absorb twice as much as when listening to a newscaster reading. The reader can choose what to study and when, read it as often as necessary and in any order, and pass the material to someone else.

Selecting the best information channel mix

Therefore, some communications efforts need audio-visual techniques (the launch of a new car, say) and some need print (your new pension scheme). Many need both in some complementary combination (shareholder updates, for example), supported by the website.

Face-to-face meetings

The spoken word, properly delivered, is unbeatable, even without visual aids, and is great for chemistry, particularly if small groups are involved. People relate to people, and if you can see the whites of each other's eyes and there is no intimidation – that becomes real communication, as feedback is instant. There are, however, certain limitations: meetings are very inefficient in reaching numbers, particularly spread across different locations, and are also heavy users of management time. Nevertheless, imagine: the chairman talks once to six people in a room... or once to a video camera in a studio... and this can be transmitted anywhere live, or, via as many tapes, CDs or DVDs as you wish, can be sent around the world, via the website.

Team briefings

Managers talk to their staffs in a cascade of information, down the organization. This is also organic and powerful and is, again, the *real thing* with great potential for feedback of information back up the chain. Limitations include the fact that briefings maintain existing pecking orders; some managers may not communicate well, some may bully, and some may retain information to strengthen their power. Some participants may not participate. Verbal messages can be misunderstood and are difficult to retain – and impossible to pass on to third parties such as other colleagues, wives, husbands and families. Therefore, all team briefings must be backed by datasheets.

Seminars/conferences

As these are extensions of the meetings technique, seminars and conferences have similar plus and minus factors. They can be very persuasive as real people are presenting. They allow the use of dramatic audio-visual support, normally inappropriate in smaller-scale meetings. Limited feedback is possible if question and answer sessions are allowed, though this can be a little formalized. They are relatively inefficient in influencing large audiences, as groups of more than 200 or 300 tend to lose the interactive dimension and become remote. They are demanding of management time as considerable preparation of presentations, set, room design, etc, are necessary to achieve impact. Seminars and conferences have long lead times and therefore are not usually suitable for urgent news.

Closed circuit television (live)

This is almost as good as face-to-face communication as real people are talking in real time, live by land line or satellite with closed circuit television (CCTV). This system can reach far more people, including those in remote locations, and often several linked together. It is very practical today as any city in the world can be linked with any other. It is also efficient in the use of time. Television adds its own little spice to some occasions; however, the mechanics can get in the way and the balance is a little less even, as one person will need to manage or chair the discussion. The method carries the same strengths and weaknesses of the spoken word, as in meetings. Today, technology allows CCTV to be transmitted direct to managers' desks via their PCs. Of course, webcasts and video clips can be featured on websites, and links or extracts sent by e-mail.

Internet

Both the web and e-mail newsletters have become powerful channels for communication. Both allow virtually instant feedback. Generally, research suggests that web channels offer good communications but not always with high credibility. One solution is to use e-mail and the web in parallel with other channels.

Company material can be accessed on websites. These can be promoted by other communications methods as well as through clips and links sent via e-mail. Particular attention must be paid to monitoring the web, as unofficial, rogue and critical websites can carry powerful material that may contradict company perspectives.

Video television (tape/DVD)

This still deals with real people but is recorded and not live. It is also persuasive. We are all familiar with television, and this technique can reach a large audience through tape copies or satellite transmission. The spoken word has power but the limitations are less severe as tape can be rerun and passed on to others. However, a professional performance is required and amateurs (most of us) look and sound less than totally convincing. Feedback is very limited, indeed, non-existent at the time of the transmission. You need a notetaker or a return tape to present reactions to the messages. Recipients also need a VCR, disc player, PC or special equipment to access the material.

Audio tapes

These relate to real people and can be effective if professionally produced. Although a little dated now, they can be economical and effective. They can reach a large audience reasonably quickly. Playback equipment is portable and readily available; this can be a factor in remote markets or with busy executives such as salespeople who can listen in their cars. Because of our familiarity with radio, this method can have a high credibility factor. Rerunning, handing on and selectivity make the method an improvement on meetings, but weaknesses include no visual element and feedback is slow and ponderous. In common with video tape, there is no certainty that messages are received or accepted.

Media relations

Communications through a third party can have great authority. Stories acquire the integrity of the medium or the journalist – if *The Times*, the *Herald Tribune*, CNN, the BBC or the *Wall Street Journal* say it, that carries real weight. Though the 'public' media are external, they are a credible way of talking to employees as they can reach many people simultaneously. However, there is no total control over the message as this is ultimately decided by news value and editorial judgement (which is why media relations efforts have credibility). Reports may carry undesired messages and there is no real feedback.

House journals

The newspaper format gives (or suggests) a news urgency; and magazines give (or suggest) an authority. The messages have some useful credibility because people tend to believe material in print, and the company has to be truthful in black and white. Certainly, credibility can be higher than verbal information alone, which may not be recorded and, therefore, difficult to challenge. The messages can reach all employees simultaneously. The quality is variable as this is dependent on the professionalism and integrity of the editor, and too many have previously proved to be compliant. Such journals work better when the editor has clear independence.

Information lines

Some companies run employee information telephone lines, virtually all of which are digitally recorded and most are updated daily or more often. They offer confidentiality as employees can choose when to call, without colleagues being aware. They are economic but their credibility can be limited. Digital systems allow simultaneous listening by almost unlimited numbers.

Notice boards

Regretfully, this method should only be used in desperation. Most are defeated by fully understandable worker cynicism. The only advantage is that management has full control of information. The minuses? Well, who reads them and who is influenced by such propaganda? Feedback is likely to be abusive or worse. One day, someone will run an effective communications scheme via notice boards and will ensure that it has credibility.

Advertising

Some managers use the safe route of advertising when they should take the riskier avenue of organic communications. Advertising reaches defined audiences with agreed messages as often as you want, wherever you want. Benefits include the fact that you can control the message and (generally) deliver it exactly where you want, in the way you want, as often as you want. Advertising can reach an enormous audience, virtually simultaneously. If it is so effective, why bother with the rest? Fundamentally, the public fully understand where advertising is coming from and who pays for it. *They would say that, wouldn't they*? This factor makes advertising good for awareness and information – but less effective for changing opinion and attitude. It also has limited feedback capability.

Leaflets/brochures

As with all print, leaflets can be read at the speed of the recipient, who can also select those items of interest or re-read those that need more study. Print can also be passed on to third parties, so messages are conveyed with great accuracy and do not get distorted. However, also like advertising they do suffer from the *they would say that, wouldn't they?* reservation on the part of most readers, so are not effective in shaping opinion. Feedback is also limited to coupons or other cumbersome options.

Integrating the mix

Most programmes will benefit from using a mix of channels, selected to be the most effective for the respective audiences and tasks. When planning, use the criteria detailed below; however, an equally important factor will be coordinating the messages and the timing of the distribution.

Selecting the best method

Make decisions about communications media with care. The best method should be developed from a clear understanding of the communications needs. There is a real danger that the wrong technique may fail, therefore damning the validity of the communications. Equally, an inappropriate vehicle can demand a disproportionate amount of time and management effort to maintain on a regular basis.

One company my organization was called in to advise was concerned about the effectiveness of their very attractive series of video news magazines which did not seem to be producing the results they expected. These were eating a sizeable chunk of the communications budget. They had been introduced as a result of a survey which suggested that only 18 per cent of employees felt satisfied with company plans and activities. Yet few attended company showings of the videos and the take-up of copies for free home use was minimal and declining!

Management, it transpired, had tackled the wrong problem with the wrong technique. The briefest of surveys undertaken showed that there was resistance to company portrayals. Some perceived these as indoctrination. However, the majority wanted to question management to discuss policy and did not seek more information alone. Also, although over half the workforce had access to a video-player, less than half of those felt they had the time or interest to play a 30-minute management tape.

Quite a proportion of those with VCRs explained that it was difficult to get access to a family television set at convenient times. Even those who felt that they could find the time said that members of the family always drifted in to watch it and often caused considerable embarrassment with derogatory, ribald and generally unsympathetic comments. We interviewed 100 employees and found only 11 who believed that video was appropriate and watched any proportion of the material available.

The solution to the company communications needs was a structured series of briefing meetings supported by simple handout

briefing sheets plus feedback questionnaires that every meeting organizer had to complete and return to the chief executive. The result
was a significant improvement in attitude – some 78 per cent later
confirmed approval of the communications with 70 per cent
recording acceptance of company policy. This success encouraged the
company to also run video briefings on an intranet site that could
only be accessed by employees.

Most communications programmes use a mix of techniques. Each
specific campaign (within the broader programme) needs a critical
path/timetable, particularly with major announcements. The mix
will probably include 'public' media, as well as private or 'owned'
channels that the company controls.

Employees respond to a statement of corporate ambition

The mission and vision statements are not the same, and neither is
essential, although both can be very helpful. Unfortunately, experience suggests that many organizations that operate without either a
mission or a vision statement have neither a mission nor a vision. It is
unwise to assume that all those the organization depends on for
success know what it is trying to achieve, therefore it helps to put the
aims into writing. A statement of the corporate ambition can be
particularly helpful to employees.

Although some resist the idea, once the point of the operation is
put in writing, that effectively becomes the mission statement. It
should embody the work of the organization, its responsibilities and
the values that guide everything it does. The purpose of this statement is to ensure that everyone knows what the organization is
trying to do and how the policies it follows are intended to achieve
this. It is important that the staff of an organization identify with and
'own' the mission. If they do not, the effectiveness of operations will
be affected; in particular, performance and delivery can become
inconsistent and drop below standards set.

The other stakeholders (customers, trade and professional bodies,
government, funding bodies and so on) should also be able to relate
the mission to their idea of what the organization is about. If there is
a mismatch between the promise and the delivery, this can be
damaging to the organization's activities, staff confidence, relationships and reputation. Therefore, the *mission* statement would
normally cover:

1. The purpose of the organization.
2. What it sees as being special about itself.
3. The values that it strives to apply to all it does.

The mission and vision statements must be consistent, though each addresses different areas. Sometimes they can be combined.

The *vision* of the organization is where it wants to be and how it expects to get there. Therefore it is essentially talking about ambition, and would normally cover:

1. The future positioning of the organization.
2. The way this will be measured.
3. How it should be viewed by stakeholders.

What makes a good mission statement?

The development of a good mission statement is about reality and truth, not theory and illusion. Every organization has a purpose, and so should be able to develop a mission statement that helps it be more effective, better understood, or have a greater chance of winning a positive and constructive reputation across all those publics that it depends upon for success. As an example of how every organization should accept this challenge, consider a company working in a sensitive service area, totally performance-driven to meet its major community and social responsibilities: a housing association.

Mick Leggett is chief executive of Cross Keys Homes, headquartered in Peterborough. He believes that communications is central to the development and maintenance of a good reputation. One of the early appointments that he and his board made was of leading journalist, Kelly Swift, from the highly respected local paper, the *Peterborough Evening Telegraph*. Her brief was to lead the company's public relations initiatives to support the service to Cross Keys Homes' tenants and the community.

Leggett explains that Cross Keys was set up as an independent company, and took over the social housing of Peterborough Council. Some of the senior management team of the new company had previously worked within the council housing department. Leggett not only had experience within the council but had also been a director with other housing bodies.

It is true that some organizations do manage without a mission or a vision statement, but I don't believe they are the most effective ones. In our sector, social housing is not just a service in a highly sensitive area; it really is a concept that needs to be put over in ways that go beyond the techniques that might be deployed in a commercial housing operation. We felt that a mission statement would bring together all the feelings and the values that we and our stakeholders believe are drivers for success.

For those struggling to pin down the reality, he recommends some simple but helpful guidelines:

1. A mission statement should say who you are, what you do, what you stand for and why you do it.
2. A mission statement is not a slogan, goal, business plan, advertising copy or public relations piece.
3. An effective mission statement is best developed with input from all the members of an organization.
4. Simplicity, honesty and frankness are essential.
5. Your mission statement needs to appeal to all your stakeholders: for example, your customers (or, in the case of a housing association, the tenants), staff, shareholders or other funders, neighbours, local communities and so on.
6. Avoid saying how great you are, what great quality and what great service you provide. Using these concepts makes you indistinguishable from the rest.
7. Effective mission statements need not set the world on fire. The best ones are direct and powerful.
8. Make certain your statement is about you and not some other company. That is why you should not copy a statement. Even if your statement is a little unpolished it will appear to have more credibility and integrity than if it portrays you as something you are not.
9. Try to relay somewhere in your statement that you understand the future of your business depends on delivering increasing value and quality to your customers, accounts and clients. This delivers a clear message of your priorities.
10. Review and edit your statement on a regular basis.*

---

*These notes are based on a document produced by the author for new housing association, Cross Keys, when he was working on a contract with marketing communications agency, Fox Murphy. The thoughts were used to help the company develop its market positioning, and are reproduced with the kind permission of the chief executive, Mick Leggett.

SOME OBSERVATIONS, IN SUMMARY

1. Employees should be considered the primary audience for they have the ability to make or break any communications plan.
2. The contribution they can make to enhancing the corporate reputation will be considerable, and often at no cost.
3. Treat your employees as your *home* team, part of the information network with a two-way role between the company and all its external publics.
4. Make sure that your public relations philosophy is professionally presented to employees, for discussion, before any external communications.
5. If you fail to win the support of your employees for what you are planning, then much of your external communications will be wasted.
6. One of the most important influences on employee attitudes to company public relations will be the attitudes your managers present...
7. ... therefore, you will need to gain the commitment of all levels of management to the plan and their support of your aims and messages.
8. Try to test this acceptance by finding out what views are expressed outside formal company situations – in other words, when the boss is not there!
9. As part of your eyes and ears, use the many external contacts that employees have as a source of useful information on external perceptions.
10. In employee communications areas, the public relations and human resources disciplines – and respective bosses – must cooperate completely.
11. Human resources must rightly be responsible for all personnel policy but, equally, public relations must handle the communications.
12. Make communications part of your employees' responsibilities; appraise them, train them and provide them with the necessary assistance.
13. Expect all employees to contribute positively to both better internal and external communications, as well as suggesting improvements.
14. Consider the use of some *meetings plus core messages* informa-

tion process internally, such as the cascade system or team briefings.

15. Use printed material for accuracy and 'transportability' to reinforce core verbal messages presented at such briefings.

16. When you cannot expand on a point (for example, because of stock exchange rules or the competitive position) explain why.

17. Above all, trust your employees for they are on the same team. People tend to respond very positively to being briefed in confidence.

18. However, make quite clear what is confidential and what is not – and what the 'official line' might be when talking to non-company third parties.

19. Build all internal communications procedures on personal briefings (face-to-face, whenever possible) ahead of any external announcement.

20. *Remember:* briefed today and in the papers tomorrow – such joy; the other way round – such grief!

21. Differentiate clearly between when you are asking for views to help decide policy and when you are asking for support for decisions already taken.

22. Set up parallel systems to feed back up to management the concerns of employees and their views on communications problems/opportunities.

23. Check on the communications flow, both ways, to identify and help those who might hold on to information to give them power over their staff.

24. People only talk when people listen, so start a listening philosophy from the top. Encourage your managers to welcome 'unwelcome' views.

25. Listening does not compromise a good manager; it helps that person to be more decisive, for the views of those affected and their likely reactions will be known.

26. Analyse the information needs of employees appropriate to their roles in the company, but create opportunities for those who require more detail.

27. Harmonize communications across divisions and across countries so that while they may be different, to suit local needs, they will be consistent.

28. Do not wait until legislation or trends force new communications efforts but undertake these voluntarily and as early as possible.

29. Make sure that such developments, trends or company employee communications policy changes are relayed to all divisions.
30. Put your employee communications policy into writing, publish it widely and include it in new staff inductions to ensure maximum support.

8

Public affairs

Set the agenda for legislators and opinion leaders

Key factors discussed

- Integrating all corporate communications.
- Influencing potential legislation.
- Using and bypassing trade bodies.
- Operating within the European environment.

PUBLIC AFFAIRS AT THE HEART OF PUBLIC RELATIONS

Today, major organizations cannot operate to full effect without a proper understanding of the political climate at local, national and international levels. Indeed, developments and trends at global levels are becoming increasingly important: national legislation often reflects global perspectives. What is happening in the public arena will have a direct effect on what can and cannot be done, not simply in the legal or legislative sense but in terms of what is publicly acceptable. The basis of public relations is that organizations can only succeed through a public consensus that allows them to pursue their legitimate aims.

Decisions in the public sector are being shaped, influenced or implemented by civil servants, politicians, government researchers, local authority members and officers, lobby groups, national assemblies, and international assemblies, such as the European Parliament, the European Commission, NATO, OPEC and the United Nations.

Oddly, much of what we describe as 'public relations' is actually closer to private relations – communications between tightly defined groups of people; these are 'defined' in the sense that the communications audiences are the 'publics' upon whose consent the organization depends for its success... though these publics could be financial analysts, union leaders or civil servants. Often, public affairs can be one of the most important elements in a broad public relations programme; it is involved with the planned management of those political and public issues that decide the future of the nation and, therefore, affect the organization.

Business leaders need to be familiar with the programmes of the main parties, particularly those in power or likely to be in power, which might influence public opinion or the shape of future legislation. Not only can legislation be a factor, but changes in employment rules, social services, investment, planning and regional policies can also have a direct impact. Increasingly, local and national governments are becoming involved in public issues such as the environment, safety, food, health and hygiene, which means that the organization also needs close coordination between its issues management plans and its public affairs activities, as these are likely to overlap.

Management needs to monitor public affairs issues in all markets in which the organization operates. This will require special local and national expertise which it is beyond the scope of this book to offer. However, the broad principles, modelled here on the UK, will still be broadly relevant.

Employing a worthwhile public affairs adviser

Public affairs requires an understanding of how public opinion is shaped, whether by pressure groups, by specific opinion leaders, through planned, focused campaigns, by special interest bodies or the media. Our legislators (and those who advise our legislators) are all influenced by the same process. You also need to remember the importance of what is happening at local level in county and city halls… and the interaction between all these and the statutory bodies that exist to manage sectors of our public life.

One of the most important and difficult tasks in public affairs is identifying what matters from the volumes of published and private information that may have *some* relevance. If a public affairs adviser is to provide an effective service to the management of the organization, then he or she must be able to sift, sort and précis just the information that is important, at exactly the right time.

To filter this material demands a full understanding of the organization's business and a clear brief on where the managers see it heading. Possible sources of information in the UK would include *Hansard*, official government business publications, trade media reports, surveys and studies by specialist associations, speeches by political leaders, party publications and summaries of the proceedings of the European Parliament and Commission. Equivalent sources are published across all democracies. Even where companies are operating in non-democratic areas, there will still be considerable published data, and channels through which to influence the legislators.

It will be essential for the management adviser to build a database of those individuals who are the key players in the movement of opinion on your topics of interest – for example, in Europe, those MPs and MEPs on committees that will promote change, those public figures, academics and researchers whose views are respected. Commercial organizations run computer services that offer a rapid analysis of experts and interested individuals, but this can be no more than the starting point for an understanding of the influences at work.

Of equal importance as knowing the information is knowing the relevance of it. The chief executive needs to be confident that the public affairs adviser has the ability to interpret and analyse the basic information that will be presented. Such analysis needs to include, for example:

● At what stage is the thinking?
● How likely is it to result in change?
● What factors may affect its progress?
● How would this impact on the organization?
● Does it involve the whole business sector?

- Are there others who may be affected who will be interested in having some input into an initiative to modify, redirect or reverse the proposition?
- Which public figures, experts and opinion leaders (who have already or are likely to air views) will carry weight?

MAKING A SUBMISSION IN THE LEGISLATIVE PROCESS

Knowing what is happening and its possible impact are only parts of an effective lobby. It is what you do about it that matters. The preparation of the programme of activity can be crucial. Direct approaches may be relevant where a key politician or official needs to know your company's view. This must be presented factually and positively.

Remember also to cover the possible arguments *against* your case. If you want support from those who may influentially argue your cause, it is little less than courtesy to run through the contrary arguments you feel they should expect to face. You will never again win the support of someone you have inadequately briefed who, in good faith, then walks into a wall of opposition, outlining points of which he or she has no idea and no ability to refute.

Third parties who will be influential – such as officials of professional bodies, even competitors – may need briefing so that they will support your views. On some major public issues, it is appropriate to 'go public' and involve the more respected and influential media. This needs careful consideration. A carefully presented case may be convincing if put privately, and public or media pressure can sometimes jeopardize this and create antipathy. This might be true, for example, where media coverage could weaken the position of a politician, or even suggest a route he or she could take which could force him/or her politically to take the opposite stance. However, once entrenched positions are established and confrontation seems inevitable, it may be sensible to appeal to public opinion – accepting that any behind-the-scenes influence has usually been abandoned by then.

The construction of the political lobby requires special skills and may well involve the employment of specialists, many of whom may not be in general public relations at all. However, whether the chief executive is running the lobby, employing a public affairs specialist or the parliamentary division of a consultancy, it is useful to appreciate a few broad principles:

1. Particular attention to identifying the right individuals is central to success.
2. An effective and carefully considered case, with evidence, must be developed.
3. The counter-arguments (and their strengths and weaknesses) need to be understood and may need to be discussed when seeking support from people who will be asked to back your case. They cannot afford to look ill-informed and be humiliated.
4. Timing of the presentations is critical. Some attempts to persuade are made too late, when views have been developed beyond the point of influence.
5. The identification of those who are likely to be supportive should be carried out early as they can become ambassadors for your case.
6. Those who need persuading from different views should be tackled before the tide is beginning to flow in their or your direction.
7. Do not overlook those who have an interest or responsibility in the relevant sector, such as constituency MPs (and MEPs), as you should receive, at least, a friendly hearing for your perspective.
8. Check out those on the special interest all-party and party backbench committees, for example, as they may already be informed on the subject matter and be receptive.
9. Mount a parallel approach to the civil servants as well as politicians at all levels; you will need the backing of all advisers behind all political initiatives.
10. The parliamentary media can often put weight behind your case if it offers an interesting story for them, but use as much diplomacy and skill in briefing them as your MPs, MEPs or civil servants. They are often easier to contact at Westminster than general press reporters.
11. As all legislation has to go through both upper and lower houses in most legislations, briefing members of the Lords or their equivalent in the upper chamber can be invaluable; some have government posts and many of the more active have the ear of government leaders and administrators. They may also have an important power to delay legislation.

12. When generating support, take advantage of all offers of help and make specific suggestions of where help will be most valuable.
13. Brief everyone involved very thoroughly, particularly if changes are necessary in strategy or tactics, explaining the reasons.
14. Keep all briefings friendly and businesslike with no more than appropriate hospitality.
15. Sometimes short office meetings with one or two people will be more valuable than long discussions over the dinner table; sometimes the converse might be true. Use careful judgement.
16. Make sure that you always advance a positive argument rather than only being critical of alternative proposals, for everyone likes reasons for action.

Make sure you say what you mean

The language for briefing must be simple and direct, avoiding jargon. The chief executive is unlikely to prepare the case for the organization, but he or she must certainly be totally satisfied with all written documents, briefing material or presentations.

This is not the place for guidelines on good communications language but short sentences and active verbs are always best. Good communicators have enthusiasm and confidence. Chairman of Normand Motor Group, Struan Wiley, presented many successful cases in the public affairs arena. No one ever misunderstood his message; he explained the simple origin of his direct style:

> My first boss checked thoroughly everything I wrote. This meant corrections had to be made. In the end, he said the best way round the problem is to keep the sentences short. Other than full stops, only use punctuation in exceptional circumstances. The result is shorter, more concise and clearer communication.

Wiley is right. In fact, the most important point in writing copy is to keep it simple and short. Make sure everything conforms to your personal style – particularly if anyone else is drafting material for you.

Do not get hung up about rules. Ending a sentence with a preposition is not something 'up with which I will not put'. You may also find split infinitives in this book, for this 'rule' is sometimes pedantry. And do not be embarrassed to start a sentence with 'and', if it works.

Any comments credited to the chief executive should be written – or approved – by that person. There are, however, a number of reasons why it may not be wise for the chief executive to direct his or her own lobby. There will be other company responsibilities and these may well take the chief executive away at exactly the time the lobby needs his or her full attention. Also, the chief executive's direct involvement does not allow the various levels of contact or provide the 'longstop' option. With a lobby run by an adviser, the chief executive can come in, wherever appropriate, as the heavyweight.

Present your case to all interested parties

There are likely to be other influential groups that will require special attention. These may include trade and professional bodies, educationalists, pressure groups and local government. To communicate effectively with such groups it is important to identify their own aims and appreciate how these might relate to the organization's aims.

Any public relations programme targeting opinion leaders will only be successful if it can create understanding between these special interest groups and the organization. Wherever possible, it should *also* be an aim to create goodwill and support. However, where the special interest group is directly opposed to the interests of the organization, this does *not* mean that no attempt should be made at communications... or that it is impossible to achieve understanding.

It is important to understand the position of all significant external groups – particularly those trying to exert pressure for change, such as a campaigning consumer body or a group of dissident shareholders. What is their case? Is it factually based? Who are they trying to influence? How are they attempting this? If there is validity in their claims then this may suggest appropriate policy changes within the organization. For this reason, a key target for pressure groups should be the public relations advisers to the organizations they are attempting to influence!

Political democracy is intended to work in the best interests of *most* people. Similarly, the information democracy should ensure that all the best arguments are presented and the opinion which emerges is in the best interests of most people.

Identifying allies, those who are neutral and those who may prove to be opponents is critical. *All* should be appropriately briefed. The aim is to reinforce the support of your allies; convert as many neutrals as possible to your cause; and to minimize the damage or mischief opponents attempt to create. At the very least, briefing them removes the possibility that they can claim they have not been consulted.

Do not rely on trade associations alone

In much of Europe, the role of the public affairs adviser is still not fully accepted. The function is far better understood in the United States, where the concept of the 'political' chief executive has been one of the key features in the development of communications over the last decade or two.

In contrast some British (and other European) businesses do not seem to recognize the need for political monitoring and political action. A few businesspeople believe that an occasional social contact with politicians, topped up by information from the media, constitutes an adequate background against which to spring into action should the need arise.

In addition, a number of trade associations claim to have a competence in political monitoring, but in many cases this barely exists. British public affairs specialist, Douglas Smith, chairman of Westminster Advisers, quotes the disturbing experience of hearing the head of a major trade association seeking to calm fears over an impending bill, saying, 'Relax, we are still squaring it with civil servants.' This comment was made blandly in the House of Commons itself, with MPs present, on the day when the bill under discussion had its first reading and all concerned knew it would be law within months. Some companies may be leaving political monitoring and lobbying to trade associations that do not have the expertise to tackle this critical area.

Much of the lobbying undertaken by some trade associations, individual companies and organizations is somewhat basic; it may make them *feel* good, but will have very little influence on the shape of legislation. Too often, the case is being presented too late and without enough authority or substantiating evidence.

An intelligent public affairs campaign should not be mounted to deal only with contingency situations. The organization should be maintaining continuous parliamentary contact and monitoring developments. You need to be aware of possible trends and political feelings at an early stage – often at the stage when ideas are being shaped in the 'think tanks' (the Adam Smith Institute in the UK and other similar influential bodies). This will eliminate the need for emergency measures at a later stage in the legislative process.

In the public affairs area in most legislations, the decision-making process has many levels, in the UK from junior to senior civil servants, from backbench MPs to cabinet ministers. The organization that wishes to influence the decision-making process will be working at all relevant levels. While the European level is of paramount importance, lobbying at national parliamentary level continues to be important.

Ministers can often be the most valuable source of contact. Their active involvement will help establish their own reputation for action, upon which their political future is based. In planning any presentation to a minister or a ministerial department, check policies and styles; useful pointers can usually be established by watching the public and television performances of the minister concerned, and reading all his or her policy statements and speeches. More substantial checks need to be made into the minister's areas of special interest; and it is also sensible to seek the advice of your local MP. An approach can enlist his or her support, although his approach is likely to differ depending on whether he or she is a member of the party in office.

Ensure constituency politicians are briefed

Probably the most important factor in developing the presentation of a parliamentary case is to understand how your national parliamentary processes work, the role of the elected representatives, civil servants and ministers and an appreciation of the importance of timing. As with so many areas in the complex world of public relations, there can be no real substitute for employing the best professionals possible to handle specialized sectors. The director with a responsibility for parliamentary affairs does not necessarily need to know how to handle all issues. However, it is essential to have the skill to know when to call in expert advice. There remain basic aspects of good communications which have an influence in the parliamentary area. These usually need to be handled by the public relations specialist as part of a broader communications programme.

Every organization should ensure that it has a satisfactory relationship with all relevant constituency MPs. This must be regardless of what their parliamentary allegiances may be. These politicians should know the company and have an understanding of the style of its senior management and what it is trying to achieve. This understanding will ensure that there will be a number of informed views on the organization within the legislative assembly; the constituency representative may not just be the one associated with the organization's head office as there will be a politician representing every depot, regional warehouse or distribution point.

Each should be briefed and should meet the senior manager at each location: in the UK, a Friday may be the most convenient as many MPs are then in their constituencies. Having established the initial contact and given the politicians the opportunity of meeting senior management as well as staff, and of seeing the organization at work, it is sensible to keep the members updated on company developments and management views on any proposed legislation. A local press picture, or a radio or television interview or news piece, are usually popular with the visiting politician.

Present the case to all key committee members

A working relationship with a constituency MP does *not* constitute parliamentary relations. In an information democracy, it is reasonable that the best case will emerge through a process of argument and counter-argument. All sides in every case have the democratic right to present their arguments in the best way they can. Consequently, it is fair to say that an improvement in parliamentary liaison by companies would help create better understanding… and, possibly, a more sympathetic climate of parliamentary opinion. In our information democracy, the principle is 'let the best case win'.

Opportunities to influence legislation exist not only for trade associations and commercial organizations but also for charities, professional groups, social bodies and societies. Perhaps the best starting point for parliamentary relations for these groups would be the party committees and the all-party committees relevant to their areas of interest. Such committees welcome input from informed organizations on current issues; it is possible to find a committee in the British Houses of Parliament on virtually any area of professional and business interest.

If the campaign is likely to involve a high degree of sophistication then it might be advisable to retain a parliamentary consultancy.

Consideration might be given to retaining an appropriate politician as an adviser, though the rules on what is allowable have been tightened. But it must be recognized that while he or she can provide guidance, very limited time will be available to help the organization. Equally important, as the elected representative has to retain independence, he or she is less likely to want to put forward the client's point of view than might an ordinary constituency MP. Public relations practitioners are advised to ensure that any special relationship is properly published. Most legislations have strict rules on paid relationships. In the UK, for example, MPs are required to declare any special interest and income where this is required, and always in parliamentary affairs.

FOCUS YOUR EFFORTS FOR EFFECTIVE EUROPEAN INFLUENCE

Member states in the European Union share a unique position in world legislative practice – the current 25 EU members are subject to both national and binding transnational legislation. And, clearly, the transnational legislation of the EU will continue to be of increasing importance.

The European process differs somewhat from some national practices, in that the European Commission – in effect, the civil service of the European Union – initiates legislation. This is first considered by the Council, then by the European Parliament and the Advisory & Economic Social Committee. Since the Maastricht Treaty came into force, the European Parliament has the power of co-decision on many matters. But even before that, in practice over three-quarters of its amendments found their way into legislation, even though its powers under the Single European Act of 1987 suggested, in theory, that it will merely be consulted.

It is possible for organizations to make direct representations to the Commission in Brussels; however, it is also possible to direct an input through national parliamentary channels.

However, it is preferable, recommends Tony Pearce, managing director of the Access European network, to operate through a European grouping or trade association, whenever possible. The Commission and the Parliament prefer to hear the views of European groupings but will, of course, listen to any organization wishing to present a serious perspective.

The UK and other national parliaments (unlike the European one) do not have enough time to debate all impending European legislation. There are select committees on European legislation across most administrations that are expected to identify all draft directives and regulations that should be discussed at the national level. An organization wishing to present evidence to these committees should arrange to discuss this with the relevant official managing the business of the committee.

Keep your Euro-MPs fully informed and up to date

In the European Parliament each MEP today has more power and influence than in the earlier stages of the assembly. Political groupings are of some importance, but do not allow the complexity of relationships to deter you from keeping close to your region's MEPs – not just for your headquarters' operations but for every location you operate.

Every organization in the European Union is within a region represented by European members of the European Parliament. Organizations should consider presenting their case to their local region's MEPs – they know how the system works, what is possible and what is not. Most will advise on the thinking of the Commission on particular issues, for this body has significant power and considerable influence.

Understand the political structure of Europe

Perhaps some companies and other organizations have not been positive enough in presenting their case at the European level. Possibly this is a result of the limited understanding of the workings of the European legislative system. Useful sources of information for would-be campaigners are published by the Commission in all official languages, as well as across all member states. For example, in the UK these include the House of Commons library (which lists all committees and party groups), the *Civil Service Year Book*, the *House Magazine* (the unofficial guide to parliamentary activities), a number of commercial parliamentary monitoring services, the European Commission and European Parliament Offices in London and other UK cities, which provide guides and information. The Public Relations Consultants Association in the UK keeps up to date with European lobbying practice, and their expertise is available through their member consultancies. The Department of Trade and Industry is also particularly helpful and will provide information and advice.

To appreciate how to influence the legislative process in the European Union, it is important to understand the structure of the inter-linked elements.

There are three 'European Communities' to which the 25 member states all belong, which make up the EU to which we informally refer: the European Coal and Steel Community (ECSC) set up by the ECSC Treaty signed in Paris on 18 April 1951; the European Economic Community (EEC), set up by the EEC Treaty signed in Rome on 25 March 1957; and the European Atomic Energy Community (EURATOM), set up by the EURATOM Treaty also signed in Rome on 25 March 1957.

However, of more current relevance are the four main community institutions, all of which play a role in shaping legislation: the Commission, the Council, the European Parliament and the Court of Justice.

The Commission

This proposes policy and legislation. The Council of Ministers and the European Parliament then discuss and, if appropriate, adopt or amend the proposals; the Commission also implements the decisions taken by the Council of Ministers and supervises the day-to-day running of European policies. The Commission is the 'guardian of the treaties' and can initiate action against member states that do not comply with EU rules. It has its own considerable powers in some areas, notably competition policy and the control of government subsidies.

The Council

This is the Union's main decision-making body. It adopts legislation on the basis of proposals from the Commission, taking into account the views of both the European Parliament and the Economic and Social Committee. The term 'Council' embraces not only ministerial meetings of the Council of Ministers but also council working groups of officials from the member states and the committee of permanent representatives of the member states in Brussels (COREPER) which prepares discussions in the Council of Ministers.

Specialist councils have evolved dealing with particular areas of policy. The main ones are: foreign affairs (including trade policy and general issues), agriculture, budget, finance, industry, the internal market and research.

Councils are attended by the relevant ministers from member states and by the Commission, which is present as of right and participates in discussions as an equal partner. The relevant national minister is usually obvious from the title of the Council. For example, the UK is represented on the internal market and on the industry and research councils by a minister from the Department of Trade and Industry (DTI).

The European Parliament

This is a directly elected body. Under the EU treaties, its formal opinion is required on most proposals before they can be adopted by the Council. Members are elected for a period of five years. The secretariat of the Parliament is divided between Brussels and Luxembourg, although the Parliament's plenary meetings are mainly held in Strasbourg and its committee meetings in Brussels. A plenary session chamber has been built in Brussels and this hosts 'mini-plenary' meetings several times each year.

Most of the detailed work is done by its specialist committees, divided by subject area, which examine Commission proposals before they are put to the Parliament. When consulted on a proposal, the Parliament refers it to one of these committees. The committee appoints a 'rappateur' for the proposal, that is, an MEP charged with preparing a report on it. The committee then discusses that report and may amend it. Each report includes a draft opinion on the Commission's proposal. This draft opinion is put to the Parliament as a whole by the specialist committee, and is adopted (sometimes with further amendments) as the Parliament's opinion.

The European Court of Justice

This rules on the interpretation and application of European laws. It has judges from each country in the Union. Judgments of the court are binding on each member state. (A *court of first instance* has been created to relieve it of some of its excessive workload.)

How does Brussels work?

The EU is not just a set of procedures and institutions but is run through a complex matrix of individuals, all with their special responsibilities and perspectives. Remember also that in all the

Union institutions there are currently 25 nationalities working together. This makes for cultural and linguistic diversity, and some quite marked differences of approach. However, all EU officials are committed to the same treaty objectives and there is therefore much common ground between them.

Virtually all EU officials speak several community languages. French and English are the most widely spoken. Written texts for internal discussion are usually produced in either French or English. More formal documents, such as draft proposals from the Commission to the Council, are translated into all official EU languages.

In addition to the formal channels of communication, there are also informal ones. Officials working in different community institutions on the same subject are likely to be in close touch with each other. There are also close contacts between officials and other Brussels-based personnel, such as the member states' permanent representatives and the Brussels press corps. It is worth being aware of these cross-currents. For example, one EU contact may well be able to introduce you to other useful contacts in other institutions.

Understand the progress of EU legislation

There are usually three stages in actually influencing decisions in Brussels:

- gathering information;
- agreeing your action plan;
- making the necessary contacts.

The Commission and relevant national departments of state have prepared helpful information and will always offer more up-to-date advice than can be presented in this book. However, the following suggestions should be useful.

The first step in any campaign to influence decisions in Brussels is to obtain clear and up-to-date information on what is happening. One thing the European legislative process produces in abundance is information. Additionally, many publishers and consultants offer newsletters and information services, drawing on the basic documents. So how do you set about establishing what you need and how to get it?

Trade associations and chambers of commerce can often help. National government departments publish information covering the current EU legislative programme, while specialist industry publications, from trade associations or elsewhere, may help the public relations adviser to stay in touch with the community issues likely to affect that person's business. Consultants with expertise in EU matters can also help with gathering and interpreting data.

Whether the organization approaches the EU directly or indirectly, it is important to bear in mind that dialogue with Brussels is a two-way process. The public relations adviser will want information from the Commission and the other institutions about their plans, and will want to influence those plans. But they, in turn, will value the information the organization can offer about its particular sector.

The Commission relies upon information from various outside sources in order to draw up its forward proposals. For any piece of legislation, there will be a list of key contacts the executive responsible for the lobby will need to make and maintain. Make sure these contacts have a written note of the organization's concerns, but do consider face-to-face meetings too.

Use European lobby specialists

The Brussels machinery is accessible and willing to listen to a well-prepared case. An efficient trade organization with a lobbying brief will concentrate on establishing effective contacts at all national levels and in the European legislative system. National and European industry or trade bodies have influence as they represent a broader constituency. The one-company lobby is not impossible but may have limited influence.

Effective lobbying cannot be undertaken on a part-time basis by a general public relations practitioner operating across a broad spectrum of company communications activities. As a consequence, the importance of the specialist public affairs consultant is increasing steadily. Some large companies (and larger consultancies) employ public affairs advisers to concentrate on this area.

The corporate influence on legislators at national and international level is an area where the chief executive will wish to be personally involved. There is considerable expertise available to help you win in the corridors of power.

Some notes on the essentials of lobbying

Douglas Smith adds to his earlier observations on treating with caution those trade association ambitions to present the business cause. Organizations need to take their own responsibility for their own presentations. He has produced for clients and others a simple guideline to the realities of effectively influencing the legislators.

'Political public relations is a key part of the broad public affairs sector. This central facet is sometimes called government relations or, even, "lobbying". It is a specialist and obviously important part of public relations for any group since the actions of governments affect their business and lives dramatically,' he comments.

What are the elements of a successful lobbying campaign? Essentially they are the same as for any campaign:

● intelligence/research;
● communication;
● pressure.

Intelligence

Monitoring and research are vital to any campaign. 'Cogito ergo sum,' as Descartes put it. Always take the time to think about:

● **Issues.** Is what you seek to achieve actually possible within the political framework on the day?
● **Timescale.** Can you act in time to be effective?
● **Procedure.** Where is the best place, or places, to move? Through the civil service? The Commons? The Lords? The European community? The World Trade Organization? Or a mixture, as is usually the case?
● **Friends and enemies.** As in any military manoeuvre, you have potential allies and real opponents. How do you identify each and realize their value or danger? For example, many pressure groups are now both powerful and dedicated.
● **The key people.** Who really matters for the issue in question? Some politicians and civil servants are more important than others.

Communication

What is the practical message you wish to convey in its most effective form? 'Politics is the art of the possible,' sensibly observed Bismarck. Agree your strategy, after:

- receiving the facts – the intelligence process;
- taking sensible soundings – testing the water with key people;
- accepting inevitable differences.

'Think like a wise man but communicate in the language of the people,' advised Yeats. Only then send out your message, which must be:

- varied to appeal to the audiences;
- well argued in a calm, balanced way;
- brief, tightly edited and clear;
- supported by the essential detail;
- and, of course, timely.

Be discreet. For example, be careful about putting strategic advice in writing, whether to the client, to allies or anyone where there may be the slightest chance of a leak.

Pressure

Rarely is any case won without it, however logical the arguments may seem. So, the issue must be fought through:

- the system, via the established political processes;
- the media, which influences politicians but requires skilful mobilizing;
- your allies, who can greatly add to the variety and force of your argument.

Media exposure can attract – and hold – political allies especially, who rarely shun publicity.

But be flexible

Because few campaigns are won outright without concessions. 'Finality is not the language of politics,' noted Disraeli. So:

- Consider reasonable offers – from government in particular, often in secret.
- Seize your opportunities. There are usually times when outside events allow pressure to be stepped up.
- Finally, play it long. Your opponents are more likely to compromise or collapse if they see you have stamina for a long fight. This is especially the case with administrators (such as civil servants).

SOME OBSERVATIONS, IN SUMMARY

1. Public affairs is all about issues in the public arena and, ultimately, what the public, through its legislative processes, finds acceptable.

2. Do not attempt to present views at the public affairs level unless they will have a consensus of support by specialists or the broader public, once they have been understood...

3. ... in other words, do not waste time on lost causes or arguments you have been unable to win elsewhere. Everything you say will be checked.

4. Structure your public affairs activities to cover local, national and (where appropriate) international politicians, civil servants and their advisers.

5. This is a specialist arena not for the amateur, the inept or faint-hearted, so the cheapest approach is to use the best advice you can buy.

6. One of the essential (but, sometimes, exhausting) activities is to monitor, sort and sift the volumes of information to what really matters.

7. From the right information must come the analysis of the implications, trends and the current state of play to enable you to plan your strategy.

8. Perhaps your best investment will be in building a reliable, up-to-date and accurate database of all those of influence on your policy issues.

9. When building your case, remember to develop the counter-arguments, as those briefed will want to know how to deal with any challenges from possible opponents.

10. Keep the language of briefing simple and direct, avoiding jargon.

11. Consider carefully when a private lobby is most effective and when it may be necessary to go public to apply pressure through popular support.

12. Use your professionals to lay the groundwork in public affairs so that the chief executive can come in at the close or as a 'longstop', if necessary.

13. Know the competition – those who will be putting counter-arguments to yours or trying to achieve the opposite to your desired effect.

14. Should your opponents be using misleading arguments, consider briefing them yourself to prevent them using inaccuracies in their case.

15. Make sure your trade association is aware of your plans and liaise closely – but do not rely on them alone to present an industry brief effectively.
16. Ensure that everything is well planned and that all who are likely to be involved are briefed to minimize the need for 'fire-fighting', should your plans be threatened.
17. Your constituency MPs, of all persuasions, expect to be briefed and can not only support the case but can offer helpful advice.
18. Party and all-party committee members should be briefed individually or in groups; be certain to give everyone an equal opportunity to meet you.
19. At your national level, present the case both to civil servants and ministers. They like winners, which strengthens their track record of parliamentary success.
20. At the EU level, you may need to use different procedures as it can be more effective to operate through a trade grouping.
21. Key influences will include members of the European Parliament and officials in the relevant directorates-general (DGs) in the Commission.
22. Cover all MEPs who have a constituency involvement with your company or the issue, using both formal and informal presentations.
23. In London, Washington, Brussels or other legislative centres, use local and specialized professionals, not your general public relations team.
24. Exchange information across your operating markets, even briefing legislators on what is happening in other countries, where this may be helpful to them.

9

Corporate/investor relations

Build a corporate reputation that becomes the company

Key factors discussed

- Investor relations and reputation.
- Winning management support.
- Trust in City and financial circles.
- Present a broad management team.
- The role of the public relations adviser.
- Planning for good and bad times.
- Making corporate messages believable.
- Corporate social responsibility.

COORDINATING FINANCIAL AND CORPORATE RELATIONS

The company reputation is significantly shaped by how it undertakes corporate communications. The bedrock of all public relations activity – community, employee, marketing or parliamentary, for example – should be the interrelationships between the company and its corporate audiences. Central to such corporate public relations must be financial/investor relations. Though this is a highly specialized branch of public relations, it is potentially so high profile and core to all company operations that it must be considered part of the broadest corporate communications efforts.

These suggestions primarily cover quoted companies; however, even private companies and non-profit organizations have a requirement for corporate, and often financial, communications and many of the points in this chapter apply to such bodies.

These notes relate to practices in the UK which are parallel to those across many open financial democracies. The principles apply broadly but may need tailoring to meet national policies, legislation and guidelines.

CORPORATE PUBLIC RELATIONS

How can public relations contribute to the achievement of company commercial aims?

Sir Robin Saxby is chairman of ARM Holdings plc and in a study was rated one of the most respected business leaders in the UK. He believes that communications can play a key role in shaping perceptions of an organization and contribute to building the reputation. Today, he explains, the communications strategy has to embrace investors, customers and employees. The company must have environmental policies, ethical policies, remuneration policies, accounting policies and so on. Indeed, it must communicate simultaneously with all shareholders with the same information. Being dually listed on two markets with different legal and accounting standards, as ARM is, presents extra challenges. The internet is an essential tool for communication with shareholders and customers. A solid marketing communications strategy, which presents the company in its true light and manages the various channels of communication accurately and effectively, results in higher shareholder value. A direct measure of this can be seen in the price earnings ratios of competing companies.

Effective corporate relations presents the company to the broadest audiences; many other aspects of company communications should be run in a consistent way under this umbrella.

Some city financial advisers do not agree and feel that investor relations should be independent of all other activity. Can financial relations realistically be operated separately from the broad public relations programme? Consider the following case:

According to an in-depth analysis by the *Financial Times* of the biggest scandal to hit the City in the decade, unacceptable communications practices were central to the loss sustained by countless institutional and private investors. Before this company, Exampleco – a top exporter and winner of several Queen's Awards to industry – collapsed so dramatically, it had made a series of acquisitions. These will somehow have to be unbundled following revelations that the chief executive published information that is now believed to be misleading. The company was being advised by David Trackman, head of Inside Track, the maverick City public relations consultancy. He is believed to have been on a contract approved by the chairman but not submitted to the board.

This information was used on good faith by analysts and respected City journalists in their reports; it not only held the share price artificially high but may have been a factor in winning some sensitive defence contracts. The City Takeover Panel has already censured the board and forced the resignation of the chairman, Lord Craskeman. All the directors could face a bar from holding future office if the criticism is sustained of their not being on top of what was being done in their names by the company public relations.

Trackman could face legal action over his alleged role in preparing statements, 'polishing the reality', as he claimed in a recent interview on BBC Radio Four's *Today*.

Central to the case being prepared by the Serious Fraud Squad is the fact that the company had no written public relations policy and communications had never been formally reviewed by the board. The earlier resignation as a director of barrister and ex-cabinet minister, Sir Paul Hilverson, has forced the prime minister to dramatically overhaul the rules on MPs' business interests; Sir Paul is believed to have played a pivotal role in recent confidential discussions on Libyan trade links.

No, thankfully, not an actual report but an imaginary drama that will hopefully never come to pass. Yet each of the elements has validity and has been seen in recent news stories.

Unauthorized control of public relations

If you were a director of a public limited company, such as the fictional case above, you would certainly want to know what the public relations policy was and what the communicators could or could not do in the company name – especially without the directors' knowledge. At the least, you might want to prevent any misinformation – particularly to make sure the company was not allowing any of those less-than-totally-ethical practices that might be undertaken by those exceeding their authority. This might prevent directors and senior executives being unknowingly involved in the fictional activities that formed the report above. Remember Exxon, Maxwell, Guinness, Polly Peck, WorldCom, Enron and many others? Did all the directors of these companies know and approve what was being done?

If a director did not know, why not? Both legislation and best-practice guidelines across an increasing proportion of business economies expect directors to know – and they will be held accountable for mispractice, even if they claim they did not know. And one high-profile, influential and significant area where every director needs to be certain he or she knows what is being done in his/her name is communications.

How can a director be certain of what is happening in the day-to-day public relations arena unless corporate communications is actively and positively directed from the board – and from nowhere else?

On a more positive note, surely one of the best services a director, executive or non-executive, can offer the company is to ensure that it operates to the best possible standards; is sensitive to the needs of all the stakeholders; and projects its case with pride and vigour. Is that not good corporate relations?

It is relevant that the report of the UK Committee on the Financial Aspects of Corporate Governance placed much stress on communications, including the feedback role that might normally be part of a formal public relations programme to support investor relations:

> If long-term relationships are to be developed, it is important that companies should communicate their strategies to their major shareholders and that the shareholders should understand them. It is equally important that the shareholders should play their part in the communication process by informing companies if there are any aspects of the business which give them cause for concern. Both shareholders and directors have to contribute to the building of a sound working relationship between them.

REPUTATION AND INVESTOR RELATIONS

Good corporate relations is part of running a good business. It builds pride and confidence and helps senior executives to sleep better at nights.

The *captains of industry* survey, by MORI, regularly asks senior directors of major companies in the UK which aspects of company business could be most affected by a strong or weak corporate image.

According to these leaders, the top factor is shareholder loyalty. Interestingly, four out of five rate customer service by far the most important factor in maintaining or improving a corporate reputation. Favourable media coverage is the next most important. In other words, behaving well (looking after customers and getting positive news coverage for good management) creates a good reputation which, in turn, helps create sales.

According to a separate study, also by MORI, a good reputation can be a tangible business asset. Seven people in ten among the general public consider that 'a company that has a good reputation would not sell poor quality products'. Whether this is always true is less important than that it should be a widely held public belief.

This overview can be an important factor in shaping corporate policy in individual companies. Indeed, what the chairman says, how the factory managers treat their neighbours, the presentation of company lorries and the courtesy of drivers can all have an effect on the bottom line. Adopting a public relations perspective on management means more than avoiding damaging mistakes; it means taking advantage of every opportunity to ensure that all comments, decisions and actions reinforce the corporate reputation.

Research confirms that this reputation (which, after all, is built from these and many other direct and indirect factors) influences buying decisions. For example, shoppers are more likely to try something new from a trusted name; people would be 14 per cent more likely to buy a new food product if it bore the name Heinz than if it were from a large but unspecified company. That 14 per cent advantage is likely to be a major factor – more than any product benefit and, certainly, far more than any price differential. Indeed, such an advantage may support premium prices.

MORI chairman, Bob Worcester, believes that familiarity breeds favour not contempt. In most industrialized countries, 9 times out of 10, there is a high correlation between how well people *know* a company and how well they *regard* it. If a company has a good reputation among those who know it, by increasing its visibility it can increase its public regard. And, he adds, at the same time the public's propensity to buy its products, invest in it, apply for a job with it, recommend its products, and so on, increases significantly.

Over half the British public believe that 'old established companies make the best products and all the evidence suggests this is a universal truth'. Unexpectedly, 40 per cent claim to 'never buy products made by companies of which they have not heard'. This is probably not so, but it is clearly how a significant proportion of the public feels.

MANAGEMENT MUST BACK CORPORATE MESSAGES

In any group, there will be a small core who will tend to lead opinions. They may be broadcasters, professionals, academics, speakers or writers or may hold office in trade or professional groups – or may simply be those that attract the attention of others when they speak. Public opinion can often be moved by a handful of people; some major decisions require only a few to tilt the balance one way or the other. For example, it has been calculated that some major takeovers have been won or lost as a result of the views of fewer than 100 people.

Yet, while thinking about those vital opinion leaders, do not forget the others within the company. In Chapter 7, on employee relations, the potential for everyone to be a member of the public relations team was discussed. Each has an influence, and although not all may be major opinion leaders, some will!

The top 40 or 50 managers in a large organization have an importance far in excess of their numbers or nominal authority. They set the mood of the business and anyone feeling their pulse will know the health of the enterprise. It is vital that they are melded into a team; they must be at least as well informed as key external audiences such as the top 20 shareholders or analysts. Serious gaps can be left in management understanding and support through relying entirely on a cascade of information from the board.

To ensure that this key group is reinforcing corporate relations, the chief executive should supplement normal management processes with direct briefings for his or her senior managers on matters of corporate strategy. These might include briefing notes, repeats of

City presentations and an annual management conference for this group. Their contacts will be widespread among corporate audiences such as business opinion formers, the financial community and the public sector. Properly briefed, they can be a formidable force, adding considerable weight and conviction to the messages from the centre among these groups.

BUILDING THE CORPORATE PROGRAMME

The chairman, the chief executive and other senior directors should form the interface between the organization and the many publics with whom it must deal – backed, of course, by a senior and united management team.

A year or two before being asked to chair the Committee on Corporate Governance, Sir Adrian Cadbury wrote an excellent book outlining the roles of the chairman in representing the company. He said:

> The chairman is the link with the shareholders; he should also be responsible for company relations with other outside groups. It is for the chairman to put across the company's aims and policies to all those whose confidence in the business is important. (Sir Adrian's comments to the author, based on his views expressed in *The Company Chairman*, Director Books)

Indeed, the chairman's responsibility for the public face of the company also means that that person is the guardian of its character and conduct. Sir Adrian adds:

> The standards in the company are set from the top. It is for the chairman to ensure that everyone in the business knows what the company stands for and what standards of conduct are expected from them.

He also observes that it is essential that companies present their past record and future ambitions positively to the outside world. The outside world judges companies not just by the kind of business they are in but, above all, by the competence and flair of the people who are running them. The chairman has the responsibility for conveying to the public the ambitions of the company and the abilities of its management. A recent City study suggested that 60 per cent of an analyst's rating of a company depends on the credibility of the chairman/CEO.

BUILDING STRONG CORPORATE RELATIONS

Just like an individual, a company needs a rounded personality. Different facets of this personality may well be more relevant to different audiences but each perspective should be part of the whole and not a completely different face. In other words, shareholders and potential investors, as well as investment advisers, will be primarily interested in the financial performance of the company; they will have an interest in the products and services, as these are the items that generate the profits.

In contrast, their interest in local community relations and environmental policies might only be to the level that it has an impact upon financial trading. However, it may be very difficult for the investment market to assess the potential impact of policy in these sectors unless this is explained by the directors. For example, a small change in EU environmental legislation, which may not be something of which investors would be aware, could have a big impact on operations and, therefore, position the company at an advantage or disadvantage in comparison with its competitors.

Similarly, a corporate audience, such as environmental regulators, might be particularly concerned about this legislation and the company's operating and environmental policies. These may be of greater importance to them than the financial position of the company, though they cannot be divorced. For example, if the company is trading profitably then it will be better able to make the changes necessary to meet the new directives. This is the situation with all corporate audiences – each will have its own particular focus but needs to have a view of the company 'in the round'.

It will be considerably to the advantage of the company if all the corporate audiences are clearly identified. A communications network needs to be set up to ensure that each of these audiences is getting a broad picture of the company, its policies and its operations. Specific focus on specific groups should be within this broader context.

Clearly, the financial and trading activities of any quoted company will remain one of central importance, simply because of the possible focus of media attention and the availability of published company information. For example, your company may be invited tomorrow to tender for an important piece of business for a major public corporation; or your son or nephew might be invited to attend an interview for a place on a graduate training scheme.

A glance at the financial columns, a quick check on one of the financial databases, or a few moments on the website will bring you up to date with the company's recent activities that might have had an impact on its trading. Yet, other important aspects such as its procurement, contract, tendering and payment processes may never get that level of media coverage and so will be unknown. That is natural and proper; however, the key point to remember is that financial communications for those companies that are quoted will always remain a central element in corporate communications.

Remember that poor performance in a minor or even esoteric area can assume major importance as a result of the criticisms of a pressure group or the probing of a specialist journalist.

CREATING INVESTOR RELATIONS

Sometimes there is confusion over corporate and financial relations. Shareholder relations, some feel, is corporate relations. But the corporation has many corporate audiences that may not be primarily related to the investment or the shareholder community. Local and national government, professional and trade bodies, suppliers, employees and prospective employees, trading partners such as wholesalers, retailers and bankers, and, above all, customers are as interested in the company as they are in its financial performance.

The company has a role in its local or national community that can be of considerable importance to many people. You do not need to be an investor in General Electric or IBM, or even a supplier or neighbour, let alone a customer, to have considerable interest in the company, its philosophies and its progress. We are all part of the corporate audience for General Electric or IBM. The direction and effectiveness of these companies' public relations demonstrate that they recognize the broad constituency that follows their activities with interest.

Many companies, charities, professional bodies and others will have stakeholders who may not be shareholders in the conventional sense and who may not be the focus of normal investor relations.

As we saw, looking at research under the setting of objectives, companies that are well known will create better customer attitudes and potential loyalties. Of course, corporate relations and financial relations cannot be realistically separated – and it may make practical sense to run these together. Certainly shareholder/investor relations will have a direct impact on the corporate reputation.

Consider the broadest corporate constituency

As noted, the financial operations of a commercial organization really cannot be separated from its trading activities. It must make sense to project the financial credibility of the company and the skills of its management, just as strongly as promoting the products and services that it offers.

The relevance and importance of financial public relations has grown in recent years. The specialists in this sector now have access to the chief executive and have become important boardroom advisers. With the interlocking aspects of the financial, corporate, parliamentary and marketing relations, there is a strong case for the overall adviser being a public relations professional. But, if the adviser is to be credible to board colleagues, then special expertise, plus courage and skill are required.

The focus of public attention on the *trading* performance of public companies and the growing understanding of the role of marketing are creating a much healthier business environment. The investment community is not the introspective group of financial institutions sometimes portrayed in television drama!

Investment advisers in the modern world not only want to know more about an organization's production capabilities, retail outlets or the services it offers, but are also looking at the market, competition and international development and, increasingly, at corporate social policies. Indeed, corporate social responsibility (CSR) is proving to be of increasing importance to stakeholders – see pages 221–230.

PROJECTING THE MANAGEMENT CAPABILITIES

More companies are recognizing the synergy between various aspects of corporate communications. The public relations adviser who combines the responsibilities of marketing communications, corporate *and* financial relations is fortunate indeed, as these are the three most important areas of an integrated company communications programme.

Many senior practitioners consider employee communications to be the fourth area for truly integrated public relations. Warren

Newman, when head of UK corporate relations for Général des Eaux Group, observed that many companies still regarded employee communications as the responsibility of the personnel people. Although finance, marketing and human resources directors are all responsible for their own ideas of activity, the corporate relations director should be responsible for ensuring that all audiences get the same message at the same time and by appropriate means.

It is not enough for a public company to be efficient and profitable. It is essential that the policies it follows, and the products and services it offers, are known and understood by the publics with whom it works. It is equally important that all financial institutions on whom the company depends are fully informed about the organization, understand the policies and respect the management capabilities.

The company cannot spend too much time on communications, but it should never attempt to present a picture publicly which is not backed up by the facts. It is essential that messages are presented in simple terms to the audience identified, but these must project the reality.

The commercial and trading activities of the company are closely linked to its financial performance. Financial advisers prefer to work with companies they know and respect; no matter how specialized the operating sector, it is important that they understand the significance of the business, the quality of its management and the potential for commercial development.

It was once a criticism of the investment community in the UK, the City, that it always seemed to be one crucial step removed from the business activities of the companies concerned. This is certainly less true today; in recent years a number of factors have changed both the financial realities and public perceptions. These factors include the growth in public interest in financial matters (for those who remember when the City pages were the City *column*), the increasing internationalization of the financial world, developments in private investment and the opening of new opportunities for smaller companies to raise finance.

Another factor is that business leaders and their financial performance have become news. People buying cars, computers, domestic appliances and many other products are interested in the companies behind their purchases. Great successes (Microsoft and Google) and great failures (WorldCom and Enron) have raised public interest in companies and those who drive them.

The financial sectors (including banking, merchant banking, broking and the major stock exchanges) are now internationally competitive, not just as a result of European harmonization, but through the development of 24-hour global trading and the geographic positions of London, New York and Tokyo, as the financial centres of the world. These are located in the three main international economic centres, Europe, the Americas and the Asia/Pacific region; by happy chance they are also spaced across the global time zones, so that trading activities are spread, almost, throughout the 24 hours.

Major companies are able to decide where to float, where to raise capital and which multinational advisers to select to help them across, say, the dozen or more financial communities that may be of significance to them. Despite some dramatic ups and downs in stock markets and confidence across the world, there has been steady progress towards more freedom, opportunity, scope and professionalism in the financial community. The financial public relations industry has also matured alongside these developments.

Most general practice public relations consultancies of any size now offer specialist financial relations advice – and those companies that concentrate solely on this area have grown in both number and size. At the same time, the public relations adviser in major corporations has found that financial relations has become an increasingly important part of his or her work, as well as one of the services in which management colleagues expect the greatest expertise and judgement. The central element in financial public relations is to create the environment within which the management of the company is best able to achieve commercial aims.

Those making investment judgements about the organization are highly professional and are working in one of the toughest business environments imaginable. Therefore, companies trying to establish effective communications with them will need to be equally as professional. This will usually involve building effective relations with four main groups:

1. The major institutional investors, such as insurance companies, international groups, pension funds and investment trusts.
2. The professionals who advise major shareholders, such as the stockbrokers, merchant banks, the corporate lawyers and accountants.
3. Private investors and shareholders (no longer always small players and, collectively, often of some importance).

4. The financial media, trade publications and commercial research and investment services that inform these groupings.

Public relations practitioners in the financial area need to be very close to the corporate policy-makers they are representing. Their activities are regulated by the law and some strict regulations – tightened since the concerns over insider dealing in New York, London and Tokyo. In the UK, these include the various Companies Acts, the Stock Exchange regulations and the takeover and corporate governance codes. The company will be judged by its performance... and much of the appraisal of this performance will result from the accuracy, candour, timeliness, integrity and overall quality of the information being issued.

APPOINTING A PUBLIC RELATIONS ADVISER

When making a public relations appointment to handle these areas the board will have to structure the adviser's role so that he or she can be on the inside, involved in policy and properly briefed, ahead of the game.

This puts a substantial responsibility on the adviser's shoulders, and explains why timid people do not thrive in this sector. It can sometimes suddenly become a fierce world where much depends on the effectiveness of both the advice and the implementation. In a takeover battle, as in any battle, there are no prizes for coming second!

Of course, companies that have their shares listed on stock exchanges have legal obligations covering the information about their performance that they must issue to shareholders. This includes the announcement of results – usually preliminary, interim and year-end. The publication of the annual report and the AGM (at which shareholders and their advisers are briefed on and can ask questions about the performance of their company) can also be significant in the financial calendar.

Notice of the announcement of results is usually issued in advance. The timing and control of the information is particularly important and the public relations executive will normally be handling the advance notice to the appropriate stock exchange, preparation of news releases, briefing relevant journalists, planning meetings with analysts, and attending any press conferences or individual interviews that might be judged appropriate.

There are also regulations relating to the issuing of information that could have an effect on the share price, such as new share issues, board changes, trading disclosures, changes in holdings, planned acquisitions, significant investments or disinvestments, major product or corporate developments, proposed mergers and other takeover activities.

A market in securities which works efficiently is necessary for the confidence of both the investors and the companies whose shares are being traded.

The responsibility of a stock exchange is not just to regulate the buying and selling of shares but to ensure that the prices of transactions are based upon reliable information and that shares are made available at the same time, and the same price, to everyone involved. Clearly, the information issued by the companies is an essential part of this communications process.

PROJECT CONSISTENT MESSAGES

Other communications relevant to the commercial performance of the organization must present consistent and effective messages. For example, information and literature that might be particularly important would include the annual report, trading summaries, background briefing documents on markets and products, bid defence documents, major speeches by senior executives, parliamentary evidence and business summaries for special audiences such as employees, customers, suppliers and so on.

Corporate advertising can be an effective public relations tool and a powerful method of putting controlled messages in front of broad audiences quickly and efficiently. However, it can be costly and normally does not involve the two-way communications element of, say, discussions and presentations; nor does it have the third party credibility of media comments. But, with the size of audience involved today in some financial communications situations, it can be effective to back up other activities.

In recent years, television has joined the press as a medium supplying business information and, even more recently, the internet has added instant, low-cost global communications to the mix. Now an even broader range of advertisers are involved, including flotation candidates, banks, insurance companies, building societies and other financial service groups. Some of this advertising is not presenting financial information but is corporate in nature, projecting the strength of the organization; equally, some of this advertising appears to be selling financial services but is really designed to do a corporate job on behalf of the advertiser – all financial advisers are also personal buyers of financial services. Advertising has often been used as a technique to inform shareholders about developments in, say, takeover battles, though its effectiveness needs to be carefully considered in these circumstances – any hint of 'panic communications' (interpreted by investors as a belated effort to cover a perceived previous lack of communications) could well be counterproductive.

PLAN FOR ALL CONTINGENCIES

Planning for potential financial crises, such as an unwanted takeover bid, should be considered alongside other crisis planning activities, even if different communications specialists would be involved. The whole of the company issues planning strategy should be coordinated: a manufacturing disaster, for example, could affect employees, investors and customers.

In some companies, financial public relations may be linked to parliamentary relations. As an illustration, there could be a parliamentary dimension to such eventualities as a bid which may need to be referred to the Monopolies Commission; significant redundancies; the exposure of international trading barriers; the opening of new international markets; and developments in relationships with those government departments that may be customers of major corporations.

Professional investment specialists are still influenced by attitudes; effective communications will not counter any evidence that they judge professionally, but *can* add an extra element. This might enable a company's shares to stand out from the thousands of others currently quoted on the stock exchanges.

BUILD LOYALTY: YOU MAY NEED IT

Until relatively recently, some public companies only recognized the importance of the loyalty of their shareholders when they were threatened by a takeover. In the past, it was not unusual to find that the public company did not even have an up-to-date record of its shareholders and so was unable to communicate with them directly and promptly.

No share register will ever be fully up to date, though modern technology brings this possibility closer. The publicly quoted company will also have a complete current list of all advisers who might influence investment. Occasions may arise during the year when the company will wish to issue information directly to them. This must be done with discrimination.

Investment professionals tend to view with suspicion any apparent extravagance, such as glossy brochures and unnecessary reports on company progress. The simplest guideline is to issue only information that is helpful to their professional decision-making; for example, if there were a significant change in the company's market, the organization might have undertaken research indicating why they should be making a particular investment. This analysis may well be of some interest; but a corporate brochure on an expensive new house style may not.

Financial advisers have to be very concerned about the loyalty that needs to be shown to the shareholders – who are able to withdraw their money at a moment's notice. As a general rule, it is safer to assume that there is *no* automatic shareholder loyalty and that investors invest only for the return they receive. Therefore, if a company wants to be able to carry its shareholders through difficulties, then it needs to communicate consistently with them over a period of time. It is of limited value taking emergency whole-page advertisements to try to establish some rapport with the shareholders. Of course, if the speed of developments requires a very prompt response, then such a technique can be used to convey information, but it must be no substitute for regular communications: certainly such actions do not always generate goodwill. Some research even suggests that such actions undermine existing confidence and support.

Equally, the chairman must never talk via advertising when the City and stakeholders might expect him or her to talk to them directly, or at the very least via the business media, supported by website messages.

Make personal meetings your first choice

Effective public relations is an essential for established and quoted companies. But it can be as fundamental to new ventures seeking not only markets, but support and financial backing.

After the hype and then the collapse of those overheated technology companies that had no real business, no real customers and no real income, investors are being understandably cautious. They need reasoned and persuasive conviction.

Vaud Massarsky is president of NPDC, a US-based venture capital firm, headquartered in New York City. This operation represents around 150 high net worth individuals investing their personal funds in new businesses. Massarsky believes that the ability of the business entrepreneurs to manage perception is vital to any strong proposition. In his experience, which is matched across the venture capital sector, this management of perception can be as significant as inspiration in maintaining momentum behind a business venture, especially a start-up. Good ideas need to be explained well and with a focus on what they can achieve, he explains. Investors and new business partners need to believe in the dream and see it converted to a reality. That takes the skills of someone who well understands reputation management, the processes behind public opinion, media interests and needs. It used to be that investors looked carefully at the marketing plan with new ventures, with the emphasis on how reputation will be established. They still do, but a sound communications plan, run by an experienced and trustworthy public relations person, adds a lot of credibility to the initiative.

With major established companies, the needs are equally important but the emphasis is different. Continuity can be important in maintaining relationships. City support is essential at all times but particularly, for example, when a rights issue is planned or a new acquisition or market development is being negotiated.

There can be no substitute for face-to-face meetings to help strengthen the credibility of the company. Many companies with strong relations in the City ensure that their chairman, chief executive and finance director hold regular meetings with advisers in City circles.

The City columns of the national and provincial press (and, increasingly, radio and television, plus electronic newsletters, the internet and key trade publications), provide an important source of information for people making investment decisions. In dealing with the media, it is essential that the person running your public relations develops a reputation for accuracy, speed and honesty in all press statements. Any blurring of the truth, evasion, exaggeration or inaccuracy will damage the practitioner's reputation.

News stories need to be sharp and short. It is essential that, in addition to the name of the public relations executive responsible for the story, the company director to whom the media can talk is also included. Preferably this should be the chief executive.

The public relations practitioner should be the bridge to the company management and never the barrier; only in special and *agreed* circumstances should he or she actually speak for the company.

Establish relations with commentators

A good reputation in financial circles is vital. Constant meetings with City journalists (not necessarily editors) and the chief executive are not normally as necessary as some chairmen feel. These are really only productive when there is a story or development that can be discussed at the meeting. This might provide an exclusive article relating to the growth of the company. Alternatively, an informal press lunch might provide an equally valuable opportunity to brief an individual editor on the background to an expansion into a new market.

Few City journalists are likely to look in much depth at most listed companies, except at the times of the announcement of the interim and final results, acquisition activity and possibly the publishing of the annual report.

The AGM is usually of limited media interest unless the chairman is making an updated statement on performance or some extraordinary activity is expected from shareholders. Briefings for investment advisers must include background on the company, its development, its attitude towards the market, future potential, investment policies and expansion plans. It would be normal for these to be presented by the chairman, chief executive or managing director. For convenience, many of these are held over lunch, but a good lunch should never be a substitute for a good presentation.

Briefing meetings can be particularly important for companies with provincial headquarters, who might not have quite such regular access to City advisers.

Good relations with financial commentators depend on corporate candour and individual communications skills. These factors help build reputation.

219

THE ANNUAL REPORT

Obviously, one of the important influences on the attitudes of both the investing community and wider corporate audiences towards the company will be the annual report. The figures are always the most important part. The emphasis should be on the clarity in presentation of the information.

The chairman's report should be crisp and factual and should not contain over-optimistic language or industry jargon. Pictures of the directors should be treated with care to avoid the suspicion that the annual report is being used as an ego vehicle! Of course, investors want to see what the custodians of their money look like, but there are both imaginative and dull ways to show them. As an example, in a study of annual reports Whitbread was commended for using small action shots of the senior people plus a quote relevant to their direct responsibilities (with, properly, all employees at all levels identified by name in the captions to pictures).

More and more companies that are considered leaders in this field are improving the quality of presentation of the annual report and accounts. However, it is no coincidence that these companies also focus as much attention on the depth and clarity of the factual information. They do not make the mistake of substituting an attractive overview of the company for a concise analysis of the company's performance; such an analysis can be helpful as it will generally go beyond the statutory information requirements.

CORPORATE MESSAGES MUST BE CREDIBLE

Some specific activities may be undertaken to project the corporate personality of the organization. These will be important for quoted companies as they can have an influence upon the investor market and, therefore, the financial performance.

Corporate activities may be of even greater importance to non-quoted companies, which generally do not have the analysts, City commentators and financial media to discuss and project their trading record and financial performance. However, the activities of many non-quoted companies can be of interest to observers and commentators – such as fund managers, analysts and financial media. This may be because the companies plan to float at some stage; or they provide data and trading information that can be benchmarked against quoted companies in their sector; or simply, they are well managed and innovative in ways that can influence the policies of their quoted competitors.

There are two aspects of a corporate relations programme for the non-quoted company. First, all activities and visible aspects of the company must be planned to ensure that they project consistent corporate messages. As a simple example, whatever a transport company's corporate policy may be, it has to remember that a very large number of opinion leaders travelling the roads of the country will be influenced (positively or negatively) by its fleet of vehicles. Should someone propose that an attractive trading tag-line might be 'Your friendly freighter', then someone had better be sure that the drivers support this concept. It will also be important that the company is employing neither policies to force drivers to cut corners to meet schedules, nor employment procedures that encourage them to be roadhogs.

The second key factor is to consider whether specific 'umbrella' activities might be considered to project corporate messages across the broadest range of audiences possible. Should this be the case, then sponsorships, community relations programmes, corporate advertising, business in the community, style initiatives, educational support and/or other activities might be considered. Any such scheme that is proposed should be tested against the corporate objectives. Ideally, activities can be planned that have a corporate support role yet also back up marketing and employee relations at the same time.

In practice, effective corporate relations can have a measurable effect on reputation. People relate to people and the links between corporate and community affairs can be particularly valuable in projecting the human face of the organization.

CORPORATE SOCIAL RESPONSIBILITY

Increasingly, the responsibility that an organization demonstrates towards the diverse communities within which it works are important in shaping the attitudes of those with whom it relates. In turn, this helps to develop and project the reputation. A key element in corporate social responsibility (CSR) can be community support, charitable involvement and the sponsorship of good causes. The following is an edited version of a CSR appraisal focused on these areas.

Setting criteria for community relations

Agreeing a policy to link sponsorship, community and charitable involvement within the corporate framework to strengthen the corporate reputation

A credible method of evaluating such activity against a corporate communications strategy is essential. The following was prepared by the company's public relations manager, with the advice of an outside consultant, to a brief from the company's marketing director. It is an example of a strategy document created for board discussion by a market leader. This was produced in advance of undertaking a number of successful activities; it ties community and charitable support into one coherent whole. As this is a confidential strategy approach for an international insurance broker, the directors have asked that the company not be identified, so for the purposes of this case study we shall call them InsurCo.

The development of a corporate reputation policy for InsurCo, with recommendations on community involvement and charitable donations

Background

InsurCo is a new kind of insurance broker with its focus on solving the most demanding risk management issues of specific businesses and industries across the globe. To achieve this, it needs to create an environment of understanding across broad audiences critical to its success. A range of communications and marketing techniques are likely to be used in an integrated and seamless matrix. The aim? To create among those publics with whom InsurCo is in partnership – clients, industry bodies, professional advisers, legislators, neighbours, employees – the feeling that 'I know InsurCo, I have heard of the company, I understand what it does, it has a good reputation and seems to be the kind of company worth dealing with/working for/recommending/buying from/talking to', and so on.

Quite a challenge. Community support has been part of the communications mix in the past. Has it worked? Does it have a role for the future? What could we learn from our experiences? What could we build on from the successes? These are among the questions that need to be addressed.

Investigation

Central elements in the investigation were a series of interviews with senior members of the management team to identify their views on the role that sponsorship might play in the future.

Policy approval process
The consultancy recommends that an approval body should be set up. This would set the policy, review the initiatives, access candidate activity, make decisions, manage the processes, and above all, monitor and report on performance. As a working title this will be the community relations committee. It should have members across all company disciplines. The chairman should be appointed by the CEO. Divisional members should be approved by the committee chairman and staff representatives should be elected by employees.

The need for policies
Sponsorship and charitable and community initiatives can be expensive. They can create positive or negative perceptions. Many companies undertake activities that reduce their commercial effectiveness. Some do not exercise tight control and so expend an immeasurable amount of money and effort that is allocated through divisional resources and budgets.

It would help everyone making policy decisions in InsurCo to have some central policy and guidelines. This would keep expenditure and activities under control, as well as measure effectiveness.

The principles
Community initiatives should not be undertaken because they are a good thing to do; because of the competition; or because of a particular interest in the activity. They must be undertaken to a defined strategy and this document sets the first approach towards such policies.

Elements
There are a number of elements to consider:

- the responsibility to the community;
- the potential to create awareness;
- the opportunities for exposure of the name;
- the 'associations' that surround the event;
- the relevance to the target audiences;
- the business entertainment provisions;
- the logistics involved in organization;
- the history or track record of the activity;
- the solus or cooperative sponsorship proposal;
- the capabilities of partners or organizers;
- the media interest and news opportunities;
- the direct and promotional costs of the activity;
- the incidental costs, including executive time;
- the cost-effectiveness project comparison.

Each of these is discussed in outline and the consensus view of executives noted, where appropriate in *italics*.

Awareness

Often a central consideration in a community opportunity will be the likely awareness that can be created by the sponsor, related to the audiences of importance to the sponsor.

Also, awareness may not be enough alone. When Gillette originally sponsored cricket, awareness was very high; however, a significant proportion of the public surveyed thought that Gillette was some long-forgotten cricketer! Therefore, the branding of activities is an important factor, as Gillette demonstrated when they increased their profile and improved guidelines on using the logo in association with this sponsorship.

The general view among InsurCo directors was that a good level of awareness needed to be a factor when considering a candidate activity. This needs to be aimed at industry and specifier levels but not at public levels.

Name exposure

A consideration will be how effectively the name can be exposed. A 2-inch logo on a racing car or a badge on the driver's overalls may equate to no exposure. In contrast, the Round the World Race seems incomplete without Whitbread and, later, Volvo, in the title. Or the Stella Artois Tennis Tournament or, from another sector, the Booker Prize for Literature. What events have the relevance, quality, value and integrity to which we would be willing to attach our name?

Any event that we support must be clearly seen as an InsurCo activity, that belongs to us and cannot be referred to properly without our name.

Activity associations

The activity itself sends out messages and can be surrounded by an environment that may be positive, negative or neutral. Speedway and dog racing are downmarket. Horse racing can be down- or upmarket, depending on the event, course and level at which it is supported. Betting shops are down and Ascot is up though, to some, over the top. Wimbledon is classy but classless, though Henley is establishment.

A county clay pigeon championship can be very upmarket, but discreet at the same time. Banger racing would be cheap and nasty. Or would it? Suppose it were a community effort supported by government to get energetic car-mad young people off the streets?… and so on.

We only want to be associated with activities that reflect that InsurCo is professional, responsible and a leader that makes a major contribution to our local and economic communities.

Relevance to audience

A hypothetical illustration: why support three-day horse trials if it has no relevance to the people with whom we work and research confirms that they see the sport as being for the privileged with too much time and money? Who are we trying to reach and what is of interest to *them*?

We are targeting decision-makers at middle and senior levels, plus opinion formers such as key editors and members of our local communities.

Candidate activities are broad, including golf, major spectator sports events, theatre, the visual arts, business education/training and social support, all with a relevance to the insurance and financial services sector.

Entertainment

Some activities may give exposure and entertainment opportunities. The Round the World yacht race gives some limited entertainment opportunities (the start and the stopover points, plus an awards dinner) but this is clearly secondary. Grand Prix racing, Wimbledon and Henley can give good entertainment opportunities without any need for sponsorship. Other activities in education might relate more closely to our employees' interests.

Opportunities for focused, limited scale entertainment in groups of 12 to 20, possibly as part of a major event. During work hours without partners but with business angle or social with partners on evenings or weekends.

Organizational logistics

There are plus and minus factors in being responsible for organizing an event. The pluses are control, quality, exploitation, 'ownership' and strong company association. The minuses are cost, diversion of management, need for special expertise. Hanging the name on an existing event is the alternative, with the opposite plus and minus factors.

No strong views were expressed on this, other than InsurCo is an insurance broker not an event organizer so a newly created activity might divert management time.

Track record of event

Sometimes a new event can create considerable news interest. Equally, a well-established activity may have had all the wrinkles smoothed out. Certainly, it is easier to assess the likely responses and results from an event that has had to deliver in the past.

If we decide to be associated with an existing event it can only be one that has an impeccable record, with organizers prepared to consider our own input. We expect to see a defined return from participating.

Solus support

The supporting company can take the sole sponsorship role or the primary role. For example, a cigarette company may sponsor a Formula One team but involve many secondary sponsors, all of whom want action and response in return for their contribution. This can cause conflict but does reduce the cost to the primary sponsor.

InsurCo should be the sole sponsor of an event designed to generate better awareness and to influence business contacts and prospects. This need not be the case should we consider entertainment or educational initiatives.

Capabilities of partners

The professional capability of the organizers of the activity can have a major influence on the results. Their efficiency might need to be balanced against possible resistance to new ideas: 'We've been doing it this way for X years', etc.

We would only want to work with a credible organization which would deliver the performance promised.

Consideration only for credible event organizers with track record and proven performance data.

Media potential

The news interest in activities can be because they are in the calendar and generate stories (Wimbledon, say) or because they are unusual (The National Chess Championship). The former type of event has stronger staying power. The latter may be relevant if an area exists that could be of public interest with the right promotion (a children's charity, say).

News coverage of the event would be useful, but is not the central criteria; media entertainment opportunities might be valuable. InsurCo wants to be associated with an event that is worthwhile.

Potential cost

- Direct event costs.
- Promotion costs.
- Incidental costs.

The true costs of any activity will include the up-front price, plus the costs of generating the maximum benefit plus the indirect costs that arise from local budgets, company personnel costs, travel, executive expenses and time. All of these should be included in the calculation of the real cost. Similarly, in the calculation of the potential budget, the corporate and divisional monies that are currently being spent should be totalled.

Views on group expenditure on the right activity ranged from £1 million per annum to zero. All were agreed that discretionary divisional spending was higher than might appear and this needed some control.

Cost-effectiveness
No sponsorship should be undertaken simply because it is the 'thing to do' or makes us feel good – though both may be valuable side-benefits. The activity should be undertaken to support corporate strategy, to specific objectives, to an agreed budget. The success in putting those messages in front of that agreed audience should also be measured to appraise the cost-effectiveness.

Some recent activities may have generated a significant audience and positive media coverage, but are not so appropriate today to reach the key decision-makers. Criteria for effectiveness need to be established.

Charitable donations

Observations
It is clear from our investigations (supported by all senior executives inter-viewed) that the company is involved in contributing to many 'good causes'. This represents a keenness to support activities that are viewed as being appro-priate by the individual managers. However, it seems likely that the goodwill is being dissipated through spreading support thinly and/or not getting recog-nition for this effort.

To help to develop a policy, it might be helpful to look at some of the obser-vations that arose in discussion.

The reasons for charitable donations
Not all donations are to official charities. Some are to good causes that are not charities but may not even be strictly organized as official bodies. This does not mean that such donations are wrong but it is worth recognizing this point.

Let us consider some of the reasons why a company might make small-scale charitable donations.

1. *It is the 'right thing to do'*
Does a company have a moral responsibility to distribute largesse? It could be argued that the company *has,* and 'sections' of the community *have not* and the wealth should be redistributed. Should an organization be filling gaps left by the government, society and the voluntary sector?

On balance, most people would agree that the company has a commercial, operational and ethical responsibility towards its customers, employees and shareholders and trading partners. If it behaves properly with respect for its neighbours and the community within which it operates, and pays its taxes, then it can be argued that the contribution that it is making to the economic well-being of the community is the end of its moral responsibility.

2. *Goodwill can be generated towards the company through supporting the right causes*

In a recent survey, some 70 per cent of business journalists felt better disposed towards an organization that has an active role within the communities in which it works.

It is difficult to measure the goodwill that is generated by such activities. Indeed, in some cases – often unknown to the company – minimal goodwill may be generated and, on occasion, this may even become ill will. For example, a local cause feels it needs £200 to achieve something and is offered £100. This can look very petty from a multi-billion-pound operation. Equally, some causes may not gain the support of management and, therefore, achieve no support. Others may win some support but are viewed as being less deserving in the eyes of the community. Clearly, this is a minefield and policy needs to be agreed.

3. *Employees will feel better disposed towards the company*

It is possible that some employees who are successful in their appeals will achieve an enhanced status in the eyes of their colleagues within the good cause they are supporting. This is not guaranteed. They may go back to a committee meeting which has expected them to raise £200 and say they only managed to raise £100. All employees will have their own social or community interests for which they might be pleased if the company were to donate, say, £1,000. Should the company donate £1,000 per employee to the good cause of each employee's choice? Clearly not, but it would be a policy of sorts.

Some possible guidelines

To develop a policy that can be agreed at a senior level within InsurCo, it might be useful to feed back some of the broad observations made by the executives that we interviewed.

If the company were to be involved in formal charitable/good cause donations, then these might be orientated towards organizations that have:

- a formal, established structure;
- local branches of registered charities or organized groups;
- educational or training bodies, particularly those aimed at the less-advantaged;
- direct relationship to communities within which InsurCo works;
- some direct connection with employees within InsurCo.

From this can be drawn the basis of a policy that would include all corporate donations.

Community involvement

Coordination
Elements of community involvement should be closely coordinated, possibly by an umbrella policy which links charitable contributions and community activities.

Corporate social responsibility can be demonstrated through community involvement, along with other activities.

Definition of the community
All seem united that the only communities that would be of real relevance would be those within which InsurCo works. There is no support for the concept that a major company has to fill a gap that is left in community welfare by the government.

There was mixed response to the suggestion that companies have community responsibilities. On balance, there was little opposition to some modest level of support and there was some positive feeling towards community activities that directly have a relevance to InsurCo.

Even with this framework, what constituted the InsurCo community was not universally agreed. The four areas that were accepted were:

- the financial services industry;
- the City (and particularly the insurance sector);
- communities within which employees live;
- communities within which InsurCo has significant operations.

The financial services sector is probably better covered through the company's normal public relations activities, particularly media relations.

The insurance community within the City clearly has some relevance but this might also be better covered through proposed sponsorship activities.

It was generally agreed that the communities in which employees lived were too diverse and any activity orientated to those areas would be spread thinly and would generate minimal benefit.

The community within which InsurCo operates was considered relevant, although there were mixed feelings over the benefits of a commercial, entrepreneurial group financially supporting a local mixed community which might be run by those with left-wing sympathies. At worst, such contributions may be greeted with hostility and generate ill will and, at best, some thought, support might be seen to be cynical or patronizing. Any backing for community involvement must be handled with great sensitivity.

Candidate activities
Those activities that involved human response were largely felt to be the most beneficial. Some of these require management time but no cost. Examples that might be supported included:

- *Facility visits* – Schools and colleges that wish to see how a large company worked might be allowed to make suitable visits.
- *Careers' talks* – Community groups that ask for an executive of InsurCo to talk to them can be assisted. Speakers could be provided on a wide range of topics, but those targeted at young people/school leavers would probably be most appropriate, particularly careers guidance.
- *Reciprocal support* – In contrast, should InsurCo ever be looking for volunteers or special assistance, then consideration would be given to local community groups. This might include buying paintings for offices from the local art college; allowing charity collectors and local artists to use the reception area.

Above all, those activities targeted at young people and with a focus on careers, particularly in insurance, would always take priority.

Some provisional criteria

Community support
1. Local communities where major facilities are sited would be preferred.
2. Activities which focus on young people and their careers will be a priority.
3. Financial contributions alone with no community involvement will not be supported.
4. Specific activities preferred, not those where the InsurCo contribution is but part of 'something in the hat'.
5. Activities where there is a personnel link with the company would be top priority.
6. Support 'in kind' would be considered. No effort to be considered in isolation but all to be related to charitable donations and sponsorship.

Charitable contributions
1. Criteria broadly as with community involvement.
2. Clearance of all projects through a suitable committee.
3. One major goodwill cause to be supported each year – possibly selected by a ballot of employees.
4. Additional budget for smaller discretionary contributions, also to be approved by the committee. Such small donations not to exceed a nominal figure to be agreed, say, £250.
5. Budget for major activity and discretionary grants to be decided by management committee.
6. Annual report on activity to be prepared by chairman of the review committee for discussion by management board.

SOME OBSERVATIONS, IN SUMMARY

1. The company reputation, according to research and common observation, is significantly shaped by corporate communications.

2. Good products and reliable customer service have proved to be factors in building a good reputation...

3. ... while a good reputation is an important element in shareholder loyalty, as people like to invest in companies of which they can be proud.

4. However important investor relations may be, it should always be considered as part – often a significant central part – of corporate relations.

5. In fact, consider the corporate public relations as the umbrella for all company communications, working to harmonious objectives.

6. The chairman and board carry the ultimate responsibility for company performance, delivering the excellence of communications to project this.

7. The directors must spell out and control what is said in the company name, and policy must be checked and approved at board level.

8. Make sure that the communications process is sensitive to the needs of each of the stakeholder groups and monitors their approval of corporate actions.

9. Corporate governance demands an intelligent two-way communications process, understood and supported by each director.

10. Guidelines also make clear the importance of feedback so that shareholders can advise the board of areas of concern.

11. The allocation of corporate responsibilities means that the chairman is the guardian of the character and conduct of the company.

12. Be sure to include identified opinion leaders from each sector in the audiences addressed by corporate communications.

13. A particularly influential group will be your own top managers who need and deserve special treatment to weld them into a powerful team.

14. Issue all briefing materials to this group and consider a regular presentation to them on the corporate position by the chief executive.

15. Each different corporate audience needs special information but make sure this is against the backdrop of the overall company position.
16. Do not allow financial communications to overshadow the many other important areas of communication with other company audiences.
17. In all activities make sure that the capabilities of your management – preferably a team of managers – are being firmly presented.
18. Build shareholder interest and loyalty through consistent and relevant communications rather than emergency efforts when you need their support.
19. Focus investor briefings around face-to-face presentations, using members of the board and top management, to demonstrate team strengths.
20. Make the annual report in the style you can control, the keystone document that identifies everything that you believe the company represents.
21. Build policies for corporate social responsibility and integrate these with corporate relations and investor policies.
22. Use the issues audit to identify areas of risk and opportunity that should be considered in corporate and investor relations programmes designed to reinforce reputation.

10

Issues and crisis planning
Use issues management to build your 'reputation insurance'

Key factors discussed

- Plan to minimize risk.
- The concept of managing issues.
- Risk and impact analysis.
- Winning competitive edge from issues.
- Prepare for potential crises.
- Building a crisis team.
- Get the media on your side.
- Test and rehearse procedures.

PLAN TO PROTECT YOUR REPUTATION

The corporate reputation is an asset that should be treated like any other. However, it is important to consider methods of protecting the reputation when things go wrong – a form of *reputation insurance.*

Many companies (but by no means all) have crisis plans which are intended to protect their reputation should an emergency arise.

Unfortunately, this is an area of public relations that is still developing; there are still some crisis 'experts' who are over-claiming for the benefits that will derive from their particular philosophies.

The argument is roughly as follows: 'You can face any disaster without much damage to your reputation, as long as you follow the advice in this reassuringly expensive three-ring crisis plan binder. This tells you that someone senior must turn up at the scene of the incident, look sympathetic and good on camera, and make the right soothing, apologetic noises.'

The reality is that companies should be planning not just to manage crises but to avoid, as far as possible, any such 'incidents'.

Look at issues before planning for crises

As touched on in the chapter of objectives, management should take one step back from contingency planning or crisis management. The board should have a clear view of all likely and unlikely issues that could be facing the company and its markets over, say, the next five years. (See the section on issue audits.)

Some argue that if public relations disciplines are being properly implemented, this may well be an effective method for getting all levels of management to take these responsibilities seriously. Significantly, organizations that have ethical policies tend to be most socially aware. The behaviour of the organization in its relations with the community in which it works is known as corporate social responsibility (CSR). CSR is an essential element, both in building a reputation and managing issues. This chapter outlines some useful management processes to protect and reinforce corporate reputation.

All members of the senior management team should participate in this issues evaluation and the development of CSR policies. There are very sound arguments why this should be run by the public relations discipline. Members of this team should be tuned into the marketplace; they will have a clear view of the broad range of perceptions of the key audiences upon which the organization depends for its success; and, above all, they should have independence of all vested interests.

FRAMEWORK FOR ISSUES MANAGEMENT

Good company policy and its related public relations is all about goodwill and building positive attitudes across the audiences that an organization depends upon for success. Undertaken effectively, this is how a good reputation is built. As discussed earlier, the purpose of a good reputation is to build the trust that will build relationships that encourage positive action to the benefit of the organization.

Public relations may not directly stimulate positive action (though it can do in some cases). However, public relations will create the environment within which the organization operates and, with a good reputation, other appeals to key audiences are more likely to be effective – whether this is in response to recruitment advertising, invitations to invest, the presentation of sales offers, participation in community events or other initiatives.

Some organizations believe that their public relations should be built around what is 'news'. However, this is translating what the organization wishes to do into what observers and commentators – particularly the media – may require. Many activities the organization undertakes are not inherently newsworthy, nor do they need to be. Equally, the messages that the organization wishes to project may become distorted by the constant focus on the news aspects. Working in an over-excited media environment can mean that too much emphasis is put on some aspects of organizational operations. At worst, this can mean corporate communicators may be tempted to indulge in manipulation of reality or become economical with the truth.

Set the tone for the communications

When Norwich City Council in East Anglia, UK, bought several hundred acres of land on the edge of its boundaries, it had a plan to create a new residential community that would be of mixed housing – council and private properties, starter homes and executive detached houses.

This was quite a challenge and involved many aspects of planning that could potentially be controversial. The council had the wisdom to decide to call in independent communications experts and they ran a competitive tender to identify the most suitable team. When selected, their recommendation was to manage the news process, of course, but less predictably to ensure that this was within a calm, objective framework. The reason for this was that the media and many other commentators – community leaders, independent architects and planners, trade and professional organizations and many others – wanted their voices to be heard. They would be inclined to simplify the arguments to be provocative and, therefore, generate public attention. The consultants' recommendation was to keep toning down the reporting of progress and to deal with any hype with a balanced, reasoned response.

Central to this process was a series of key professional partner and public meetings. The presentation of the concept was summarized in a professionally produced audio-visual presentation. The development was to be called Bowthorpe, the name of a nearby hamlet. The consultants recommended that the titling of this audio-visual presentation should be low key to set the tone of all that would follow. They proposed *Bowthorpe: a pleasant place to live*.

This was considered by some councillors to be massively understating the significance of a 600-acre development, which would represent the biggest investment ever undertaken by this or any other comparable local council. To the credit of the councillors, after the rationale had been debated, they agreed with the logic of the approach. The campaign went ahead.

The result, after the initial 12 months of the campaign, was virtually 100 per cent community acceptance of the project; it has since been completed and gone on to become a highly successful residential area. One result was a significant and measurable improvement in the council's reputation.

Interestingly, it did achieve the combining of the mixed types of housing with a good level of success. In fact, on the completion of the first phase of the campaign, one of the leaders of the council who had been most vocally opposed to the low-key approach commented to the director leading the campaign team: 'As you know, I had my doubts. However, I think the approach was correct. People do not want to live in a social experiment. We have achieved with Bowthorpe exactly what we wanted and that is we have produced a highly acceptable and pleasant place to live. My own view is that we would not have done this without this intelligent public relations approach.'

Before planning news, consider issues analysis

A good public relations person does not have to be loud or assertive. In some cases this may be a necessary approach but more often it would be inappropriate. Public relations practitioners often feel under pressure to impress their bosses or their clients and one way to do this is to promise headlines – which may not be achievable or, if achievable, may be presenting distorted messages. This can reduce the potential goodwill, which is essential to the success of the project.

An intelligent starting point for the creation of an effective public relations programme is not to look at the news but to look at the issues that are involved. From this, the organization can then decide the stance it wants to adopt towards each issue. In some cases this will also mean a change of policy – or the development of new policies because of the nature of the issues that are identified in this process. Having developed the stance, the organization (with its public relations advisers) can then begin to formulate the activity and the related messages that need to be projected.

An issues audit will identify the issues that need to be considered and research will identify the perceptions of the audiences that need to be addressed. The potential positive or negative impact on the corporate reputation can be assessed, and suitable policies for dealing with each issue can be developed. These brief notes give an outline of how to plan and run an effective issues audit and develop policies from it.

THE PLATFORM FOR RELATIONSHIP DEVELOPMENT

The organization that is on top of the issues and ahead of the competition is in a very powerful position. It is the way to create leadership and to generate interest across the key publics.

In some circumstances this will give media opportunities but, as discussed earlier, in a more controlled and more manageable manner. Many publications and broadcast programmes are looking for interviews or opinion pieces from managers who have credibility and authority. Editorial articles that analyse trends and look at future potential developments are also of considerable interest to editors and features editors. The great advantage of using this material is that the originator has control over what is said – subject to the normal editorial policies of the publication concerned. Though such pieces naturally have to be a summary of the key points, they can be presented in an intelligent and rational manner without any hype.

The broadcast media do not usually use such features but they do need professionals who can speak with authority about key sectors. The issues audit and the policies that are developed from this will provide many opportunities for radio and television comment –

either in their specialized business programmes, in local and regional features or on general news programmes.

The public relations programme can also use the results of the issues evaluation process to produce material that is relevant directly to the market in which it is operating. These can be customer briefings, seminars, white papers and many other effective communications techniques.

At the industry, trade and professional level, trade, government and professional bodies will be interested in the views that are built upon this analysis of issues. It is the responsibility of the public relations professionals to convert opportunities into reality.

THE NATURE OF ISSUES

Issues have a major impact on both brand and corporate reputations. Any reputation management programme must consider this area, and have policies and strategies in place to deal with all situations.

The word 'issues' has a number of meanings. The dictionary defines an issue as a 'topic of interest or discussion or an important subject requiring a decision'. A more helpful definition might be something along the lines of... *a significant factor that is likely to have an impact on individuals, groups or organizations*. Whatever definition is used, it is important to remember that issues have no angles, side or spin. They are what they are. They do not exist to add advantage or disadvantage – though they can be managed to create benefits or mismanaged (even, more usually, ignored), which can result in disadvantage.

Issues are often presented as being problems, but this is a misunderstanding of the term – and could lead to a misapplication of the concept of issues management. Clearly, an issue has potential to be beneficial to the organization – or otherwise.

Issues may not always mean problems

The most helpful way of looking at issues is to consider that they can be potentially positive, negative or 'neutral'.

A potentially positive issue is one that gives direct advantage to the organization – and possibly all its competitors in that sector. For example, a building products manufacturer that is using aluminium for doorsteps, sills, window ledges and other areas that are subject to wear, may find that concerns over the use of non-renewable hard-woods gives them a theoretical advantage. However, issues are rarely that simple. *Please note that the following is not based on facts but just suppositions to illustrate the case.*

An analysis of this position might confirm that the forestry industry is moving rapidly into sustainable hardwood production. Suddenly, the advantage is not as strong as it first appeared. Equally, aluminium may not be such a benign and environmentally accept-able material. It too comes from a non-renewable source. Perhaps the pollution caused by the production of the finished aluminium weakens its environmental case. The bauxite ore sites from which the aluminium is manufactured may be in poor third world countries where workers are not getting a fair return for their efforts, and are employed in substandard conditions. The issues audit will look at all these factors to see whether this potentially positive position can be sustained.

As another example, a major international company manufac-turing double-glazing products once approached the author to promote its case that double-glazing reduced fuel consumption – and this, in turn, reduced global pollution. An evaluation showed that this was simplistic and not entirely defensible. In the course of the audit of the environmental issues, it became clear that the company was a massive user of hardwood in many of its products, all of which were sourced from non-renewable sites. Of equal importance, the greenhouse gases generated by the manufacture, transport and processing of the glass and aluminium severely weakened the envi-ronmental case. The consultant pointed this out to the management and was promptly fired from the project; a more compliant public relations adviser was soon appointed.

As a result, the company went public on its dubious claims. These were briskly exposed by environmental pressure groups and chased up by the media. This company has since ceased trading. This was not entirely due to making such a serious miscalculation, but prob-ably was due to the opportunistic and weak management that allowed such a doubtful policy to be promoted.

Similarly, a division that was part of Unilever wanted to promote chemicals that were manufactured through processes that had low environmental impact. The evaluation of this opportunity quickly identified that while this was true, the raw materials were produced in poor environmental circumstances and were causing massive local pollution.

The employment conditions of those producing the materials nowhere matched the employment conditions of those in the industrialized nations that were converting them into finished products. The case simply did not stand up. Hearing the consultant's appraisal of this situation, the management accepted the argument; they used this as a lever to improve the environmental standards at the point of production of the raw materials and the employment conditions of those working for the contractors that were supplying these materials.

Examine the strength of the issues case

Although the initial audit may identify issues as being potentially positive, further evaluation would establish clearly whether this is sustainable. Positive issues should be used to give maximum benefit to the organization. Clearly these benefits are stronger if the issue is analysed, evaluated and promoted ahead of the competition.

Some issues have the potential to be negative that is, to the disadvantage of the organization. Again, a deeper appraisal is necessary to see whether this assumption is correct. Sodastream, then a major soft drinks subsidiary of Cadbury Schweppes, manufactured a range of drink concentrates that were heavy in sugar content. Some of these products were targeted at children. A survey had shown that parents, health advisers and other groups were concerned about the impact upon their children's health, particularly their teeth. Also, there was much concern over the rising level of obesity in children. The issues audit looked at this and also identified, through discussions with children's groups, that there were considerable concerns over certain additives that were approved at the European level but which were suspected of being harmful to children.

The result of this study of a potentially negative issue created a significant positive marketing opportunity. The company introduced a range of low-sugar, high-fruit concentrate drinks in which all unnecessary additives were removed. In some cases, this meant that the colour of the products was not quite what might be expected. Rather than conform to consumer expectations, the company used this as an opportunity to explain these products were better for health and that the traditional colours previously used by the company, and still in competitors' drinks, were unnatural. The result was a popular, top-selling range with serious claims to be healthier. Not only did this increase sales and profits, it met understandable concerns and confirmed the company's policy of listening to its customers.

Although the potential for issues to be positive or negative is clear, the most interesting area is those that could be described as 'neutral'.

A neutral issue might be one that could have the same impact upon every organization within that market sector. This might be a global trend, say, towards more concern about the health and safety of organization employees. Another example might be legislation proposed by national or other governments.

Water heater and shower manufacturer Heatrae-Sadia was concerned about proposed EU legislation that related to warranties on electrical products. Their public relations adviser had an effective monitoring process in place and this move was detected at an early stage. One suggestion considered by the consumer services division of the Commission was that warranties should be harmonized across the member states of the European Union for two years, as standard. This caused considerable concern within the company and among other organizations producing electrical products in the UK where the normal warranty period was one year.

The technical, development, marketing and finance professionals within the company looked at this as an issue. The public relations adviser was also asked to take part in these discussions. He recommended an evaluation audit on this specific issue and spent some time with the relevant executives, including the production director. This revealed an extremely interesting point that, until then, no one had spotted.

Together, they looked at the product failure levels to see what the impact of a two-year warranty might be on repair claims and replacements. In fact, the initial failure level of products was below 2 per cent – and this was almost always within a few days of leaving the factory. The reasons for this were either some minor manufacturing fault or damage that might have been caused in transit or installation. Once any faulty products had been replaced, the failure rate dropped to virtually zero. What proved extremely interesting was that the products were so robust and well made, that failure rates did not start to be of any significance until around year seven. Raising the warranty level from one year to two years would be of no real significance.

When these findings were presented to management, the recommendation was that consideration should be given to an extended warranty period – ideally a period of time greater than that likely to be recommended by the European Union in its proposed legislation. The management had the confidence to set this at five years.

The marketing, sales, advertising and public relations functions were all invited to discuss how this might be presented to the marketplace. Though the original concept had come from the public relations end of the business, the advertising agency performed a superb job in converting the idea into a strong proposition. They developed a concept: *the best feature of this range of products is tied on with a piece of string*. The illustration in the advertising showed a five-year warranty tag attached to the product.

Sales, marketing, public relations and advertising all worked together to promote the concept, which had a predictably immense impact upon the marketplace. Competitors were caught on the hop. Many of them were still debating whether they should move ahead to two years – but now the leading player in the marketplace had made all of their discussions and plans meaningless.

A direct and valuable benefit above the sales generation was that the reputation of Heatrae-Sadia was enhanced. This factor could help improve relations with all stakeholders, as well as adding capital value to the brands.

That is the power of intelligent issues auditing.

IDENTIFYING POSSIBLE ISSUES

In summary, issues may be potentially positive, negative or neutral. The skill is to: maximize the benefits of those that could be positive for the organization; minimize risk and possible damage from those that could be negative; and, through an early-warning system, recognize and manage those that affect everyone equally (the neutral issues) to win the best competitive edge. And remember those that are neutral are likely to far exceed the positives and negatives added together. Neutrals provide the best opportunity to enhance corporate reputation *and* marketing advantage.

The process for identifying the issues and their potential impact is a lot simpler than might be thought. General management may question whether the public relations professionals have the expertise to identify these issues; obviously they usually do not. But the simple approach is for the public relations professional to interview those who do have the expertise.

In virtually all cases, every issue of any consequence will be known within the company and it is simply a process of interviewing the heads of department to get a full list together of all those issues that might be of concern. It is wise to also undertake check interviews with trade and professional bodies as well as with relevant government departments, pressure groups and others prepared to cooperate. One method of gaining their cooperation is to offer participants a copy of the summary report – suitably edited to take out anything of a confidential or commercial nature. These approaches need to be handled carefully to ensure that competitors are not alerted to the initiatives being undertaken.

PROCESSES FOR THE AUDIT

Analyse present perceptions

What reputation does the organization have? The aim of the issues audit is to identify opportunities to lead business thinking in important business sectors, while at the same time ensuring that strong policies are in place to minimize the risk of damage to reputation by potentially negative or threatening issues. Therefore, the first step is to evaluate the quality of the reputation, including its strengths.

Interview those who know

Part of the audit process is to talk to all those professionals, both within the organization and outside, who have expert knowledge. Particularly helpful can be government departments, professional bodies, pressure groups and academics. The organization should have relations with university departments that specialize in their areas of interest and the senior academics within these departments can often be extremely helpful.

Survey the market

It is sensible to try to identify where the organization stands in relation to issues, particularly in comparison to competitors. The competitors' situations in the marketplace need to be monitored. In some cases it will be advisable to bring in specialized consultancies or research companies to assist in this work.

Clearly it's important for the organization, when developing its policies, to understand how far ahead or behind the competition it lies. Being behind the competition is not necessarily the disadvantage it may at first appear. It is better to be second with a sound understanding of the factors than it is to be nowhere at all.

Obtain contrary use

As with all aspects of public relations, it is important to know who might be your allies and who might be your opponents. In many cases there will be those who take neither side and who can be converted to allies or opponents, depending on the skill with which the communications are undertaken. Even opponents can sometimes be converted to allies or, at least, partially neutralized through being involved in the evaluation process.

Therefore, it is important in the audit to get the views of all of those who may adopt a stance that opposes the organization. Such individuals and bodies will include the single-issue pressure groups as well as industry experts, activists and possibly some academics or government advisers. Their ability to damage the organization is reduced through their being involved in the evaluation process. The organization takes its stance and is prepared for an investment analyst, a politician or a journalist to check this position and other views. It would strengthen the argument of an opponent if it was able to claim it had not been involved in this process.

Structure for presentation

The issues evaluation process can generate a useful volume of data, electronic information and paper. Management will require a summary. The ideal (and it is usually achievable) is to summarize each issue onto a single sheet of A4 paper. These can be indexed and bound together or submitted in electronic form. Any supporting data or documentation can be held separately or added as appendices. Even if the arguments are convincing, some in the organization will want to check the broader data from which the deductions have been made.

The framework for the summary needs to be consistent across all issues, and the chosen approach should be followed by the public relations professional or other project manager to present the information in the most useful form. As an illustration, the single A4 page might be divided by cross-heads that summarize the elements of the conclusions. For example, the potential impact of the issue; the likelihood of its occurring; a summary of its key points; the suggested stance for the organization; the likely costs of changing policy, and so on.

Prioritize the issues and the stances

Some method of setting practical priorities for the issues will be essential. Experience confirms that every thorough audit will identify far more issues than management can cope with at one time. Therefore, those that are most likely to be of significance, most likely to occur, or have the most influence upon the organization should be considered as top priority.

In this process, it is useful to identify some type of category heading. For example, the top priority might be described as... *an issue requiring immediate action and a new/revised policy and related communications plan*.

Therefore, some suggested issues categories might be:

- immediate action, priority announcement;
- immediate action, delayed announcement;
- immediate action, no announcement;
- delayed action, short term;
- delayed action, long term;
- industry action;
- no action, immediate announcement;
- no action, no announcement.

Sources for information and informed perspectives will include:

- internal divisional heads;
- internal operational staff;
- competitors and industry partners;
- media, analysts and industry commentators;
- trade and professional associations;
- pressure and single-issue groups;
- government departments and statutory bodies;
- academics, standards bodies and industry experts.

The resulting evaluation will produce a snapshot view of the issues and, ideally, some recommendations on how each might be addressed. However, this is of little value to the organization unless it adopts policies relating to these issues. Such policies will be the result of management decisions within which the public relations adviser or other project manager should be an active participant. In practice, it is usually helpful for this executive to make recommendations that will be based upon the public relations advantage or disadvantage that might arise from the different options. Such recommendations should be tested with other executives directly involved in each area.

CREATE ADVANTAGE FROM THE OPPORTUNITIES

The results of the issues evaluation should be applied to all policies across the company, wherever there is a risk to be reduced or an advantage to be won. As noted, the aim is to protect, enhance and project the corporate reputation.

The organization that is ahead of its competition will have significant advantage. The biggest benefit may be that it can control the agenda, make its comments and force others in the market to respond to the points it has chosen to lead on. This is an effective way to establish market leadership and authority. Academics, analysts, editors and others will be more likely to want to seek the views and to cooperate with the pacemaker in the market. It can also be a good platform from which to win greater market share and convert issues leadership into sales leadership.

The wise organization will not rest upon the results of the audit and evaluation. It will maintain a constant monitoring focus on the issues and the stances of other interested parties. The idea is not just to take the discussion leadership but to maintain that position as views are added and the evolution of opinion unfolds.

Finally – though the process has no end – the policies should be regularly reviewed and updated. This information will be fed back into management, which creates the eternal circle – information shapes the thinking; this new thinking stimulates the market, which generates new information through responses from others; this shapes fresh thinking... and so it goes on.

Clearly, the company has to have a stance towards all issues, some of which it will be able to control and some of which will be external. As a simple example, a company manufacturing small domestic appliances may see public concern about packaging and be encouraged to shift from plastics to recyclable paper or card-based alternatives. The company may decide to go with this trend or to evaluate alternatives that are currently not recyclable. Many plastics are environmentally more friendly than their supposed recyclable paper and cardboard alternatives.

How might specific issues enable a company to develop its reputation as a leader? One key is to identify opportunities (and potential problems) ahead of the competition.

Some US electrical equipment manufacturers have taken to packing all products shipped to store in non-food-grade popcorn. It is an effective alternative to polystyrene beads, is cheaper when produced in quantity and has at least as good an ability to absorb shocks as the plastic material that it replaces. After use, this 'packaging' can be fed to chickens, pigs or even pets. Alternatively, it can simply be composted.

In this example, such companies clearly have a high level of control over the stance they wish to take towards this opportunity, and the results they might consider following. However, they may have little or no influence over moves towards legislation suggesting bubble insulation for small domestic appliances and the elimination of the earth cord. Other safety standards, service back-up, replacement and guarantee policies may also be affected by legislation. To maintain its reputation for being an industry leader, the company must constantly monitor issues and refine its policies.

IDENTIFYING POTENTIAL OPPORTUNITIES

External legislation may be a factor over which the company has limited control. However, by auditing issues, alternative approaches to each issue can be developed, and from this might spring a crisis management plan to deal with contingencies or emergencies that issues might create.

An effective reputation management strategy can play a key role in keeping line managers on their toes and, to some extent, acting as devil's advocate. To take an example, the issues audit process discussed earlier can often identify potential crises before they occur. Consider Townsend Thorenson and the disaster that struck it when one of its ferries put to sea with the bow doors open and nearly 300 people were drowned in the ensuing sinking of the vessel. The crisis management was appalling, but even if it had been brilliant it would not have brought back any of those victims. However, if an issues management system had been in operation, perhaps the hazards associated with a procedure that allowed (indeed, encouraged) ships to sail with bow doors open might have been treated more seriously.

How could a non-technical public relations person, or any other professional adviser, prevent a marine tragedy that could not be prevented by the marine specialists? Quite simply. Marine specialists knew the hazards but had failed to get the company board to override the commercial pressure to turn the ships round quickly. Commercial needs appear to have taken precedence over safety and, indeed, the decent values by which a company should be run. The public relations adviser has no line loyalties, no concern about seniority, no axe to grind. But he or she can and should bring such issues to the attention of top management. 'If what I understand is correct, chairman, the recent issues audit suggests that we may be accepting practices that would appear to be unwise, if not seriously risky...'.

PREPARING FOR POSSIBLE CRISES

The adviser should be responsible to the chief executive (or equivalent) and this means advising him or her of any company practice that could be damaging to the company's reputation. If the adviser had been running an issues management programme, then all the senior directors and managers would have been interviewed regularly to identify anything on the horizon that might have an impact upon the company and any practices, trading activities, competitive influences that could similarly affect the corporate position.

It was clear from the inquiry on the Townsend Thorenson disaster that many senior managers within the company were extremely concerned about the conflicting pressures on turning ships round quickly in harbour and maintaining the highest safety standards. It is not unreasonable to believe that a strong public relations professional, with the backing of management to take responsibility for issues management, would have become aware of this. The chief executive would have been asked to give this important area immediate attention.

This process is sometimes called 'reputation risk management'. This is defined as the discipline designed to protect the reputation against threats. In other words, packaging trends and public concerns may be issues over which the manufacturer could have a good degree of influence. Industry legislation and competitive activity may be issues where it has not. To take one of these as an example, the traditional metal electric kettle market was wiped out almost overnight by the introduction of a new product design – the plastic jug-type kettle.

This innovation was only partly due to the development of a plastic that would be unharmed by boiling water; the more important factor was the vision of the designers and marketing professionals who knew there was a better material than metal and a better design than a saucepan with a spout and a lid. Manufacturers even with dominant positions in secure markets need to be constantly looking at everything that could endanger their position.

A sensitive monitoring system is absolutely essential for an effective crisis management programme. The media information network is likely to be at least as effective as the company's and quite likely to be quicker to react. Remember, too, that some threats to the reputation may begin quite modestly while others can have a dramatic and immediate impact.

Crises can arise where there is no obvious 'issue' that might have given indications on how to avoid the problem. The key is to have the processes and resources to respond rapidly to minimize damage to the corporate reputation. In such cases, when handled properly, the media can be an ally. A few days after the fatal crash of American racing legend Dale Earnhardt at the Daytona 500 in February 2001, NASCAR, the US motor sport body, held a news conference where comments were made that suggested that a seat belt separated and caused Earnhardt's death. This was devastating news for Simpson Performance Products, manufacturer of Earnhardt's belt. Simpson retained public relations counsel Epley Associates and before the five o'clock news, issued a simple but factual statement: 'If seat belts are installed according to manufacturing specifications, the belts don't fail.'

The media reported this statement. NASCAR responded to repeated news inquiries about installation by saying only that 'we are investigating further; we are not blaming anyone'. In the meantime, there was an unnecessary doubt put into the marketplace about the integrity of Simpson equipment. But NASCAR's integrity was also called into play by the media. As a result a respected newspaper, *The Orlando Sentinel*, took action and won a court order for a nationally prominent pathologist to review the autopsy photos. His report refuted the claim on the cause of death and showed that the belt breaking did not cause the fatal injury to Earnhardt. NASCAR backed down from its earlier statement.

Despite lengthy stonewalling, independent experts concluded that the belt was not defective and met all industry standards. They also found that the belt was not installed according to specification. The findings of the independent experts were advised to NASCAR, well in advance of a nationally televised news conference announcing the results of NASCAR's investigation of the wreck. The motor sport body refused to acknowledge the detailed information from the independent experts hired by Simpson. The public relations professionals took the bold step of directly briefing the media, which, by now, was concerned about the facts being presented and was sensitive to the seat belt manufacturer.

Simpson Performance Products, highly respected within the racing community, is a small organization dedicated to manufacturing safety products. It could not afford to sit back and have NASCAR unfairly and inaccurately imply that its product was defective. By quickly providing credible data to the public, balance was given to the story. Of even greater importance, NASCAR could not continue its unfair claims and many journalists felt that Simpson had fought hard and well to protect its reputation from unfair comments.

Apologize promptly, when appropriate

One difficulty in crisis situations is that it can take time to establish the facts... and when the media spotlight may be glaring on an organization, time is not in plentiful supply.

Understandably, there is a strong instinct to play for safety. Indeed, some legal and insurance advisers would prefer the company to say nothing. Any comment, they argue, can have an effect on any future legal claims or court actions should negligence or misdemeanours be suspected. Yet, to offer no comment can destroy a company's reputation by making management look indifferent to the hazard or actual harm that might be created by an incident.

If the company reputation is to be protected, early and sensitive comments are essential. Remember the concept of the corporate personality? Would an individual retain much respect if no comment was offered on a tragedy in which he or she was involved and may have been responsible for?

From his own experience, Sir Jeremy Morse, banker and past chairman of the Institute of Bankers, contends that apologies are an important part of public relations for large organizations.

He recommends prompt apologies for particular errors and omissions. However, the company needs a policy issue on what to do when things go wrong in a bigger way – accidents, catastrophes, and major management failures. Such cases are complex and there is a natural temptation to hide behind the complexities while sorting out the problem. But, in fact, he maintains, it almost always pays to make an early apology: something major has gone wrong; we don't know all that is involved; we shall sort it out as quickly as we can; meanwhile, we apologize to those affected, etc.

This may lead to the organization being blamed for matters that turn out to have been someone else's fault. He explains:

> Nevertheless, there are two central reasons why this is usually the right course. First, externally, the public respect an apology freely given rather than one that comes after a considerable period of stonewalling. Second, internally, an early apology frees managers to sort out the problems far more effectively than if they are still maintaining an outward front that nothing is wrong.

An affective procedure planned in advance is essential to minimize damage. It can even pay dividends. Black & Decker produced a substandard product, yet the company's prompt and open handling of complaints actually saw sales increase for the replacement model.

Similarly, General Electric recalled a potentially lethal range of lighting products with such efficiency, candour and speed that not a single negative news report appeared. Indeed, public recognition of the company's caring stance saw sales rise to cover what might have been the crippling cost of the no-quibble recall and rectification process that had been set up within 24 hours.

A market of some $200 million was protected. The product recall cost $5 million and, clearly, during this period, sales dropped to zero. However, the reputation of the company and its products was so enhanced that, when the lights were reintroduced, sales peaked significantly higher than before the problems. The loss was recovered in less than six months. Behaving responsibly is good for the reputation. It can also be profitable.

ESTABLISHING A CRISIS MANAGEMENT TEAM

The company needs to form a crisis management team well ahead of any anticipated problems. Ideally, this will be composed of experts who have been trained and know how to work together. The company will need more personnel allocated to this team than are actually necessary. When a crisis hits, some are certain to be away on business travel, even ill or on holiday.

Equally, there needs to be more than one leader of this team to cover such an eventuality. The crisis management team should encompass a range of skills other than communications. These might include senior executives from within sales, marketing, customer care, operations, personnel or industrial relations. Ideally, these should be personnel at the most senior level.

The advantage of having such a mixed team is that they bring a range of expertise and improve the chances of various aspects of any crisis being well covered. Also, each member of the team needs an understudy.

Establishing incident rooms at each location

An incident room should be established at every company location. Quite often this will double as some other function room, such as a reception, canteen, briefing or interview room. However, it is helpful if it is equipped to deal with the emergency – for example, a locked cupboard containing all essential items.

Note that each location may need more than one incident room as one can be closed off or inacccessible when the incident is, for example, a fire or an explosion.

One recommendation worth serious consideration is the two-room contingency suite. This uses an inner and outer room. The inner room is the quiet area for the top crisis management team which focuses on policy. The outer room houses the operational staff who receive and manage all incoming data, analyse and present an intelligent summary to the crisis management team in their inner sanctum.

Establishing a training and policy manual

The issues management team, ideally well ahead of any contingency, should develop a crisis manual. This is a practical document full of essential information, not only to help the team in handling the incident but in providing background material that can be used to deal with enquiries. Copies of this manual need to be available at every incident location and it is particularly useful if this can be in electronic form on computer so that high-speed print-outs of background to various products, situation, safety records and other items can be available instantly. Much of this data may need to be issued to the emergency services, the media and others.

The three-ring crisis handling plan – which details exactly what should be done in each incident and is often prepared by specialists with minimal company input – is extremely unlikely to be used and will sit on the shelf gathering dust. A document that has helpful and immediate information is much more useful.

Copies must be kept by all members of the crisis team both in their offices and at their homes. Members of this flying squad are also advised to hold in constant readiness a packed bag with any emergency items that may be necessary, such as a change of clothing, portable telephone, spare batteries, the crisis manual, a company telephone list and a key media list. Direct telephone lines, a television and video recorder with blank tapes, computer terminals with modems, and so on, should be available in each incident room.

In dealing with a major incident, your company spokespeople will need to be able to handle the media effectively. In many cases, the media will be aware of the incident before the company. The most credible company spokesperson will always be the most senior. There are some basic guidelines that should be considered when dealing with journalists in an incident situation:

- Ensure that spokespeople are fully briefed and trained.
- Establish a media relations strategy as early as possible and ensure that all are fully briefed on it.
- Give the media the fullest information possible. Even if you do not have full details of the incident, useful background on the company, its record and trading activities will be helpful to journalists.
- Make sure that everybody is as helpful as they can possibly be with the media, dealing with all questions they can cover and logging those they are unable to answer so that the media can be called back.
- Honour all such commitments to the media. If information will not be available for, say, half an hour, then make sure that it is and that it is disseminated to those who have asked for it.
- Get on top of the situation early and maintain control. Decide the agenda and manage the media information to that.
- Use pre-prepared information. With television journalists it is extremely useful to have available maps, plans and aerial photographs of the location where the incident has happened.

- Get the information out as quickly as you can, even if this means supplying it part by part.
- Ensure that you are disseminating information through other channels of communication: e-mail, telephone and fax should not be forgotten. Pre-prepared video material on products, processes and locations may be helpful.
- Release information simultaneously to all stakeholders, so that other audiences such as employees, shareholders, neighbours and governments are not totally reliant on the media for their understand of what is happening.

MAKING PERSONNEL AWARE OF THEIR RESPONSIBILITIES

Many companies do not follow such simple but vital procedures. As noted earlier, Townsend Thorenson suffered a tragedy that should have been anticipated. The public fury over the inadequate response ensured that its name could never be used again. The press office was not staffed at the time of the tragedy and it took the company precious time to respond. The news was instant. It was on radio and television while company officials tried to gather a response team. When they did eventually do so, it was not impressive. Television showed us press officers handling distraught public enquiries, writing phone numbers in the margins of newspapers. The chairman eventually arrived at the scene, back from holiday. In one of those horrific examples of misjudgement, he was interviewed wearing a distressingly inappropriate straw summer hat.

The death of the passengers through maritime malpractice was a shock. The way the management seemed to have prepared for the possibility of an accident was unforgivable. And they were not forgiven.

This catastrophe helped improve industry standards, best-practice guidelines and legislation. It also raised industry awareness of the need to be prepared, and of the potential damage to reputation that can be caused by a contingency for which the company is not prepared.

The company responsibility is clearly to minimize risk, hopefully to the point of eliminating it. But any company running ships, coaches, buses, trains or planes would be considered recklessly casual if it were revealed that it had no adequate plans to handle a major incident. Even if it were not the company's fault, lives could be threatened through terrorism, sabotage or suicide.

As noted earlier, when a British Midland plane crashed on a motorway killing many passengers, the speed with which the company reacted brought out the maximum public sympathy at that awful time. The chairman, Sir Michael Bishop (then plain Mr Bishop), was on the scene in less than an hour, personally directing a well-drilled contingency team. As well as assisting the emergency services, he talked openly to the media so that anxious members of the public could be as fully informed as possible. The support operations behind the scenes were equally as efficient. British Midland was able to recover and is, today, one of the leading and most respected independent airlines of Europe, renamed bmi. It may not be entirely unrelated that Sir Michael has since moved on to major roles in public life.

THE EMERGENCY ROLE OF SENIOR PERSONNEL

When the oil tanker *Exxon Valdez* split open in Alaska, spilling millions of gallons of oil, senior executives were slow to visit the scene until forced by public pressure. Some 30,000 customers sent back their company charge cards in disgust. The reputation damage to the company was enormous; the financial damage incalculable, although an immediate indicator was a collapse in the share price, which never fully recovered.

Perhaps the best-known crisis management programme that recovered a frightening situation was some years ago but still a text-book case study. Johnson & Johnson acted decisively following the malicious poisoning of their Tylenol product. This had been the best-selling analgesic, contaminated by someone with an irrational grudge; at the time of the crisis, a survey confirmed that 94 per cent of consumers were aware that Tylenol was associated with the cyanide poisonings.

The details of this horrific incident have been well reported, but it is useful to note that the strategy Johnson & Johnson adopted involved a total recall and a new product relaunch. The company policy was one of total honesty and this clearly resounded well with the public. This recaptured its market share and, eventually, additional sales because of the goodwill generated towards the company. It was a clear example of turning a potential disaster into an opportunity. Obviously, in this case, the company was not negligent or at fault in causing the original problem, which was the work of a deranged blackmailer.

This illustrates the more important point that the public do not automatically view every company problem negatively. Their opinions and attitudes are very much shaped by the response of the company. Johnson & Johnson wasted little time in recalling millions of bottles of its Tylenol capsules, and spent a million dollars warning physicians, hospitals and distributors of the possible dangers. As the *Wall Street Journal* said at the time, 'The company chose to take a large loss rather than expose anyone to further risk.'

The company adopted a worst-case approach to the problem and insisted on a total recall, even though the original problem was only in the Chicago area; the testing of all recalled products actually confirmed that only 75 of some 8 million tablets were contaminated, and these were all found in one batch.

Perhaps one of the keys to the prompt and responsible approach adopted by Johnson & Johnson was that the company had a well-published credo, which identified its primary responsibility as being towards its customers. A company may safeguard its reputation by adopting a policy that will help employees make such decisions.

An aftermath to the crisis was that Johnson & Johnson examined its responsibility to customers. As a result, the firm introduced the first truly effective tamper-proof packaging, which has since become the standard for pharmaceuticals, and indeed for many food and drink products.

One visible action that the public can recognize is the seniority of the managers allocated to deal with crisis. A criticism of the Exxon company was that top executives did not immediately respond and it was some considerable time before anyone in authority actually arrived at the scene of the *Valdez* disaster in Alaska.

In contrast, Warren Anderson, chairman of Union Carbide, immediately flew to Bhopal when his Indian subsidiary suffered an unimaginable manufacturing accident. This produced a poisonous gas cloud which, in one night, had killed 1,200 people – and the death toll was rising hour by hour. He knew he risked almost certain arrest and an obviously hostile reception but believed that it was his responsibility.

He defied the advice of some legal colleagues not to accept responsibility – and expressed both regret and concern. This established Union Carbide, equally, as the victim of this tragic disaster. It also positioned the company as the leader in establishing what went wrong and what needed to be done to rectify the tragedy that had been created.

Union Carbide may have mismanaged some aspects of the tragedy, but they did have the sense to respond promptly, calling a press conference at their head office on the very first day. This contrasted with, say, the Firestone Tyre & Rubber Company officials who claimed that nothing was wrong when Firestone 500 tyres first began disintegrating.

Later this same company so mishandled the problems over tyres supplied to Ford (and got into an unhappy dispute with its customers) that its reputation was irreparably damaged. We are unlikely to see this brand name again.

Media interest had been created rapidly in a battle between two motoring giants. Each seemed more concerned about allocating blame than protecting the public. The story became even more shocking when it emerged that executives had been aware of the problem but tried to keep it quiet.

THE SPEED OF THE MEDIA

It is important to remember the speed of response of the media. Journalists can often be the first to be aware of many incidents – sometimes even ahead of management. The famous case of the Flixborough chemical factory explosion illustrates the dangers. The news was around the world in minutes because a radio journalist happened to be cycling past the plant at the time.

When the Gulf tanker, *Betelgeuse*, unloading at Bantree Bay, caught fire and exploded at 1.00 am on a January night some years ago, a senior journalist from the *Irish Times* was actually watching the shipping in the bay through his binoculars from his holiday cottage. The ship literally blew up before his eyes. News of the disaster was being flashed around the world on the wire services within minutes of its occurrence. It was over an hour before the public relations people were advised.

What starts as a small story can also become a very big story, even if no direct single tragedy or accident is involved.

Some years ago, a small (and what should have been an insignificant) contamination incident affected the Coca-Cola sold in Belgium, the Netherlands and parts of northern France. School children became ill after drinking the product and the scare rapidly escalated, exactly as anyone might have anticipated. Perhaps equally predictably, later tests showed that the contamination gave the product an unpleasant taste but was harmless to health.

This incident proved not to be so insignificant as the managers obviously imagined it was. For days no senior executives from the company took any key role in addressing public concerns. The media had a field day with nobody from corporate headquarters to address the issues and perhaps to have managed the situation and, even, to get some different perspectives. Perhaps the bosses in Atlanta were not moved to prompt action because the region represented only 2 per cent of global sales. The mistake that they made was that the problem represented 100 per cent of global media interest. Nowhere in the world where Coca-Cola was sold had media that was indifferent to this global brand and unconcerned about contamination in their region.

The problems that the media identified at the time included the claim that company policy did not allow executives on the spot, in the region, to take control and manage the situation. A rumour circulated, probably malicious, that the senior responsible executives in Atlanta discussed the problem, one asking, 'Where's Belgium?' Possibly this was not true, but it illustrates the problems that can be exacerbated by media comment, particularly where journalists know that no senior, credible company spokesperson will challenge such assertions.

This was one of the world's largest and most sophisticated companies, managing one of the best-known and most valuable brands. Their inaction resulted in severe damage to the reputation and made the company an even more interesting target for media criticism. The insignificant contamination that became a highly significant disaster is being quoted in marketing and communications courses around the world. It finds its way into countless articles and books, such as this one. But the end results were somewhat worse than making the directors feel bad. This incident cost the company billions in sales, in reparation activity and in damage to the share price. It was not good for some senior careers. No professional manager wants to be seen to be responsible for a damaging incident that was clearly out of control.

SUBJECTIVE COMMENT CAN CAUSE IRREPARABLE DAMAGE

Lever Brothers had enjoyed a high-profile multimedia launch of its advanced detergent, New System Persil automatic washing powder. A report by the National Eczema Society throwing doubts on the product, quoted in *The Guardian*, was the start of a major problem. This was picked up by the *Sunday Mirror*, later the *Daily Mirror* and virtually all the national UK publications. Market share collapsed.

It is important that the management should remember that many new products will have potentially critical audiences. Journalists are also interested in manufacturers' problem stories.

In the case of the Persil powder, research eventually undertaken suggested that only 1 in 10,000 people might have had a dermatological reaction related to its use. However, that was too late and the damage had been done. Better warnings on the packet and more detailed explanation over its enzyme base might have prevented the problem in the first instance. This proved to be a case where an issue audit before the launch might have identified the risk – it would certainly have prepared the company to deal more promptly with a problem before it could cause such damage.

The original and potentially world-beating sweetener to replace sugar (but with none of the disadvantages of saccharine) was cyclamate. Its credibility was severely undermined by an extremely negative report from a small US research institute which linked the product with claimed carcinogenic properties found in tests it had undertaken.

This led to massive media exposure of the supposed risks. These reports took the company by surprise and it was very slow in response; the damage was so severe that the product was withdrawn. Eventually, some serious reservations about the research were recorded but, by then, it was too late.

The makers of aspartame – perhaps most famously known under the Searle brand name NutraSweet – were much more careful in the preparation of the market. The information they produced for journalists and other commentators minimized the possibility of any such damaging and possibly irresponsible reports. It has swept on to become a billion-dollar seller with minimal negative comment and a strong brand reputation.

CHECK PROCEDURES WITH REALISTIC TESTS

An emergency exercise is an excellent way to test the procedures. A simulated emergency will be agreed among a very small group of people – the smaller the better. To make this an effective test, other members of the emergency and crisis teams must be able to react in exactly the way they would with the real thing.

The testing will be a good way of evaluating how effective training has been. No set of procedures can work perfectly and any test will identify a number of areas that, hopefully, will only need slight adjustment but, occasionally, may need major reorganization.

Past-head of public relations for British Airways, Peter Jones, had considerable experience of developing and running crisis management systems. On a number of occasions – sometimes the real thing and sometimes tests – he was able to check out practice against theory. One critical factor, he believes, is that you must contain and separate the incident. The rest of the business has to continue or you will have no business.

From his experience, you might use only 50 per cent of whatever the crisis manual says, but you will never be able to tell in advance what that 50 per cent may be. However, the one constant factor is that the speed of modern media gives you an absolute maximum of 60 minutes to get the incident communications under control. Broadcasters can be on air in seconds and on many occasions they may be the first on the scene. The tone of those early broadcasts can set the tone for the whole incident.

While the natural focus is on external communications, it is critical not to forget to keep your own personnel and your business partners fully informed. For example, if a plane is involved in an incident and your counter staff are not briefed, then they cannot adequately deal with the naturally concerned enquiries of other passengers. 'Believe me,' added Jones. *'I don't know equals I don't care.'*

Communicate simultaneously to all audiences

Managers need the ability to see the crisis from the public perspective. For what is now Aventis's biggest facility in the UK, we helped run an exercise to test emergency procedures. The aim was to check communications alongside essential rescue and containment operations. The company had simulated an explosion on site in which a number of people had been severely 'injured' and perhaps some may even have 'died'. The test allowed company personnel to identify any weaknesses, sharpen their skills and check coordination with emergency services. It ran well and identified some areas where improvements could be made to minimize problems should, heaven forbid, the real thing happen.

The senior site manager was a masterly example of command and authority as the unnerving 'incident' unfolded. Just one factor caught him by surprise. He had dealt very effectively with a 'local radio reporter' – in actuality a member of my staff – who had grilled him on the incident. He had forgotten that such comments could be broadcast locally within minutes – indeed, factory neighbours would have heard or seen a real explosion. He was very disturbed when the next telephone call was from a tearful and very worried local neighbour, convinced that her husband, who was working on that shift, had been killed.

The management, in dealing with the accident and emergency services, had remembered their responsibilities to the media but had forgotten that telephone lines would be instantly jammed with calls from anxious friends and relatives. Emergency procedures were adjusted in this and other areas as a result of this experience. Although the woman calling was only a member of the consultancy team, the adrenalin had been running so high that the plant manager was genuinely shocked by the thought that in reality this could be the widow of someone on his staff, a colleague or friend, who had been killed.

On another occasion, during a similar test, the consultant posed as an aggressive television reporter and grilled a hapless employee of a leading distributor of hazardous materials at its Thameside plant. He challenged the executive over the hazards of the butane stored at one of their facilities. He bullied the man into admitting that he lived 20 miles away and that he was glad that 'I'm not a factory neighbour, because my family would never feel safe.'

An executive from the nuclear-waste reprocessing plant in Sellafield, Cumbria, casually commented after a leak of radioactive vapour: 'This sort of thing happens every day in industry.'

An official in the steel industry protested about what he felt to be unfair reporting of a fatal accident with the comment: 'Our industry is improving standards all the time. The media exaggerate these incidents. We have only killed four people this year.' Hardly comforting news for the widows and not very impressive to those who are not thinking in statistics but in human terms.

The moral is to think about what you are proposing to say. Run through it. Review your plans and, above all, test any procedure – for every incident has the potential to create new problems and from these come the lessons that bring constant improvement.

Testing the emergency media procedures
Make sure all are brief and supportive to ensure positive results

Whitbread, the major UK food, drinks and leisure group, has an effective and well-tested crisis plan. It has helped the company through a number of situations that could have been damaging to its reputation. Usually everything runs smoothly, but not always – and it is the odd hiccup that comes from running the procedure that helps keep everyone on their toes and sort out such wrinkles.

Marketing director at that time, Stephen Philpott, recounts a crisis well handled with only positive media coverage, but it could have been otherwise.

The company markets Heineken beers in the UK. During one normal business day, he received a call from the company in Amsterdam. This advised him that around 240,000 bottles of Heineken Export that Whitbread had sold in the UK might contain tiny glass particles. They had to run an instant product recall.

The crisis came in the middle of a holiday period, as might be expected, when news was quiet; the recall attracted more news interest than it might have done at a busy time. The company was pressed from all quarters for interviews. The public relations professionals of Heineken and Whitbread agreed that Philpott should calm concerns by undertaking a series of interviews. Most ran as planned, including the main BBC news, ITN news, and most of the nationals.

Breakfast TV were keen for a special piece to run in their national morning news programme and a late-night situation was planned. Philpott and his public relations adviser would meet the television crew and interviewer at around 11.30 pm to carry out an interview at one of the Thresher wine merchants' shops in central London. All arrangements were made with the manager, but when they arrived the shop was closed and no one was to be seen!

After a couple of telephone calls, they found that the manager had received counter-instructions from his area manager who had told him not to get involved. The Whitbread team were unable to find anyone at that time of night with the authority to persuade the shop manager to go against his boss's instructions.

By now the interviewer was getting impatient, the crew tired and irritable. The potential for disaster was considerable; the interviewer could have commented that he and his crew were denied access to the shop to film the potentially hazardous product. Philpott could have been filmed regardless in circumstances that were far from ideal.

Happily, while the options were being discussed, an enterprising colleague negotiated the use of a nearby office. Due to the openness of the Whitbread team, the interviewer was level-headed and accepted the situation in good humour. The result was a fine and fair interview.

Stephen Philpott's advice after the experience is to check and double check every detail. Anticipate everything that could go wrong and have an alternative available. As Philpott ruefully adds, one other lesson from this incident is that all personnel attending any such crisis situation or interview now carry with them all necessary personnel and emergency telephone numbers. They are not much use in a directory back in a drawer in the office or on the PC on your desk.

SOME OBSERVATIONS, IN SUMMARY

1. If it helps to persuade colleagues to make the commitment, consider your crisis plan as part of your reputation insurance.
2. Be cautious in appraising the potential contribution of recommendations as there is considerable over-claiming for some simple solutions.
3. The best crisis plan when running any organization is one that minimizes the chances of incidents causing risk to life, property, business trading and reputation.
4. Before planning any crisis or contingency plan, analyse all the issues that could affect the organizer's reputation.
5. Brief your public relations personnel to prepare the issues audit or, if necessary, appoint experts to help them.
6. The senior executive allocated to pilot this project through the company must have direct and easy access to the chief executive or chairman.
7. The first step in any issues audit is to start with interviews internally, as most potential issues will be known to specialists within the company.
8. Next, look at external audiences – an independent view is one good reason why public relations people may be best suited to manage this project.
9. Before making judgements on issues, produce an index of these for circulation and comment within the company.

10. Following such comments, develop a corporate stance on each issue, involving input from your specialists but endorsed from the top.

11. Remember the competitive position when you review issues which are to your advantage (positive), to your disadvantage (negative), or neutral – the latter are likely to be in the majority.

12. An intelligent issues audit will not only solve potential problems, it will identify many new business and marketing opportunities.

13. Your crisis plan should spring out of the issues audit, reflecting the mission statement or the corporate objectives relating to its key audiences.

14. This plan will cover more than communications – it will need to involve safety, marketing, human resources, personnel and other disciplines.

15. The final plan will have to be signed off by the chief executive or chairman after discussion, amendment and a formal presentation to the board.

16. Concentrate on the principles and not the terminology – for example, issues/crisis planning is sometimes called reputation risk management or contingency planning. The policy and the plan are what matter, not the titles.

17. The central element in the plan, if it is to be of practical use, will be the early warning system that monitors issues and identifies potential crises.

18. Agree with your legal and insurance specialists the stance that you will adopt should a crisis arise. Never play down your position for legal safety.

19. Apologies and expressions of regret are the least that might be expected; they can generate understanding, and ease the pressure on executives trying to find out exactly what happened.

20. Intelligently and sensitively phrased, such apologies do not need to be an admission of liability.

21. Parellel with the development of the plan, establish teams to handle such crises and ensure that they have the essential range of skills.

22. Create an appropriate incident suite at each location, plus a spare one on a different part of the site in case an incident should make the first inaccessible. Use the inner and outer room concept.

23. Ensure that these rooms have the necessary facilities that, at a

moment's notice, can be brought into operation for the team dealing with the crisis.

24. Train your flying squad; make sure there are back-up personnel for each member; and that all are equipped and prepared to depart at a moment's notice, with bags packed, a pre-prepared currently dated letter of authority from the chairman, passports ready and so on.

25. Ensure that the crisis plan tightly integrates the communications, human resources, marketing and safety disciplines.

26. All personnel on the crisis team need appropriate media training, plus familiarity with the basic company information for use in interviews.

27. All line management (to a level to be agreed) need training in crisis handling so that an incident is not vested in the hands of a few specialists.

28. Remember that many personnel such as security guards, lorry drivers, secretaries, and telephonists may be closely involved and need both empowerment and briefing.

29. All personnel need to know how to behave, the extent of their authority, the lines of communication and their responsibilities.

30. Prepare standard company information on such areas as products, manufacturing processes, safety records, shipping, distribution procedures, employment, management structure and so on.

31. Ensure that this information is available in hard copy and, above all, electronic form at each of the incident rooms.

32. Do not rely on public communications but ensure that the team is equipped with mobile phones, laptops, shortwave radios, transmitters or portable satellite dishes, as may be appropriate.

33. Ensure that all communications is targeted at all audiences and not just at the media, with appropriate contact lines or enquiry personnel.

34. Above all, run regular tests, checking safety response and media handling; consider using your public relations people as 'hostile journalists'.

35. Use your website and industry sites and chatrooms as an integral part of your communications network. Be certain to be as up to date as possible with all data and communications. Ask for responses, check these and reply promptly.

36. Set up debriefing meetings with all members of the team to improve procedures; invite the emergency services to attend and comment.

11

Personal skills

Develop your own expertise to communicate effectively

Key factors discussed

- Deciding the corporate message.
- Building two-way communications.
- The value of good media skills.
- Creating platforms for comment.
- Understanding how journalists work.
- Techniques to win positive coverage.
- Interviews, articles and opinion pieces.
- Personal presentation skills.

ESTABLISH HONEST MEDIA RELATIONS

The chairman, chief executive and other senior directors should use professionals to help plan the programmes of reputation management and run the associated communications programmes; but they will need personal skills if they wish to lead from the front. In this chapter we are looking at business communications skills rather than interpersonal capabilities, although they do have some elements in common.

Just as the chief executive is really the chief financial officer, he or she is also the chief custodian of reputation and therefore the chief public relations officer for the organization. The chief executive may delegate the day-to-day management to a professional or may ask for professional advice, but he or she must ultimately take personal responsibility for the effectiveness of communications and therefore the management of the company's reputation.

USE OF LANGUAGE

If you want to communicate effectively, it is reasonable to expect that you will have a grasp of the language. Many who would seek their fame and fortune in the worlds of public relations and other communications disciplines have neither this capability nor an interest in acquiring the skill. One young applicant for a job with my firm showed me an example of his work. He had used apostrophes inconsistently. I felt this might be an area where he could learn the simple rules so he did not make such mistakes. Whatever you do, I explained, you cannot be right if you spell a word in two different ways in the same piece – or use an apostrophe performing the same function but also in two different ways. He looked at me blankly. 'Who cares?' He did not get the job, and I suspect never got a job in public relations – although that cannot be certain, judging by some of the news releases written by so-called professionals.

John Humphrys, celebrated broadcaster and presenter on the flagship BBC Radio Four *Today* programme tells a similar story in his book, *Lost for Words*. He quotes the experience of a professor who underlined spelling errors in an undergraduate's essay. When the student read this, he commented, 'What are you? Some sort of spelling fascist?'

Wisely, Humphrys believes the rules can be broken but you need to know them to appreciate when you can go off the straight and narrow. As he says, 'An awful lot of people despise pedants. My friend and former editor, Rod Liddle, is to pedantry what a dog is to a lamppost. He can certainly not see a rule without wanting to cock his leg against it. He was fired from the BBC for writing rude things about the government (editors of the *Today* programme are not meant to do that) and is a born iconoclast. Show him a sacred cow and he will slaughter it on the spot.' So when Lynne Truss wrote her admirable book on punctuation, *Eats, Shoots and Leaves*, Rod naturally wrote a column attacking it, remarks Humphrys. It was, as you would expect from Rod, clever and funny. It was also virtually unreadable because, apart from full stops, he used no punctuation. His point was that we would understand what he was saying perfectly well. Indeed we did, but it wasn't half hard work. The great strength of commas in the right place is that you don't have to pause and think. They do the job for you.

As I know John Humphrys a little, through my own and my clients' appearances on *Today*, I asked him if he would like to write the foreword to this book. I explained that he could be as independent as he felt, as the idea of this book was to separate good, ethical professional practice from the more typical, which is frequently abysmal. Sadly he declined, as he is uncomfortable about both public relations and the jargon too many business leaders use. I trust he will not find too many examples of the sloppy use of English in this tome, nor too much management-speak either!

CONVEYING THE KEY MESSAGE

The chairman, the chief executive and other top managers need to have the understanding and the skills to present the organization to all stakeholders. And if much of the day-to-day liaison with media, MPs, analysts and others is undertaken by the public relations team, the senior managers need to be controlling what is being said in the name of their organization.

The spokesperson needs to represent the organization properly, but information is also needed to convey the message: company plans and aims, the state of the market, competition, audience perceptions and public expectations, for example. The message will become confused unless it can be communicated in simple terms.

One central point in preparing much material for business communications is the need to eliminate anything peripheral and to get briskly to the message. For example, at a seminar or a staff briefing, the message has to be in the first sentence. If it is not, the audience will listen impatiently and hypothesize on what the key message will be. Fairly soon, they will get bored or irritated and you will have lost them.

Some research suggests that a speaker has as few as six seconds to capture an audience. Even being generous, you will have no more than half a minute to get them interested before irritation sets in.

A press interviewer may accept just a little of the preliminaries, but a radio or television interview cannot waste a second. You need to develop the skill of condensing complex arguments into simple points that retain the essential truth, without distortion.

A news release needs to have the major point in its first sentence. And in a similar way, the main message in a radio or television interview must come as close to the beginning as possible. A sound piece of advice is to start with your conclusion. What is the single most important message you want to put over? Then weave that briskly into your first sentence or answer.

ALWAYS TELL THE TRUTH

Indeed, there is a very considerable skill involved in living by the truth. While it is true that fabrications require much greater powers of memory, it is also true that the truth imposes its own burden.

In business there are constant pressures to bend, fudge or obscure reality. For example, lawyers may tell you that too much candour might strengthen legal claims against the organization. The insurers might urge you away from anything specific to avoid compromising the policy. The marketeers sometimes insist that too much information will erode the competitive edge. The financiers can detail the City regulations and conventions that inhibit openness. Even those lovers of truth and transparency, the public relations advisers, may occasionally press upon you the wisdom of the truth, nothing but the truth, but… not necessarily the whole truth.

But all this advice creates considerable problems. The director who says nothing may not be lying, but could later be accused of negligence for not having said what needed to be said – being economical with the truth, as they say.

Yet again, the truth, the whole truth and nothing but the truth could leave the company without any customers, investors or employees. How do you strike a balance?

The answer is not to view this as a moral problem but simply as a practical one. There can be no arguments over the morality. It has to be truth, nothing but the truth and (as close as humanly possible to) the whole truth, as may be appropriate at the time. Where secrecy or confidentiality dictate, it is often the best policy to make it quite clear that there are elements that cannot be disclosed, and explain the reasons.

But where the truth may not be acceptable to the stakeholders the organization has only one option: change whatever it is doing that is not acceptable. Under no circumstances use communications to try to disguise the reality or mislead those who rightly expect to be told the truth.

Always question and test advice

There is another matter that complicates these decisions. Sometimes, advisers advise as if the organization were working in a vacuum and it has total control over all decisions that it makes. For example, your marketing professionals may ask you not to announce the major export order that the company has just won; there might be a second one in the pipeline and they don't want to alert the competition to this opportunity. It sounds logical and sensible but, in reality, it is a flawed argument. The organization placing the order with you may be quite pleased about it and may have its own reasons for wanting to talk – officially or unofficially.

Other business people involved may see aspects of the deal and may talk about it within your industry, which might include shippers, handling agents, secretaries, telephone and fax operators, insurers, bankers and countless others. They may also discuss it with friends in the media.

There is another weakness in this argument: it makes the assumption that you only obtained this order because your competitors were not aware of the opportunity.

It is very probable that any intelligent buyer placing a major order will be as aware of the competitive position as you are. After all, it is in his or her interest to obtain quotes from as many competitive sources as possible. Therefore, there is a strong possibility that the competition are already aware of this potential business. Even if they were not, the winning and delivery of such a major order is bound to come to their attention sooner or later if they are the sort of competition you ought to fear. And if they are not the sort of competition you ought to fear, why all the secrecy?

Early comments can win maximum attention

The truth is that when you make the announcement you win

bonus news points in the media, with your employees, with government, with suppliers and business partners, with your shareholders and with everyone else who is interested in your success. As any such news story can only be issued with the support of your customer, you actually strengthen this relationship with the announcement – and improve the chances of a follow-up order.

On the other hand, hold the news until it has become common knowledge and you not only lose these opportunities, but you run the risk of irritating people who wonder why they were not properly informed.

Try ringing a trade journalist about an order you should have mentioned three months previously and you might receive a very chilly 'I heard about that ages ago from your competition; it's a pity that you didn't tell us at the time you signed the deal because we could have given you the front page on that!'

When presenting messages, be sure that you can live with the results that may come back in seconds or in years. Be certain of your facts and never improvise or speculate. John Humphrys is one of Britain's most respected broadcasters and was once described as a national treasure. In his deeply disturbing book, *The Great Food Gamble*, he cites the example of one of the most painful examples of a leader's words coming back to haunt him.

At the time of the scare over the safety of eating beef, the then Secretary of State for Health, Stephen Dorrell, had said in a television interview that there was no conceivable risk from eating British beef. Just four months later he had to tell a stunned parliament that a link between the cattle disease BSE and the appalling human variant of Creutzfeldt-Jacob disease (CJD) was the most likely explanation for the rise in the number of tragic victims of this incurable fatal condition. Five years later on the BBC *Today* programme he admitted to John Humphrys that he wished he had never given that interview because he had got it wrong. Though he was relying on a brief from technical personnel, he still carried the responsibility.

Tackle bad news as vigorously as good

As good news is best divulged early and honestly, this is even more important with bad news.

Your legal advisers may ask you to say nothing about the accident in which a number of workers were injured. Any apology, they may claim, might be interpreted as an admission of guilt and this could be used in the action the injured or others could take for damages against the company.

What heartless, pathetic nonsense. If you are not sorry for injuring someone you employ, then you should not be employing people. Whether the accident was due to some fault on the part of the company, some negligence, or simply the inattention or carelessness of the person concerned, the company still carries some responsibility. If the company is proved to be at fault, you want to make recompense voluntarily, speedily and vigorously and not rely on the pressures that might be produced through the legal system – with all the negative associations that that will create of a company that neglects its responsibilities and has to be forced to behave decently. Even if the accident later proves to be no reflection on company safety standards, common decency requires some expression of concern over the harm done to colleagues.

You will want the legal advisers to check over the statement, but never allow them to prevent you from making any comment.

LISTEN BEFORE SPEAKING

If you have been successful in your career, you have had to be decisive. Perhaps, on occasions, you have had to make a decision before you were fully comfortable and certain that you had all the facts. The risks from delay had probably reached the point where they would soon exceed the risks from some small element of misinformation.

But are you sure you are always told what you need to know? The decisive leader is often not the one that colleagues want to risk challenging with a contrary view. In all areas of business, listening is important but in communications it is vital.

As noted earlier, I was once asked to organize some key media interviews for Howard Schultz, a distinguished US management adviser who has been interviewed around the world countless times. I would rather upset any client than have him or her appear foolish through not being properly briefed. On this occasion, I decided I would explain the whole principle of media interviews, on the basis that UK media may be somewhat different from those in the USA.

After a polite start, I was a little surprised to see him begin to take notes. 'Fascinating,' he said later. 'Very helpful.' It turned out that he had never had the opportunity to discuss the basics and some of the points were new to him. All the other advisers with whom he had worked over many years must have made the same mistake that I nearly did.

The point of the story is not to make assumptions. At the very least, test them. You need to know the other person's point of view. After all, you learn nothing when you are talking, only when you are listening.

TEST YOUR CONVERSATIONAL INVESTIGATIVE SKILLS

Try the club test. Next time you are in relaxed circumstances with a few friends raise an interesting topic. If possible, select something you do not normally discuss, say, the influence of television upon social behaviour.

The opening stages of the conversation will probably fall into a pattern of which there are only the two main versions: you will start with a statement or with a question. Either way, the intention will be very similar. Usually, you want to gain some idea of the other people's points of view on the topic. This could be either because you have no views or because you have strong views.

If you have no views, it may be that you want to know if they have ideas that might be of interest. Or you may feel not very well informed about the subject and wish to test whether they have better knowledge.

If you have strong views, then you may want to test if they agree with your views or not. If they agree, then you can discuss the various points of the issue. If they disagree, then you can have a lively debate challenging each other's views, gathering up evidence and clarifying your thinking.

If their arguments are not as good as yours, you may try to persuade them and enjoy that satisfaction. If their arguments are better than yours, you may be persuaded or, at least, may modify your own perspective.

We all do this, all the time when 'off duty' with friends or family. But it is a natural approach that can be effective at work. You may find that you do something instinctively in social conversation that we sometimes completely omit in similar situations in our businesses. That is the fundamental fact-finding phase that should always come before the development of a point of view or case. There are few conversational debates that do not feature one of these approaches at the key start point.

You say, 'I think that violence on television is having a terrible effect on the behaviour of young people,' and you pause to see whether your friends will agree or disagree with this assertive statement. You will then adjust your comments accordingly.

Alternatively, you may say, 'Do you think there is any link between violence on television and the behaviour of young people?' You will wait to see whether they agree with the implication within the question, or not, and adjust the rest of the conversation accordingly.

Whether you want to know what the others think because it will affect how you think, or whether you want to know what they think so that you can adjust the argument to have the most influence over their thinking, you are undertaking simple but valuable perceptions research. Similarly, test company arguments you wish to advance with someone you can trust to be confidential and candid.

PRACTISE AND EXTEND YOUR MEDIA SKILLS

This book cannot cover the detail of how to prepare, write and issue news: there are many excellent publications on that subject. But these can be useful skills for any director, not only as insurance for the occasion when he or she might be thrust into the limelight but also as a positive attribute that can help to project the company and its values. Of course, an incidental benefit will be improved skill in judging work by others submitted to the executive for approval.

The simplest guidance for dealing with the media is to treat all journalists as you would like to be treated. To do this, you need to imagine yourself as a journalist. If you believe that journalism is an interesting, worthwhile and professional function, then you will have no problems.

David Gregory, when he was public relations manager of Microsoft in the UK, neatly summarized the way to work with the media: 'Treat journalists as customers. Know them. When they ring you – ring them back. Proactively brief them on issues; be open and honest with them. Keep them close and in a well-thought-through relationship.'

Many people derive great satisfaction from criticizing the media. This is particularly true when the media attack our own organization or something that we hold dear. But remember that, in a democratic society, journalists are often the only independent group employed to expose lies, fraud, deceit and dishonesty. They may all get it wrong sometimes – or some of them may get it wrong sometimes – but on balance they do an effective job in helping to protect freedom, truth and integrity within our society.

It might be superficially attractive to wish, say, *The Sun* or *USA Today* to disappear, but who is to decide which media should be allowed to survive and what they should be allowed to cover? Censorship is still censorship even if it is intended to be benign; history tells us that an imposed will (such as some form of benign censorship) soon ceases to be benign if it is unaccountable. In other words if you want a free media then you have to accept the simplification of issues by the popular media. You must also accept that some journalists might get it wrong sometimes. But their competitors will be just as keen as you to prove them wrong.

If you favour some form of control over what the media might publish, perhaps through some independent body, then which side might they have backed when Shell miscalculated its reserves and tried to disguise the facts, or the government began double-counting investments in social services, or Jeffrey Archer played out his life of deceit?

The role of the journalist is clear. *A journalist has to produce news that is of interest to readers, listeners and viewers.* If 'industry' gets bad media, then perhaps one reason may be that industry is not particularly effective in putting over its case. And if that is true, then industry gets the media coverage it deserves.

Understanding the job of the journalist

If you want the best possible and fairest reporting of your company then it is essential you treat journalists as if you understand the job they have to do – and not only understand it, but support it and try to assist them.

Obviously, you are aiming to build a good reputation among the public but you must start by building a good reputation among the media. You need to be respected for the speed and efficiency of your approach, the integrity of your information, the candour of your answers to questions, the access that you allow to facilities and personnel and, above all, the equal vigour and integrity with which you tackle bad news and good news.

Every company has its disappointments as well as its successes and nothing impresses a journalist more than a chief executive who is candid about the problem. It is simple psychology. If the chief executive can be open and honest about bad news, then perhaps the journalist can have a little more trust in the good news he or she is given at other times. With journalists, respect is like love: give a little and you get a lot in return. Certainly, it is very short-sighted to irritate a journalist.

A managing director of a leisure company is well known for hating the media. After the inevitable row he would have with each journalist that his benighted press officer lined up for him, he used to triumph, 'Sorted him out. Won that argument.'

But, as the equally inevitable ensuing coverage demonstrated, he lost every row – at least in the eyes of the readers, who were the only ones who counted.

As entrepreneurial film-maker Lord Puttnam comments, remembering his own occasional combats with journalists, 'I have always shared Oscar Wilde's view that a man cannot be too careful in the choice of his enemies.'

LOOK FOR PROGRAMME OPPORTUNITIES FOR YOUR ORGANIZATION

The ability of radio and television to reach an audience can be appreciated from the cost of the advertising! Advertisers spend this sort of money because of the audience it delivers, the attention it achieves and, most important, the results it produces. Yet both radio and television are available media for good editorial ideas: too few of these come through business channels. In the UK, for example, both *Any Questions?* and *Question Time* have difficulty in finding enough businesspeople with views and the ability to express them directly. They find plenty of politicians, showbiz types and wannabes, but not so many business leaders. Even those that do make themselves available often speak in an oblique, arcane or jargon-ridden manner, as the editors on *Today* regularly complain.

The effective public relations adviser working on behalf of the company should be creating broadcast news opportunities, and it is necessary to know how to handle a radio or television journalist when approached to provide information or facilities. As you may be the object of the story or the subject of the interview, it is wise to understand the fundamentals:

- Check the programme content.
- Will it be live or taped?
- Will the contribution be edited?
- Who else will be appearing?
- Who will conduct the interview or discussion?
- What topics or questions will be covered?
- Will there be a live debate to counter any misunderstandings or damaging assertions from other participants?

Despite views to the contrary, a live interview is *always* the best option.

A contribution that is to be edited will give the person being interviewed a little more time, even an opportunity to correct any blunders. Also, the interview can often be arranged at a more convenient time – even in your own office – thus avoiding an inconvenient journey to the studio.

However, it must be remembered that you do not control the editing. Maybe the answer when you got it wrong, or the embarrassing mistake, will make better television. Have you never seen an interview and wondered why on earth such an experienced person said such a thing? Maybe the interview was run for 20 or 30 minutes to get the key 30 seconds they really wanted.

Can you be confident that they will use the response where you explained the errors in all their 'facts'? Also, will your comfortable office be an ideal setting when the interviewer starts asking about your third world markets or possible redundancies?

It may not happen to you, but why take the chance? Live appearances are always preferable to recordings, believed Sir Anthony Cleaver, when he was chairman of IBM UK. While apparently more demanding, you have an equal chance with the interviewer. He also adds the practical recommendation that you should always have in mind the three key points you wish to convey. Make sure you express them regardless of the questions asked.

His experience is fairly typical of what can happen in a pressured situation. Sir Anthony remembers being interviewed on a number of occasions on an agreed topic, when the discussion suddenly moved into an unexpected area. In a pre-recorded interview, this shift can be edited out making the interviewee sound hesitant and lacking confidence. However, in the live interview, the viewer or listener can appreciate the sudden change. With experience, you can deal with these firmly and take them in your stride, winning the support of the audience.

'Always go for the live opportunity' is sound advice. Start with the point you wish to leave with the listener or viewer. It will give the interview punch and guarantees that whatever else may happen, you have at least stated your most important point.

Sam Whitbread, director of Whitbread and past chairman, adds two simple rules, well worth remembering, that he has followed from his earliest days in business. He recalls being given instructions he did not understand at the time, because his boss had forgotten the young man's inexperience. *Hear what you say through your listeners' ears. See what you write through your readers' eyes.*

CONSIDER THE JOURNALIST'S POINT OF VIEW

Journalists are people. They are moved and motivated by the same things that move and motivate all of us. They respond well to being treated properly; they like being treated with consideration; and they do not expect to be fawned over.

You do not need to be a personal friend of a journalist before he or she will write a fair story. Even if you are a personal friend, he or she would be a fairly useless journalist if this affected his or her news judgement and you did not get a bad press when you deserved it.

There is no great need to wine and dine a journalist – though many people make this a hobby. On the other hand, it helps if you are on passable terms and, if the way to discuss business in a busy day is over lunch or dinner, then so be it. However, never organize a lunch just to get to know a journalist; if you waste that person's time, he or she might never spend so much valuable time with you again. 'Getting to know the journalist' meetings with no news angles are usually counterproductive exercises. It is perfectly acceptable to set up such a meeting if you have one or, better still, two or three good stories to discuss.

Good stories are not what your public relations department or consultancy issued as a news release the previous week. Good stories are items that the journalist may not be able to obtain from other sources – early warnings or items in more detail, those that may have a personal slant or give some background of which the journalist will be unaware.

Off-the-record comments should be strictly for novels and television dramas, and never used in real life. Remember that 'who gossips with you, will gossip about you'. If you avoid keeping something 'off the record' it will be a great advantage, as the chances of being misunderstood will be minimized. In other words, assume that everything you say is intended to be used by the journalist. This means that you must be particularly careful with those things that you might say after a few glasses of wine.

Never use phrases such as: 'You can quote me on this.' They are pretentious, corny and the sure sign of an amateur. Leave the journalist to decide what is to be quoted, as he or she is expecting to be able to quote you on everything. Most things said after such a phrase are usually utterly uninteresting, such as, 'We are the 14th largest manufacturer of widgets in Western Europe.'

Michael Grade, UK television entrepreneur and now chairman of the BBC, is one of those rare media professionals who is also as adept when he is the subject of the news – as he has often been in his career. He has summarized a few rules of his own that he has learnt over the years:

● Never complain to journalists who criticize you. Never thank them if they are complimentary – just be accessible and friendly at all times.
● Never, never lie to a journalist, any journalist. Always remember that journalists have a job to do – try to help them to do it.
● Always correct factual errors, either by seeking a right to reply or by letter for publication, or with a personal note direct to the journalist concerned.
● Much public relations is about perception. If the perception of your company, or you, is just plain wrong, you have to take a long-term view about correcting it. It could take years to turn attitudes around – you have to keep plugging away with your own message, over and over again.
● Oh, and remember, journalists are no different from you and me – they can't keep secrets either.

Develop angles relevant to the journalist

Is your news something you would want to and expect to read in the publication you are briefing? *Plastics & Rubber Weekly* may be more interested in your widgets than *24 Hours*. If your topic is neither newsworthy nor directly relevant to the readers (or listeners or viewers) then why are you briefing the journalist? Is it hopelessly inappropriate or can it be developed to be appropriate?

Your plant extension being opened may not even be of interest to the local newspaper. However, a thousand new jobs may be of relevance to a far wider range of media. Ten new jobs in a new sector or against a background of redundancy may be news. An opening by the 100-year-old retired pensioner may be of genuine human interest. An opening by the world's most famous talking parrot may be mildly amusing, but may be seen as a gimmick and may not generate a positive reaction.

Many companies get themselves into a mess by trying to focus on creating positive media coverage for those things that they consider to be interesting. They lose sight of – or do not even consider – what may be interesting to the journalist. What interests the journalist? What interests the public for whom the journalist is writing? The journalist is a hero if the 'scoop' proves to be correct; but slipping down the greasy pole if it's wrong!

When it comes to comparing what the organization feels and what the journalist feels, then it is a million to one that the journalist is likely to have a better idea of what is of news interest than the organization's chief executive. The key question a business manager should ask is: If I were a journalist, would I consider this of news interest to my readers/viewers/listeners?

It is usually a weak approach to attempt to create good news when it suits the interests of the organization. The wiser position is to make public relations a permanent, continuous, strategic part of business management. In other words, your organization should make serious efforts to build relations with key audiences (including the intermediaries, such as the media and analysts) that encourage them to talk with knowledge about your operations, and to see your organization as a source of useful, authoritative information.

If you do this, you will not only gain much respect but any bad news will seem a lot better when you are obviously trying to help rather than conceal.

The managing director of Laurence Scott (at that time the UK's largest manufacturer of electric motors) once asked his public relations adviser to minimize the possible negative local media coverage following a most horrific accident. A crane operator had swivelled his unit, touched overhead power lines and had been electrocuted. The inquest established that to do this he had removed an important safety lock but, none the less, he had been a company employee, and was now dead, with a widow and young children. The company remained technically guilty of the offence.

The chief asked his young public relations adviser to talk to the editor of the newspaper local to the regional head office about the report that was due to be published on the accident, in a major but distant city, and to get the story into perspective; as he explained, the company had a good safety record with very few serious accidents.

Nervously (and regrettably), the public relations officer duly spoke to the newspaper; the editor had missed the fact that an inquest had taken place 200 miles away and thanked him for that information. The editor then ran a major story, highly critical of the company, drawing attention to many other accidents the company had sustained across various plants. (That foolish public relations person was, in fact, myself!)

What I should have done (but experience and courage failed me) was to have convinced the managing director that, together, we should draft our own news story. This would have spelt out all the facts, our apologies and the actions that we had put in hand to prevent the occurrence of any similar accidents – as well as steps we had taken to ameliorate the tragic circumstances for the dead man's widow and their children.

It would still have been a big story but at least it would have been more sensitively handled. The company would not have seemed so callous, or manipulative, trying to use its public relations people to suppress the publication of a story that was genuinely in the best public interest.

The moral of the story is: think twice before trying to do deals with the media. Is it worth it? Why bother? Be tested by standards you can support.

I learnt from that experience a lesson that public relations people only need to learn once. If you know something is not right, then you can be certain it is not in the best interests of your company or client, and your only duty is to say so. You can never complain later that you were unhappy about a decision if you failed to say so at the time. And a good boss must learn to appreciate advice even when it is not what he or she wants to hear.

LEARN SOME PRACTICAL MEDIA SKILLS

Commercial media exist to provide news that is of interest to their readers, viewers or listeners. This simple statement of fact should be obvious, but it means that any company spokesperson must be strict in the application of critical standards to the preparation and issue of news material.

Some journalists seem to believe that a news sense is a very rare quality. In truth it is largely common sense. Bad news is not the only news; however, it is the exceptional that is the definition of news. If one taxi driver sets fire to his or her vehicle, then that is news; the fact that several thousands others do not, is of no consequence. The first naked football fan running onto the pitch may be news, but the 500th will not. There are two main reasons why bad news gets better coverage: first, it is more exceptional (murder, hijack and fraud are not yet the norm); second, people experience morbid curiosity in disaster and tragedy, perhaps because of the relief that they are not the victims.

Companies can use this 'new is news' factor to their own advantage. The first woman to chair a public company may be news. The first major contract for the sale of an unlikely consumer product (such as electric kettles) to Tibet is news. A survey showing that the average man has three (or 30!) pairs of underpants is news. A 63-year-old cleaner being invited to open a new high-technology laboratory is news. The winner of a travel scholarship who has never been abroad is news. The invention of a safety device by an apprentice is news. The invitation of all company pensioners to the launch of a new product is news.

It only takes observation of how the media work to recognize that central to any effective media relations campaign must be a hard core of news. And it is perfectly legitimate to create news. If it is new, has never been done before, is interesting and relevant... it could be news.

Obviously, what is news in an engineering publication may not be news in the parish magazine. What is news for a local radio station may not be suitable for national television news. Let us look at some practical guidelines. You may not use them as often as your public relations advisers but, even so, it helps to understand the principles.

News releases

You should only issue news to those journals that will have a direct interest, unless you want to damage your media reputation. Do not scatter stories to all. Always provide a contact name and telephone number. Be certain that the telephone is properly manned, 24 hours a day, 365 days a year.

It takes many years of training and experience to be able to present information in the concise and direct style necessary for news releases to be used by editors. A basic writing ability is essential. But, with care and practice, an average writer can be developed into a good news writer. There are some guidelines that may be helpful:

1. Develop your writing skill. Draft, redraft, edit, polish and perfect the copy. Read publications and understand what makes news and how it is put together. Analyse the writing skills of good journalists. Understand the good; criticize the bad.
2. Always ask who, what, why, where and when and be sure that these questions are answered in every news story. Train yourself to eliminate as ruthlessly as you add. If material does not answer one of these questions, what is it doing in your story?
3. Write stories to suit the style of the publication. If, for practical reasons, your story has to go to a wider range of media, always draft it in the style to suit the most popular of these. Better still, produce different stories for different types of news outlet.
4. Always keep the copy tight, concise and factual. Never fudge an issue or create a misleading impression. Substantiate any claims. Separate fact from belief by putting the latter into quotes. (Research chief John Brown confirmed the vehicle exceeded 200 mph. 'We believe it's the fastest in the world,' said … , etc.)
5. Write a story from the point of view of the journalist. Although it is a statement from your organization, it should be presented so that it can be used directly in the publication with the minimum of editing. Comment, observation or speculation can only be included in a story in quotes or footnotes.
6. Get the main news point into the first paragraph and preferably the first sentence. Organize the paragraphs so that the most newsworthy are at the top. This will allow the journalists to edit for length from the bottom. The paragraphs you can most easily afford to lose should therefore be those towards the end of the story.
7. Keep sentences short; use positive and not negative; use active verbs; avoid subordinate and inverted clauses; and omit any subjective material or superlatives. Keep separate points in separate sentences, and break each collection of points into separate paragraphs.
8. Put the copy into modern journalistic style. Eliminate any old-fashioned phrases, formal or pompous language, jargon

peculiar to the industry, clichés or colloquialisms that are not accepted as standard current English (or appropriate language).

9. When you have written your story, check through and make sure that it meets these criteria. In particular, be certain that the news is at the beginning. Draft news releases can often afford to have the first two paragraphs deleted!

10. Go through your copy, tighten, edit, improve, check all spelling and punctuation. Get someone else to read it before it goes for release. Ask them to criticize and query. Avoid becoming sensitive about your own copy. Learn to be self-critical. Push yourself to the highest standard possible.

Letters

Publications like to receive authoritative letters on topics of interest to their readership. Be sure your company writes where relevant. Agree a corporate policy.

Review carefully whether you should respond to a negative comment about your organization from another correspondent. If it is serious you may have to, if only to prove that you challenged the view. But if it is trivial your letter might simply extend the debate. And it only takes one other letter (regardless of how unrepresentative this might be) to prolong the agony even further.

Interviews

Make sure your public relations executive has prepared briefing notes, arranged a convenient time and place for the interview, provided travel arrangements, lunch or other facilities that would be hospitable but no more. Well in advance, train yourself in media techniques. Trust journalists and get them to trust you. Say nothing off the record; however, never lie or hide the truth. If the timing of a question or discussion is not convenient, then explain why you cannot help; offer to give the journalist a story as soon as possible, and keep any such promises.

Editor meetings

Make sure you meet regularly with the key editors for your industry. They should know you well enough to be able to talk to you at any time they wish. Make sure that your meetings with them cover some items of substance and are not merely social occasions. Therefore, pick up a strong news story for each editor meeting, then follow it up every 6 or 12 months, as may be necessary.

Be prepared to make comments on issues of the day. Always be available if asked, as that ensures invitations will come. Saying no might mean the journalists will find a more reliable and consistent source.

Articles

Many publications carry authoritative articles. Make sure your executive is monitoring all publications relevant to your industry. If you see a news story that is contrary to your company's views, suggest an article as a follow-up. If you see a trend in the industry that others might not be aware of, suggest an article. Use the findings from issues audits for trend or opinion piece suggestions to editors.

Planning

At all stages the executive responsible for planning the public relations activity needs to check the corporate communications objectives with the sources of information available to these audiences. Across the world, the news scene changes rapidly: new publications, radio, television and other media opportunities are constantly arising. The result has been a major increase in outlets for broad distribution of news. At the same time many audiences are bombarded with information and becoming more selective.

The effective media relations executive should be able to balance the need for broad news distribution with targeting communications at narrower identified audiences and opinion leaders.

RADIO AND TELEVISION TECHNIQUES

Company executives sometimes put too much weight on the influence of print media – mainly because their coverage can be held in the hand, copied and passed on. Yet recent research suggests up to 90 per cent of news information may be received by most people via broadcast media. These are powerful channels and should be used. One television news slot can reach more people than all the popular national press combined.

Programme opportunities

Local stations are desperate for local news. In the UK, national radio programmes such as *You and Yours, Science Now* and *The Food Programme* regularly use commercial news items. Television programmes such as *Panorama* also use commercial news items, presented in the right way.

Local and national radio and TV can reach millions. Programme-makers are all in the ideas business. The sheer volume of radio and television currently being broadcast in the UK means that there is a massive demand for good material.

In the UK, the annual, *Who's Who in Broadcasting*, will help identify the people who put programmes together. A news release may be an acceptable method of putting a factual news story in front of the news editor, though the personal approach is nearly always best.

Radio and television are immediate media. Stories will not last, timing is critical, and news stories need to be presented quickly to editors. Facilities for interview, location, recording, studio guests and so on must be provided immediately they are required. Deadlines are tight and, with electronic news gathering, are becoming tighter. Live material from remote locations can be directly slotted into news bulletins.

Timing is, however, important in another sense. The presentation has to be crisp, immaculate and professional. The radio or television audiences have the ability to switch off or change channels instantly. As a result of this, broadcasters are constantly working to keep a high level of immediate interest in their output.

The chief executive and the public relations adviser should know how to handle a radio or television journalist when approached to provide information or facilities. The public relations adviser has also to decide who will represent the company. Should it be the top executive? If it is important or strategic, perhaps yes. Or should it be a specialist director relevant to the issue under debate? And does that director have the necessary skills? Never assume that an articulate senior executive has what it takes, unless he or she has been tested... or, better, trained.

Senior executives will have varying degrees of natural aptitude for handling broadcast interviews, observed Peter Middleton, chairman of GTL Resources plc, former chief executive of Lloyds of London, Thomas Cook and Salomon Brothers. Very few books on management pay attention to the fact that managers have talent and what they achieve cannot be learnt from studying techniques. However, to handle a key radio or television interview on instinct alone without some professional training would be foolhardy. It could put the whole corporate reputation at risk, he suggested. 'I went to my first TV training session unconvinced of the value of spending this time – but within three minutes of the day's first interview, I changed my mind.' Middleton was managing director of Thomas Cook at the time and, the travel industry having suffered a number of accidents affecting holidaymakers, he had been interviewed and simply had not anticipated the questions. When asked if he was content to let his customers die, he recalls that he 'dug a hole so deep it could have accommodated all London's refuse for a year!'

Training

There are many excellent training courses available to help you or your colleagues present your organization's case in the best possible way. Make sure that all senior executives who may be required to broadcast are trained in the techniques. Decide whether you are going to speak on behalf of the organization.

Even the most experienced presenter needs familiarization with media and the essential techniques. Never should an interviewee be composing the answer to a question live in an interview. That is a high-risk approach.

Radio interviews

These tend to be less aggressive than television, but this does not necessarily make them easier. The listener will tend to be concentrating on other things – driving the car or digging the garden. The power of the spokesperson's personality has to come over positively. Gestures (or a fine face) will not help. The speaker has to make his or her words and voice sound interesting. This is a skill that can be developed.

Ironically, although the speaker cannot be seen on radio, the studio situation can be surprisingly confusing. Often there is only a short informal build-up to radio interviews. The interview subject can be seated and, in seconds, be broadcasting live over the airwaves.

Always take advantage of any rehearsal opportunity. Run through the points, checking tricky questions, but remember that the interviewer reserves the right to ask you anything. This might include subjects that have not been discussed in the briefing session. If the interview is taped, the interviewee can refuse to answer; the silence will have to be edited out, although that is a bold and sometimes reckless approach. Some interviewers will respond aggressively.

Television studio interviews

On television, the focus of the attention is on the small studio area where the guest and the interviewer will be sitting. Therefore, it is easier to concentrate on the subject in hand. However, the surge of adrenalin can help some people sharpen their performance but stuns others into mumbling incoherence.

There is no substitute for experience. Watch television and see how it works. See how people deal with questions. Tape as many interviews as possible and rehearse your own answers to questions. Learn to identify the effective techniques and the irritating habits.

News and feature programmes

Learn the differences between the types of programme presented. News items are highly condensed; feature items might be slightly longer; while full-length investigative-type programmes can often be hostile.

You need to be very clear and, if necessary, firm with the programme-makers to avoid unhappy situations. Every seasoned public relations professional will recount personal horror stories. Most arise from a simple misunderstanding over the objectives of the programme-makers; they want to make interesting, relevant programmes, not promote your vested interests. Most will play this straight but some may be devious; all will put their viewers' interests ahead of yours – as you would in their place.

Special interest programmes

Both radio and television present special interest programmes. These tend to be less aggressive because the broadcasters are working in the same industry week after week. These feature programmes are dependent on the degree of cooperation received from people who work in the special interest sectors, such as gardening, antiques, motoring or leisure. This does not stop the broadcasters from hitting hard, but it does ensure that they are reasonably accurate and fair in any criticism.

Be sure you know what the broadcaster is aiming at before you, or one of your executives, agree to cooperate. Ask for the names of the other guests who will be appearing. Sometimes the name of the programme will indicate the angle quite clearly.

Location interviews

There are a number of ways in which interviews can be organized. With major news events, a participant may be stopped and confronted by a camera or microphone. Be sure you are not caught out by such situations. If your organization is in the news, then you or an executive might find yourself being 'doorstepped'. Think beforehand about what to say. If this is limited by the situation – for example, a takeover negotiation – construct something that will still give the broadcasters a piece of useful television or tape. However, remember that you are in charge. It is quite acceptable to make a polite excuse and break away when you have said all you wish.

Telephone interviews

On occasions, your organization will be asked to give a telephone interview: if possible, this should be resisted. The quality will be bad and you have no control over the editing or usage of the material. The viewer or listener may even get the impression that it was not important enough for your company representative to go to the studio.

If your executive is in a studio interview, he or she may well have a down-the-line interview – in fact, talking to a studio monitor. Your executive must appear to be taking part in a real-life conversation with the interviewer. The best advice is to ignore the electronics and talk to just one real person. The same principle applies on down-the-line radio interviews, where that 'real' person may be a microphone in front of the studio guest.

Panel discussions

Advanced preparation, as always, is essential. Consider the points you would like your executive to convey. It is not always a good idea to be the first person to reply in a discussion. Equally, the executive should not let the discussion go too far before he or she starts to make points.

Make sure you express your organization's views effectively. You should be quite prepared to put normal politeness quietly to one side. Do not be browbeaten by the chairman; the interviewee must answer the question in the way he or she would prefer.

Syndicated radio interviews

In the UK, there are several organizations that will produce an interview on tape, syndicated to local stations. The basic principles still apply. However, as your organization is paying for the service, you will receive more help in the preparation. Remember that the final radio tape has to meet broadcast standards or it will not be used. The syndicating companies will not allow the interview to become 'soft'. They, and you, want good usable material. So treat the interview with full professional seriousness.

Studio interviews

Face-to-face interviews are invaluable because your speaker is not competing for attention, though he or she is competing for the time. If the interview is live, then the duration of the interview will be known, and for that reason there is likely to have been more discussion beforehand about the areas to be covered. If the interview is filmed and edited, its length may depend on the amount of interest the speaker is able to generate. Avoid a 5-minute interview that will be cut to 30 seconds on screen.

Consider carefully the points you want to make. You may need to anticipate the questions that are to be asked in order to weave these into your answers. Always treat the interviewer as a professional trying to do a professional job, but remember that he or she is unlikely to know much about the sector you are discussing.

PLAN YOUR INTERVIEW

Never bluff. Handle naive questions politely. If the interviewer is asking a simple question it is because the viewers or listeners would like to ask the same simple question. There are many ways of presenting the truth but avoid misrepresentations. Listen carefully to the stance that the interviewer is taking. If you need to challenge an assumption ('Many people believe...'), do it firmly but politely, using evidence where possible: 'I can understand you believe that, but our research shows that 80 per cent of the public…'

You must put adequate preparation into what you or your spokesperson is to say. Do not rely on being a spontaneous speaker. Concentrate on the good news and avoid temptations to justify yourself. Do not allow the interviewer to get on top of the situation. Keep cool and concentrate on essentials. Do not be diverted. Learn to convert technicalities into simple lay language. Do not say anything on-air or off-air that you would not want to see used or might regret later. Prepare for yourself or for your executive a brief on the main points you wish to cover.

Do not drink (in any circumstances) before the interview. Wear clothes appropriate to the situation. Avoid annoying mannerisms. Concentrate on what you want to say, not on what they want to say. Think of interesting ways of illustrating your points. Keep it enthusiastic. Avoid jargon. Talk through the interviewer to the audience. Do not allow yourself to be interrupted. Correct any inaccuracies in the questions.

Look honest, sound honest and be honest – then you and your organization might be believed.

Preparation is really the key. When you are planning an interview always take time to get your messages clear. Often, the number of messages that you will get into an interview will be three. As Sue Bohle, president of the Bohle Company of California, advises, it is wise to memorize these messages. You can express the points in your own words relevant to the question and the situation. But you need to be certain you remember the points!

Bohle suggests that your public relations professionals work on trying to create messages that will capture the interest of the media. She quotes an example of promoting a new digital video recorder that featured the ability to skip commercials. The key message her consultancy developed for CEO Ken Potashner of SONICblue was: 'This is the product the networks don't want you to own.' The consultancy used this everywhere and the media picked up on it. An article in *Business Week* was listed in the table of contents as 'The Replay TV 4000 video recorder broadcasters don't want you to see'. A memorable phrase like this can summarize in a few words what might take a precious minute or two of explanation.

Most businesses are organizing themselves to handle media investigations in a professional way. For many years journalists had free rein and could inflict considerable damage. The fault lay in the lack of awareness by many organizations of a need to prepare for such situations.

Investigative television reporting will continue to become better and fairer as organizations become better equipped to cope with the special requirements of the medium. These media will continue to increase in importance in projecting the organization's messages.

Factors in a media training day

Notes for Denplan support for member dentists*

1. Background

The public relations department of Denplan proposes to support the local promotional initiatives of Denplan member dentists, through offering supportive media training. These notes cover some key factors in planning such training opportunities and some suggestions that might help such events be successful.

2. Aims

The purpose of such training should be to:

- Help each delegate develop an active media campaign for his/her practice.
- Give him/her a clear, constructive perspective on how journalists work.
- Demonstrate the interviewee techniques that generate the best results.
- Confirm Denplan expertise and ability to offer practical help to members.
- Build relationships through creating an enjoyable/challenging experience.
- Develop material that supports practice marketing and reputation initiatives.

3. Delegates

Media training works best with a small group of compatible people; they tend to spark off each other and create a friendly, constructive environment. Three to four delegates are the ideal numbers. Beyond four, each individual will not get enough time or attention, so a second trainer would be advisable.

---

*These notes are based on a paper prepared by the author and Fox Murphy account director, Tom Oxley in cooperation with Brian Davenport and Emma Slater of Denplan as part of their client professional support programme.

The solo training session can work well with the right participant through being intensive; but the attention on one delegate is not suitable for those who need a more measured pace or who do not respond well to pressure.

4. Mood and environment

A degree of pressure helps the performance and equates to the situation that the participant might face in real life. However, the progress from the start to finish must be seen and recognized by each delegate. Equally, the course leaders must encourage the participants, never embarrass or humiliate them and steadily raise their confidence – but not to reckless levels.

Criticism must be clear but constructive, firm but sympathetic, specific but encouraging.

5. Location/venues

Caution should be taken over running an event in the client's premises. The chances of interruption are much higher. Also the atmosphere is not correct where the participant is comfortable and knows he is the boss. It is not like that in the studio, newsroom or the interview chair. A suitable hotel room is acceptable but a radio/television production suite is best.

6. The interview approach

Also, even for print-type interviews the recording of each interview improves the experience and delegate performance to such a level that it is almost an essential. The video allows the delegate to see his or her performance. It also allows the tutor to run a tutorial on the playback, building on the good points to lead the interviewee to an understanding of what works and what does not. Finally, it provides a record of progress over the session.

The best progress is through the tutor or an appointed professional inter-viewer undertaking interviews and debriefing on these through a tutorial approach, as outlined above. Scenarios need to be planned to allow the interviewee to talk about areas with which he or she is familiar – as would happen in reality. A dentist is unlikely to be interviewed on transport issues!

Interviews and the tutorials should be end-to-end with no breaks. Coffee and a sandwich lunch are taken on the run. No discussion is allowed other than on the training and the topics for interview.

7. Timetable

A suggested programme for the day might be as follows, assuming one or two candidates. There is considerable flexibility over such a schedule but it is important that there is a 'progression' over the period of training. A half-day can be practical but training should not be less than three to four hours long.

10.00	Start. Brief on the types of media and their different approach.
10.20	Trial interview for newspaper. Slow and no pressure. Recorded.
10.30	Debrief on positive points and dangers that should be highlighted.
10.45	First radio interview. Soft feature item, live around 10 minutes.
11.00	Debrief; suggestions on getting over messages, interview 'ownership'.
11.15	Second radio interview. Tougher, live, key news issue, studio, five minutes.
11.30	Debrief. Review of the level and quality of messages delivered.
11.45	Third radio interview. Studio discussion with domineering guest.
12.00	Review of success in control. Also techniques for awkward studio guest.
12.15	Fourth radio interview. Live, doorstep aggressive, on a crisis, two minutes.
12.25	Debrief, particularly on start/finish, listening for cues, keeping ahead.
12.45	First television interview. Studio, discussion, 10 minutes.
13.00	Review of television techniques, preparation, control, message delivery.
13.30	Second television interview. Doorstep, crisis and aggressive. Three minutes.
13.40	Full tutorial on strengths/weaknesses. Learn from and avoid mistakes.
14.15	Second television interview. Live, doorstep on issues. Three minutes.
14.30	Tutorial covering message preparation and delivery, plus self-appraisal.
15.00	Studio debate. Live. Other guests with their own agendas. 20 minutes.
15.30	Step-by-step tutorial on performance and techniques taught in the day.
16.00	Questions and overall review. Assessment of the difference, start to finish.
16.15	Close.

8. Course notes

The delegates should be supported with full course notes, presented page by page through the day. These build to a binder to act as an *aide mémoire*, reinforcing the points taught and practised.

Making the company behave properly

Demonstrating the damage to reputation of negative news reports

How do you tackle a difficult situation positively? A leading manufacturing company for which I worked had a safety record that was the envy of the industry. However, one of its facilities in the UK seemed to be having a number of industrial accidents and, as public relations manager, this worried me considerably.

As I was also the editor of the in-house company newspaper, I had seen the safety reports, which seemed to suggest that something was wrong and, sooner or later, one of the accidents might not be so small.

After discussion with the safety director, we felt we needed to take further action. He had explained that as this was an older plant, it needed updating and a lot more spent on safety procedures. The safety record would have been even worse if it were not for the quality of management – but the potential for a rise in incidents was worrying. I wrote a report for the chairman on the damage to the company reputation that could be created by a poor safety record.

Arguments about doing the right thing because it is right, or treating people the way you would like to be treated, do carry some weight. These arguments have added significance if a bottom-line impact can be demonstrated. Damage to reputation is bad for sales and bad for the share price. As all good public relations practitioners know, you can never rely on bad news keeping itself discreetly quiet.

The most powerful argument to the chairman was that there were countless sources by which the poor reputation of the company could become public knowledge. One of these could be a disgruntled employee. One of these might be through a crusading national television programme.

As these arguments were not winning the day, I decided to put it to the test. I commissioned a friend of mine, who was a freelancer regularly working for one of the more sensational national dailies, to write a story – on two conditions. The first was that this was strictly confidential and would not be published anywhere. The second was that she would only use her normal sources and normal reporting methods to create her story. She would get no help from me, other than the initial point in the right direction.

The brief was deliberately minimal. Imagine, I told her (as might well be the case), that an employee or trade union official phones you off the record to tip you off.

With her assurance that she would not use this inside information to create her own news story, I asked her to check out the safety record at the plant in question. If anything of interest was found, she was to let me have the sort of story that she would write for, say, the *Daily Express*.

The story arrived on my desk two days later, making me feel I had been over-generous in the fee that I had allowed her in our negotiation!

However, when I read the copy I could see she had earned every penny. It was sensational. It was terrifying. A pencilled note on the top of her copy advised me that if she had submitted this as a normal news story she believed that it would have been very big indeed – possibly even a page-one lead.

The headlines, as I recall, read:

How many more to die?
Lifetime worker killed by fiver economy measure

The story then went on to describe how maintenance standards had been compromised as a result of a company directive to minimize maintenance costs, as the profit forecast that year was looking depressing.

During construction, unknown to the company and in a period when the plant did not belong to the group, a subcontractor had installed a safety valve of inferior design. This was below the capacity required. It had been installed in a key piece of plant with a result that a maintenance worker had been killed by exploding machinery when the valve failed.

I read the story with horror. After a few moments to compose myself I went upstairs, just a couple of flights to the office of the chairman.

He had an open-door policy and we had already established a direct and constructive relationship. He looked up as I approached his desk. I kept a straight face.

'Please read this. It appears in the *Express* tomorrow morning.'

He was one of the most enlightened and positive bosses I had ever had. Yet, as I sat for those few seconds watching him read the story, I felt that maybe I had gone too far...

'Hell, Roger. We have to do something about this. It's not fair. It's gross.'

'Hold on. I think I can stop this,' I responded.

'How? Do you know her well? Can we talk to her and put this into perspective?'

'I am sure we can,' I hesitated. 'But, to tell you the truth, this story is not appearing in the *Express* tomorrow.'

'You've stopped it already?'

'No, sorry. Even my public relations skills cannot stretch that far. The reality is that this is not a genuine story. I asked a freelance friend of mine to write it. It is what *could* appear in the *Express* tomorrow.'

'How dare you,' he exploded. Then, after a moment of tension, he laughed. 'Point made. If we behave this way, this is the kind of story we could expect. Why not use the simple route? Why not tell me?'

'I tried,' I murmured. He had walked round the desk and slapped me on the shoulders, none too playfully.

'Well, you won't have to worry about things like this any more because you're fired!'

I gasped.

'Just kidding,' he grinned. Next morning a new safety procedure was installed across the company though I never understood how it arrived so coincidentally out of the blue.

Appendix 1: The role of professional bodies in developing an effective public relations structure

Some years ago, I was invited to chair a new body. This had been set up by a group of concerned public relations professionals to help develop standards on accountability and the responsibility of practitioners towards their employers and the publics that these employers serve. The Public Relations Standards Council (PRSC) has taken a low-key approach and has no role in education training or the industry, or professional matters covered by trade and professional associations such as the Public Relations Consultants Association, the Chartered Institute of Public Relations, The Chartered Institute of Marketing, The Marketing Society (all of the UK), the Public Relations Society of America, The International Public Relations Association and similar bodies.

The following code is in draft only at the time of updating this book and comments and amendments are invited. The final version, with any modifications, will be published as a set of guidelines intended to contribute to the development of the business discipline of public relations.

Public Relations Standards Council Checklist

Management strategic public relations checklist, April 2005

1. This updated document has been prepared from comments made by members of the steering group of the Council and interested external parties.
2. This copy includes factors relevant to the public sector as well as business communications, academic and charitable and other not-for-profit organizations, plus references to brand support and internal communications.
3. Trade and professional bodies will be invited to print this in their own publications with any editorial comments they feel may be appropriate.

Purpose

All organizations need to maintain effective two-way communications with the many publics upon which they depend for success. Communications are needed to build awareness, create goodwill and support and stimulate positive action. Public relations should reinforce reputation, strengthen the corporate name and enhance the brand values. The planned activities to achieve such aims will normally be coordinated through an appropriate public relations function, employed or retained by the organization.

Public relations is *strategic* in that it must have an influence upon policy. It should be concerned about what the organization does as much as about what it says; public relations should carry the responsibility for relations with both internal and external audiences. Good policies, well presented, sensitive and responsive to stakeholder needs and expectations help to build the good reputation that is central to the role of effective public relations.

These notes have been prepared to help managers and commentators identify whether an organization has public relations operating at such a strategic level and with appropriate supporting resources.

The public relations role

1. The organization should have a written and published public relations policy, setting out the objectives, accepted by the heads of all departments.
2. An appropriately experienced public relations professional should direct the function, reporting to the chairman, chief executive or, in the public and non-commercial sector, the appropriate senior manager.
3. The public relations professional has a duty to advise all disciplines within the organization and should expect to be properly briefed on all relevant policies.

4. He or she should have input at an early stage to all relevant policies and strategic plans.
5. The job description of the senior public relations professional should require him or her to advise management on the public relations implications of all proposed policies and organizational activities.
6. The organization must require and allow the professional to advise candidly, without threat, intimidation or penalty, even where such advice may not be to the liking of management.
7. The corporate social responsibility and reputation management policies of the organization must be reviewed and regularly updated by the head of public relations, who has a responsibility to management to ensure that best practice is followed in these areas. All activity must be in line with written and agreed CSR and reputation policies.
8. The head of public relations is not only responsible to the board for what the organization says but must advise on what it does where this affects or could affect reputation; policies that the organization pursues on activities that can have an impact on reputation and goodwill must be consistent with the values identified in the CSR and reputation policies.
9. The head of public relations should have custody of the public relations policy but, in developing this, must involve all other professionals in the organization whose disciplines have an impact upon reputation.

Professionalism
10. All communications messages must be consistent across all audiences. While different aspects of the organization's policies, products, services or activities may be projected to special interest audiences, such messages must not be contradictory.
11. Internal and external audiences should be addressed with equal commitment and honesty.
12. The manager of the public relations function must ensure proper coordination of all public relations activities, integrating the efforts of all other disciplines that affect public relations.
13. All senior public relations staff must be on an active programme of continuous professional development.
14. Personnel must have the appropriate level of knowledge of their employing organization and must be following acceptable procedures to keep this knowledge up to date, with the active support of the management.
15. The public relations function should have the manpower and budget resources appropriate to the responsibilities allocated to it and appropriate to the size and complexity of the organization.

Accountability
16. The public relations programmes of activity must consider all the relevant audiences affected by the activities of the organization; specific

campaigns can target specific audiences within the overall corporate activity.

17. All public relations activities must be truthful, honest and never misleading, by commission or omission.
18. The ethical or integrity standards to which the organization conforms should be identified, with due sensitivity to the diversity within the communities in which it operates.
19. Communications normally should be proactive, taking the initiative with all audiences and all issues: a reactive approach should be the exception rather than the norm.
20. All public relations activities must respect the interests of the audiences involved, as well as of the organization.
21. All enquiries to the organization must be dealt with honestly, openly and promptly.

Performance
22. All public relations activity must be consistent with company missions and visions and with all other communications including advertising, marketing support, statements of brand values and policies, reports to shareholders and other stakeholders.
23. The public relations plan must have written, measurable objectives. The criteria for the measurement of the effectiveness of all activity must be agreed in advance.
24. Public relations performance should be reported internally to relevant management. This information should be available to employees where appropriate; where relevant to the public interest it should be available on request externally.

The code of the PRSC is complementary to the professional codes of a number of bodies in communications and marketing. The following is a sample code from the Institute of Public Relations, the lead professional body in this sector in the UK.

The CIPR Code of Conduct

The Chartered Institute of Public Relations*, as the lead professional body on public relations in the UK and a significant influence internationally, operates a code of conduct. This is supported by a professional practices and disciplinary committee.

In an introduction to the Code, the Institute states that in an increasingly

---

*The Institute was awarded its charter in March 2005. This copy of the Code was downloaded from the website in April.

competitive world in which consumer power dictates market strength, investing in good public relations is necessary for success. As the service industry continues to grow the Institute of Public Relations (IPR), as the voice of public relations professionals, has an important role in ensuring that the trust and confidence of consumers is gained in the boardroom and on the high street.

The IPR operates a Code of Professional Conduct and disciplinary powers to which all members agree to adhere. The Professional Practices Committee of the Institute has occasion to handle complaints brought against members of the Institute who are thought to be in breach of the Code.

In regard to the supply of public relations services, the Code emphasizes that honest and proper regard for the public interest, reliable and accurate information, and never misleading clients, employers and other professionals about the nature of representation or what can be competently delivered or achieved, are vital components to robust professional practice.

In March 2000 the IPR Professional Practices Committee issued a member consultation on the review of the IPR Code of Professional Conduct. The rationale for taking a fresh look at the Code was largely borne from the fact that the Professional Practices Committee had on several occasions of disciplinary investigation encountered difficulties in interpreting the complex arrangements set out in the Code. Procedures for the investigation of cases were often slow and resource intensive and the language of the Code, somewhat outdated and draconian, could not have been described as user-friendly.

Although the many cases (on average six per annum) that had come before the PPC over the years had been successfully resolved, usually by mediation and letters of guidance, none necessitated/resulted in termination of IPR membership. This led to a general perception among the membership that the PPC, and the IPR, had 'no teeth' and that the Code was outdated and not conducive to the expedient and decisive investigation of cases.

The PPC prepared a consultation paper focusing on the incorporation of new IPR activities (e.g. CPD) into the code and the rephrasing of the Code as a document of best practice, rather than retaining a 'thou shall not...' approach.

Following extensive consultation, and comparison with several codes of other professional and public relations bodies to ensure broad consistency, a revised section A of the Code was ratified at the IPR's October 2000 AGM.

The IPR can only investigate complaints made against its members.

All complaints remain confidential. Announcement of a complaint outcome is at the discretion of the Professional Practices Committee and subject to the endorsement of the Council.

Complaints arising mainly constitute breaches, and alleged breaches, of the IPR Code in respect of business management issues, for example contractual disputes, payment by results under dispute and late payment.

IPR Code of Conduct

IPR Principles

1. Members of the Institute of Public Relations agree to:
    i.   Maintain the highest standards of professional endeavour, integrity, confidentiality, financial propriety and personal conduct;
    ii. Deal honestly and fairly in business with employers, employees, clients, fellow professionals, other professions and the public;
    iii. Respect the customs, practices and codes of clients, employers, colleagues, fellow professionals and other professions in all countries where they practise;
    iv. Take all reasonable care to ensure employment best practice including giving no cause for complaint of unfair discrimination on any grounds;
    v.   Work within the legal and regulatory frameworks affecting the practice of public relations in all countries where they practise;
    vi. Encourage professional training and development among members of the profession;
    vii. Respect and abide by this Code and related Notes of Guidance issued by the Institute of Public Relations and encourage others to do the same.

Principles of Good Practice

2. Fundamental to good public relations practice are:

Integrity
- Honest and responsible regard for the public interest;
- Checking the reliability and accuracy of information before dissemination;
- Never knowingly misleading clients, employers, employees, colleagues and fellow professionals about the nature of representation or what can be competently delivered and achieved;
- Supporting the IPR Principles by bringing to the attention of the IPR examples of malpractice and unprofessional conduct.

Competence
- Being aware of the limitations of professional competence: without

limiting realistic scope for development, being willing to accept or delegate only that work for which practitioners are suitably skilled and experienced;

- Where appropriate, collaborating on projects to ensure the necessary skill base.

Transparency and conflicts of interest

- Disclosing to employers, clients or potential clients any financial interest in a supplier being recommended or engaged;
- Declaring conflicts of interest (or circumstances which may give rise to them) in writing to clients, potential clients and employers as soon as they arise;
- Ensuring that services provided are costed and accounted for in a manner that conforms to accepted business practice and ethics.

Confidentiality

- Safeguarding the confidences of present and former clients and employers;
- Being careful to avoid using confidential and 'insider' information to the disadvantage or prejudice of clients and employers, or to self-advantage of any kind;
- Not disclosing confidential information unless specific permission has been granted or the public interest is at stake or if required by law.

Maintaining professional standards

3. IPR members are encouraged to spread awareness and pride in the public relations profession where practicable by, for example:

- Identifying and closing professional skills gaps through the Institute's Continuous Professional Development programme;
- Offering work experience to students interested in pursuing a career in public relations;
- Participating in the work of the Institute through the committee structure, special interest and vocational groups, training and networking events;
- Encouraging employees and colleagues to join and support the IPR;
- Displaying the IPR designatory letters on business stationery;
- Specifying a preference for IPR applicants for staff positions advertised;
- Evaluating the practice of public relations through use of the IPR Research & Evaluation Toolkit and other quality management and quality assurance systems (e.g. ISO standards); and constantly striving to improve the quality of business performance;
- Sharing information on good practice with members and, equally, referring perceived examples of poor practice to the Institute.

Appendix 2: Useful organizations

AA Advertising Association
Aberford House, 15 Wilton Road
London SW1V 1NJ
Tel: (020) 7828 2771
E-mail: aa@adassoc.org.uk
www.adassoc.org.uk

ASA Advertising Standards Authority
Mid-City Place, 71 High Holborn
London WC1V 6QT
Tel: (020) 7492 2222
E-mail: enquiries@asa.org.uk
www.asab.org.uk

BCC British Chambers of Commerce
65 Petty France, St James Park
London SW1H 9EYU
Tel: (020) 7654 5800
E-mail: info@britishchambers.org.uk
www.chamberonline.co.uk

CAM   Communications, Advertising and Marketing Education
Foundation
Moor Hall, Cookham
Maidenhead, Berkshire SL6 9QH
Tel: (01628) 427120
E-mail: info@camfoundation.com
www.camfoundation.com

CBI   Confederation of British Industry
Centre Point, 103 New Oxford Street
London WC1A 1DU
Tel: (020) 7379 7400
E-mail: enquiriesdesk@cbi.org.uk
www.cbi.org.uk

CERP   Confédération Européen des Relations Publiques
Rue des Petits Carmes 9
B-100 Brussels, Belgium
Tel: (01032) 2511 2680
E-mail: public.relations@achelis.com
www.cerp.org

CIB   British Association of Communicators in Business
Suite A, First Floor, Avriga Building
Davy Avenue, Knowlhill
Milton Keynes MK5 8ND
Tel: 0870 121 7606
E-mail: enquiries@cib.uk.com
www.cib.uk.com

CIOM   Chartered Institute of Management
3rd Floor, 2 Savoy Court
Strand, London WC2R 0E2
Tel: (020) 7497 0580
E-mail: enquiries@managers.org.uk
www.managers.org.uk

CIM   Chartered Institute of Marketing
Moor Hall, Cookham
Maidenhead, Berks SL6 9QH
Tel: (01628) 427500
E-mail: membership@cim.co.uk
www.cim.co.uk

COI   Central Office of Information (COI Communications)
Hercules House, Hercules Road
London SE1 7DU
Tel: (020) 7928 2345
E-mail: mike.wheeler@coi.gov.uk
www.coi.gov.uk

CPRF   Council of Public Relations Firms
100 Park Avenue, Suite 1600
New York, NY 10017, USA
Tel: (1-212) 351 5048
www.prfirms.org

CPRS   Canadian Public Relations Society
Suite 346, 4195 Dundas Street West
Toronto, Ontario M8X 1Y4, Canada
Tel: (416) 239 7034
E-mail: admin@cprs.ca
www.cprs.ca

EPO   European Parliament Office
2 Queen Anne's Gate
London SW1H 9AA
Tel: (020) 7227 4300
E-mail: eplondon@europarl.eu.int
www.europarl.org.uk

IABC   International Association of Business Communicators
One Hallidie Plaza, Suite 600
San Francisco, California 94102, USA
Tel: (1-415) 544 4700
E-mail: service-centre@iabc.com
www.iabc.com

IBE   Institute of Business Ethics
24 Greencoat Place
London SW1P 1BE
Tel. (020) 7798 6040
E-mail: info@ibe.org.uk
www.ibe.org.uk

IOD   Institute of Directors
116 Pall Mall
London SW1Y 5ED
Tel: (020) 7839 1233
E-mail: enquiries@iod.com
www.iod.com

IOE   Institute of Export
Export House, Minerva Business Park
Lynch Wood, Peterborough PE2 6FT
Tel: (020) 8361 8026
E-mail: institute@export.org.uk
www.export.org.uk

IPA   Institute of Practitioners in Advertising
44 Belgrave Square
London SW1X 8QS
Tel: (020) 7235 7020
E-mail: info@ipa.co.uk
www.ipa.co.uk

IPR   Institute of Public Relations
The Old Trading House, 4th Floor
15 Northburgh Street
London EC1V 0PR
Tel: (020) 7253 5151
E-mail: info@ipr.org.uk
www.ipr.org.uk

IPRA   International Public Relations Association
1 Dunley Hill Court, Ranmore Common
Dorking, Surrey RG5 6SX
Tel: (01483) 280 130
E-mail: iprasec@btconnect.com
www.ipra.org

ISBA   Incorporated Society of British Advertisers
Langham House, 1b Portland Place
London W1Y 8AE
Tel: (020) 7291 9020
E-mail: tracid@isba.org.uk
www.isba.org.uk

ISP   Institute of Sales Promotion
Arena House, 66–68 Pentonville Road
London N1 9HS
Tel: (020) 7837 5340
E-mail: enquiries@isp.org.uk
www.isp.org.uk

MRS   Market Research Society
15 Northburgh Street
London EC1V 0JR
Tel: (020) 7490 4911
E-mail: info@mrs.org.uk
www.mrs.org.uk

MS   The Marketing Society
1 Park Road
Teddington, Middlesex TW11 0AR
Tel: (020) 8973 1700
E-mail: info@marketing-society.org.uk
www.marketing-society.org.uk

NPA   Newspaper Publishers Association
34 Southwark Bridge Road
London SE1 9EU
Tel: (020) 7207 2200

NS   Newspaper Society
Bloomsbury House, 74–77 Great Russell Street
London WC1B 3DA
Tel: (020) 7636 7014
E-mail: ns@newspapersoc.org.uk
www.newspapersoc.org.uk

PCC   Press Complaints Commission
1 Salisbury Square
London EC4Y 8JB
Tel: (020) 7353 1248
E-mail: pcc@pcc.org.uk
www.pcc.org.uk

PPA   Periodical Publishers Association
Queens House, 28 Kingsway
London WC2B 6JR
Tel: (020) 7404 4166
E-mail: info@ppa.co.uk
www.ppa.co.uk

PRCA   Public Relations Consultants Association
Willow House, Willow Place
London SW1P 1JH
Tel: (020) 7233 6026
E-mail: pressoffice@prca.org.uk
www.prca.org.uk

PRSA   Public Relations Society of America
Maiden Lane, 11th floor
New York, NY 10038-5150, USA
Tel: (1-212) 460 1400
E-mail: hq@prsa.org
www.prsa.org

SE   Stock Exchange
10 Paternoster Square
London EC4M 7LS
Tel: (020) 7797 1000
E-mail: enquiries@londonstockexchange.com
www.londonstockexchange.com

UKECO   The UK European Commission Office
Jean Monnet House, 8 Storey's Gate
London SW1P 3AT
Tel: (020) 7973 1992
E-mail: ian.barber@cec.eu.int
www.cec.org.uk

WF   The Work Foundation
Peter Runge House, 3 Carlton House Terrace
London SW1Y 5DG
Tel: 0870 165 6700
E-mail: contactcentre@theworkfoundation.com
www.theworkfoundation.com

Index